A Gift of Meaning

12-01

A Gift of Meaning

Bill Tammeus

UNIVERSITY OF MISSOURI PRESS
COLUMBIA AND LONDON

1201 1995

For

Marcia, Lisen, Kate, Chris, Dan, Katy,

David, Karin, Barbara, Mary, my wonderful

readers, and the late Tom Duffy, who never let

me forget how much words matter.

Copyright © 2001 by The Kansas City Star

University of Missouri Press, Columbia, Missouri 65201
Printed and bound in the United States of America
All rights reserved
5 4 3 2 1   05 04 03 02 01

Library of Congress Cataloging-in-Publication Data

Tammeus, Bill.
  A gift of meaning / Bill Tammeus.
    p. cm.
  ISBN 0-8262-1366-9 (alk. paper)
  I. Title.
PN4874.T22 A25 2001
814'.6—dc21   2001053439

⊗™This paper meets the requirements of the
American National Standard for Permanence of Paper
for Printed Library Materials, Z39.48, 1984.

Text design: Stephanie Foley
Cover design: Vickie Kersey DuBois
Typesetter: BOOKCOMP, Inc.
Printer and binder: The Maple-Vail Book Manufacturing Group
Typefaces: Palatino and Vladimir Script

Contents

Preface

It has become a cliché in our often-vacuous culture that humanity is engaged in a desperate but unsuccessful search for meaning. This quest sometimes has struck me as the equivalent of an ignorant child standing in a field of ripe wheat searching for grain but seeing none.

Meaning—often deep, profound, and eternal—is everywhere around us. We need nothing more than eyes to see, ears to hear, hearts to understand. What I try to do when I write newspaper columns is simply to draw out the meaning of events, people, seasons, landscapes, and other phenomena, and to offer that meaning as a gift to readers. Theologians who study holy writ have a word for this process of extracting meaning. They call it "exegesis," and it's hard work to do it right. The temptation is not to spend all that effort but, rather, to settle for the less-demanding work of eisegesis, which is putting one's own meaning into the text. I try to avoid that seductive approach, though I'm not always successful, partly because the demands of daily journalism can be so heavy that sometimes I knowingly take the wrong approach just to fill the required space.

The text from which I try to draw meaning is, as I say, simply the world as it passes before my wondering eyes. Sometimes I tell the people who ask that to write the kind of columns found in this collection, I try to look at the world through my theological lenses. By that, I don't mean that I always try to see things in the way Presbyterians like me tend to see them. Rather, I mean that I try to be sensitive to an eternal perspective and that I try to have an appreciation for the sacred all around, something the ancient Celts were so good at noticing. In fact, mostly what I try to do is simply notice, simply pay attention. I try to do what the Buddhists suggest we all do, which is to be mindful.

The columns in this book, however, are not sermons. And I hope you won't see them that way. Rather, they are my attempts to point to some important, lasting meaning. (Sometimes I find that meaning; sometimes, like grace, it finds me.) It's a great joy to me when readers tell me that my words said just what they had been thinking but hadn't been able to put into words.

In the end, the job of any columnist is to get people to think. If these columns cause you to do that, you will have given me a gift.

Acknowledgments

If the columns in this book carry meaning for you, I am not entirely responsible. More often than I can count, these wise editors saved me from myself: the late Jim Scott, Rich Hood, Virginia Hall, Karen Brown, Rhonda Chriss Lokeman, Tom McClanahan, LaJean Keene, and Kevin Catalano.

Journalism—even the seemingly solo variety of column writing— is a team game. I'm grateful to have had these skilled colleagues on my team, as well as the discerning editors at the University of Missouri Press. I'm also grateful to the New York Times News Service, which syndicated my work for ten years, and to Knight Ridder/Tribune Information Services, which syndicates my work now.

Bill Tammeus
Kansas City, Missouri
April 2001

A Gift of Meaning

Family, Faith, and Plumb Lines

Pain Inevitably Comes into Our Lives
June 9, 1996

WOODSTOCK, ILLINOIS—The morning we prayed over my mother and buried her, the air was the kind of noticeable clean it gets only after a serious rain scrubbing.

In fact, it had been raining for days. The countless nearby fields, freshly planted with corn and soybeans—rich, black Illinois earth like that my parents grew up on and loved—had done their best to sponge up wave after chilly wave of spring storms. But, finally, it was all too much. Brackish, turgid water filled the hollows of fields, an unwelcome, untidy guest.

My mother liked guests, but not the kind that make a mess. Not the kind you have to waste precious time cleaning up after. Time, to her, was too valuable for that. She preferred dainty guests who would nibble on hors d'oeuvres, praise her pot roast, and leave at a decent hour.

Mom has passed along to me her preference for decency and order, which may explain why it is taking me so long in this piece to get past the weather and to ponder the brusque reality of having just become, at age fifty-one, an orphan.

My three sisters and I joked a little about being orphans as we gathered with our families to wish Mom Godspeed and to lower her into the muddy earth of Oakland Cemetery here next to my father, who had died in 1992. But, in the end, it is no joke at all, this orphan business. It is, rather, the harsh and inevitable way of a world infected with sin and evil, disease and death.

I do not want you to think for a minute that I believe the world is nothing but pain and gloom. No, no, no. We are given almost

1

unspeakable gifts of grace and beauty, joy and insight, kindness and love. And a life well lived, like my mother's, will be weighted toward those reasons to celebrate.

But we are Pollyanna fools if we don't recognize the part pain plays in our lives, the part evil does, and heartache and disappointment.

So I say it plainly. I am an orphan now and I don't like it. And I wish there were some other way.

Still, as these things go, I've done better than I had any right to expect. My father lived until age eighty-two and—save for his last two years or so, when senile dementia veiled his active mind with bewilderment—his life was full, productive, and fat with purpose.

And Mom, Bertha Amanda Sofia Helander Tammeus, had turned eighty-three in March. She, too, lived a remarkably productive life until Parkinson's disease and other ailments put her in a wheelchair and in a nursing home a year and a half ago. And as often as not in this frustrating time, she was confused about things.

So I have very little room to complain about being left parentless at my age. And yet this is a bad business at any age. It is a pure squealing shout about our own mortality. It's a stern reminder that someday my own daughters will be orphans.

The natural way of things is to be born roughly into this world, shocked—after the comfort of the womb—by the relentless, inhospitable air that grabs us. But after our initial reaction to this rudeness we are soothed to cooing by the loving touch and embrace of the one who gave us birth.

At the other end of life, however, the natural pattern is to go out an orphan and, as we go, to create yet more orphans. Even for those of us deeply convinced that a loving God welcomes us home at our death, this seems like bad planning, a bad design. The psalmist (in the New Revised Standard Version of Psalm 90) was right: "Our years come to an end like a sigh."

So there we were, four orphans saying farewell to their old mother under a spring-blue dome of sky. Fresh flowers did their important work of beauty on her casket. But flowers, too, soon fade and blow away. And the truest thing I can think to say about all this now is that the world simply works this way. And no one—not even an orphan with three orphan sisters—can change that.

Family, Faith Make a Person Whole
June 23, 1996

WENONA, ILLINOIS—My late mother's first cousin Connie, born Karen Ingeborg Sophia Jonsson, is holding court here in Bethany Lutheran Cemetery, where her mother no doubt would have been buried if only she had survived past age thirty-four in Sweden.

Under insistent clouds, from which a frail mist occasionally slips, Connie is talking about what made her strong. Her audience is kinfolk gathered for a family reunion. We are making a cemetery stop on a bus trip, taken to see the various nearby farms my grandparents' generation occupied. (Because we are a family that gets to the point, we call it the Manure Tour.)

Connie's mother, Hilma, who was my grandfather's sister, died of complications from her seventh childbirth when Connie was not quite five years old. So my great-grandmother, Lisen Helander, helped Connie's father rear her and her four surviving siblings for several years.

But finally it was too much for an old widow and a younger widower, and all five children came to America in 1925 to live with aunts and uncles, who already had settled here on this luscious north-central Illinois farmland.

It grew bumper crops of both grain and family.

"I remember waving goodbye to an old woman in a babushka," Connie is saying to a small knot of relatives. "And I remember wondering why we were leaving her." She was talking about her grandmother, my great-grandmother.

People today, Connie says, talk about all their childhood trouble and use that trouble to explain why they're now weak and wounded.

"But I went through so much as a child," she says with a matter-of-factness tinged with pride. "And it made me strong."

What was it about all this difficult history that gave her strength? In a word, family. Connie's Aunt Sofia and Uncle Ed, who had no children, took in the bewildered girl and helped her understand the truth about herself—that she was family, that she had family, that she could count on family.

One of my indelible childhood memories is watching the casket bearing Sofie (we almost always called her Sofie) being lowered into her grave right here in this pastoral cemetery on the edge of Wenona in 1955.

I was ten years old, the very same age Connie was when she waved goodbye to her Swedish grandmother. Sofie was eighty-three, the very same age my mother, her niece, was when she died just a few weeks ago. Sofie, like her mother, rejected fanciness in favor of the simplicity of a babushka.

Sofie died a slow, bloated death. Her illness required that, on occasion, I be brought into her aching presence in the back bedroom of her small Wenona house next to the cookie factory. My job was to wish her well and, I suppose, reassure her that a younger generation was being groomed to take her generation's place.

Watching Sofie's casket sink into the rich earth in 1955—in effect, I was waving goodbye to an old woman in a babushka—unnerved me somehow, just as waving goodbye to an old woman in a babushka had unnerved Connie as she left Sweden in 1925. The night of Sofie's funeral I couldn't get to sleep in my assigned bed at my grandparents' house, where we were staying.

Twice I got up and came downstairs to be comforted by the adults whose out-of-focus voices were murmuring through closed doors. And when I lay in my bed alone, in the east bedroom, I kept my eyes locked on the cracked-open door to the hallway, absolutely certain that somehow Sofie's ghost would come through it to speak to me.

Well, Sofie's ghost didn't find me that night. But in an odd and healing way, forty-one years after her death, I sensed Sofie speaking to me here through the voice of Connie, who is herself now fast approaching the age at which both Sofie and my mother died.

Connie, in her long life, has discovered that family rooted in eternal values—family acting out its faith and principles—can catch defenseless children in loving arms and give them time and space to become whole. Her words, "It made me strong," ring almost defiantly through the headstones.

In a way I've never quite grasped before, I know Connie is right. These tough Swedes buried here—Sofie and her brothers Oscar and Alfred and Charles and Axel and Axel's boy Ralph and on and on—planted themselves deeply in the rich soil of family and faith.

They grew strong. And they helped those of us who followed grow strong so that, when it comes time—as it inevitably does—we, too, can take our turn waving goodbye to old women in babushkas, and not be afraid of whatever is to come.

An Angel Gives Love to Those in Her Care
November 11, 1991

She's now in her middle forties, this angel of a woman, and life has pushed her around from the start.

When she and her year-older brother were still in diapers, difficult family circumstances separated them from parents and other siblings. A minister and his wife adopted the two of them, though they were nearly teenagers before they knew the story of their origin.

Their adoptive father eventually lost his mind and died in an institution. When that happened, their mother essentially withdrew from life and for years was an invalid. I visited their mother not long before she died a few years ago and found that she possessed the same combination of toughness, near-anger, and love that distinguished her when, as a boy, I spent countless hours playing at her house.

The mid-forties woman I now speak of, who spent much of her childhood trying to disown a nickname she despised, left high school early to marry and have babies.

Since then, in her extended family, she has seen divorce and death and crippling accidents. She has seen her precious grandbabies move far away. She once lived in a house out in the country for more than a decade and "hated every minute of it." (Now she's back in town.)

She has worked hard, too. For twenty-three years she labored in a large factory that, a few years ago, closed its doors and threw her and many others out of work.

But for a year now she's been working at a wonderful nursing home as a medical secretary, or some such title. The truth is, her job description more accurately might be "angel" or "friend" or "caregiver" or, simply, "lover."

She's not required to do all she does. But what she does must be done if the elderly patients are to retain a sense of self-worth and dignity.

She hugs them. And kisses them. And laughs with them. She straightens their clothing and brushes the hair out of their eyes. She talks to them about people they know—or used to, before their minds began to play cruel tricks on them.

She gets a list of their children and grandchildren and asks them about each one by name. She listens to their stories—often rambling, utterly discombobulated sentences that surely, in some other world, make sense to someone, so sincerely are they rendered.

She watches for signs of change in them—when they're better, when they're not—so she can say something to the family or the nurses or doctors. She asks if they're chilly or too warm and opens or closes a window in response.

In short, she loves them.

She is, physically, no raving beauty. She laughs about trying to lose weight. She laughs a lot, in fact, for though she is well acquainted with many of life's absurdities, its unreliable twists and turns, its pain, its heartaches, but also its joys, she has not let that knowledge exterminate her sense of humor. I'm not sure anything could surprise her anymore.

It is clear that she has learned—and lives—a lesson as deep and profound as it is simple. It's a hard lesson at least as old as these upside down words from Jesus, recorded in Matthew's gospel: "Whoever desires to become great among you, let him be your servant." And these, also from Jesus through Matthew: "The last will be first, and the first will be last."

That oddly contrary sort of moral principle is obvious in the way she lives her life, and the beauty of it warms and comforts my heart—especially because I know she is there now for my father when distance means neither I nor my sisters can be.

Words That Carry Emotion So Very Hard to Say
June 7, 1992

COLUMBUS, OHIO—Because Father's Day this year will be the first since my own father's death, I've been thinking about the unspeakably awkward way sons and fathers relate to one another.

There are exceptions, but I believe most fathers and most sons (at least those over thirteen) don't know how to talk to each other. They don't know how to say words that carry emotion's heavy freight. Men stumble over—choke up at—even the words *I love you.*

We fathers and sons are emotionally constipated. Some men find the only laxative for their feelings is liquor. But when it finally works, they either can't recall what they wanted to say or they think what they are saying is sensitive and revealing when, in fact, it is sappy, embarrassing, and closer to what real laxative produces.

Why can't fathers and sons talk to each other? Why is it so terrifyingly difficult to speak of love and hate, of hopes and fears, of faith and death?

I don't yet know. I know only that my own father and I weren't very good at that kind of talk. And now it's too late. The only such talk now possible for us is imaginary. I can visit his grave in Illinois and—painfully aware of the loneliness of my own voice—say things to him. I haven't done that. I'm not sure I will or even want to. I mention the possibility only because if Dad and I are to talk now, that's how it will have to be done.

The notion of dead air between fathers and sons, their failure to expose their vulnerabilities to each other, is being noticed and discussed more and more widely. One recent evening here in Columbus, at the annual conference of the National Society of Newspaper Columnists, the speaker was Ralph Keyes, who has edited a new book on the subject, *Sons on Fathers.*

Keyes says it took him years to convince a publisher that this subject was worthy of a book. Well, it's worthy of more than one book, and Keyes's volume, in which various sons write of their fathers, is a good start.

Maybe there have been father-son communications problems in all cultures, in all history. Maybe Nero couldn't talk to his father. Maybe Plato couldn't. Maybe Freud.

It would be worth knowing. If this is just a twentieth-century problem, perhaps sons and fathers can yet find a way to recover the ability to speak with each other.

Some fifteen years ago my father and I talked at some length to each other—but it was in a structured, goal-oriented way.

We did—long distance—an oral history of his life and work. Maybe, I now think, it was my attempt to hold conversations we'd never held. I'd write him questions and he'd answer on a cassette tape recorder. When I finished transcribing the tapes, we had 222 pages.

What especially strikes me now about Dad's words in that project—words I've been rereading since his death in January—is that he often seems not to know what he thinks and how he feels about certain personal matters.

"I think this question is a little bit too profound for me to answer," he said when I tried to get at whether, in the Depression, he felt like a pawn of an economic system he believed in.

And when I asked about his and Mom's plans for children, he said such questions really never "came to mind, and I don't remember if I ever discussed this with Mom or that we had any preplanned notions as to that."

It was as if he was so busy just surviving, working, doing all those ten thousand little things fathers must do, that he never really talked to himself much, either. This sounds harsh, but maybe he never challenged himself to think through what he thought about marriage, fatherhood, faith, life itself.

So perhaps he and I never could have talked about these matters because he had very little to share that was examined, very little he really owned.

My regret as I think about Father's Day this year is that I never pressed him to hold that conversation with himself, never asked him if he understood a need to.

We sons are free to reject our fathers' experience, wisdom, and values, but first we must know what they are. We can—and in many ways I did—surmise and assume our fathers' wisdom and values by watching and participating in their lives.

But how much better to have their help interpreting what we are seeing. How much better if they would just tell us—and we them. How much better if we'd just ask—and ask when someone's still there to answer.

Fresh Vision Opens World of Possibilities
September 21, 1997

WOODSTOCK, ILLINOIS—After my mother's death last year, my three sisters and I sold the house in which we grew up.

At the time of the sale, I never imagined the humbling lesson this wonderful old home eventually would teach me. But through the agency of imaginative new owners, I have seen again the need for new eyes to show me possibilities that escape me because of the enfeebling forces of habit.

I first learned this truth about reinvigorated vision as a child. My midwestern family and I arrived fresh-eyed in crowded India so my father could help teach agriculture as part of a university team.

Everything we saw was new. Much of it was unimaginable. Every street beggar was a wonder.

One day well into our stay, Dad came home to eat dinner and, between bites, complain about an American missionary couple who had been in India for decades. He was working with them on a project, but they had stayed so long in India, Dad complained, that they no longer could see the problems. And without a good view of what's wrong, they had no hope of finding solutions.

When he said that, it occurred to me, at age twelve, that I no longer was astonished by the Indian street scenes that had astounded me the year before at age eleven. I, too, even as a child, had begun to suffer the same diminished sight that afflicted our old missionary friends.

Over the years I have tried to remember that lesson. But my obvious failure struck me hard when I saw what the gift of new eyes was doing to the house of my boyhood.

The couple that owns it now brought with them none of my blindness. So they have begun to remake the place according to a vision I lacked.

It is a marvelous old house—nearly 115 years old—that sits on an acre of ground not far from the downtown of this small northern Illinois community in dairy country. The garage is an actual barn, in which horses once were kept and, when I was a boy, chickens. Behind the barn is an apple orchard.

The house itself, when I lived there, had five upstairs bedrooms. After my sisters and I grew up and moved out, my parents turned one of those bedrooms into a bathroom, which made a total, then, of two. Nice timing.

The upstairs also contained a dark (and packed) storeroom the size of a fairly roomy bedroom.

All the home's interior space still is there, but it's been rearranged. Walls that I thought were inviolate have been knocked down.

The old storeroom has become a laundry area with an attached bathroom and dressing room. The old utility room downstairs, where my family washed tons of clothes for tons of years, now is a computerized office. The wall enclosing the back stairway that leads from the kitchen to the upstairs is mostly gone.

The side door of the house (used 90 percent of the time, versus 10 percent for the front door) has been covered over and a new door cut into the new office that used to be the utility room. The kitchen has been remodeled and rearranged.

In short, someone else looked at a house I had seen year after year, decade after decade, and saw wonderful new possibilities I never did.

For some reason, when the new owners allowed my wife and me to view what they were doing, I did not become angry or defensive. Nor has that been my reaction since then. Instead, I am grateful that we have found people who genuinely seem to love a spot of Earth that, in some odd and maybe even visceral way, will always be home to me.

And I am grateful for the reminder about the need for new eyes. What I don't yet know is whether I can carry this lesson into other parts of my life—the ones I've been looking at the same old way for decades. I hope so.

What We Really Need Is Each Other
December 14, 1997

PEKIN, ILLINOIS—Not far from the nursing home where my aunt (my late father's sister) has been working on recovering from illness, a shopping mall is offering the sort of high-energy, low-satisfaction Christmas available at malls everywhere.

In front of the JCPenney store a small train gives rides to kids after they've visited Santa, seated on his throne a few yards away. Santa wasn't busy when my daughter and I walked in, so he waved to us and extended season's greetings.

Not far away a Radio Shack salesman (who obviously hasn't yet earned enough commission to pay for a shave) offered to give me 10 percent off an IBM Aptiva computer if only I'd apply for a charge card and put the whole system—a mere $1,498 plus $199 for a printer—on credit. I declined.

And on it went, store after store filled with the sometimes necessary, often ridiculous stuff that, when wrapped and bowed, too often passes for Christmas in our culture.

The people at my aunt's nursing home don't need any of this stuff. A computer—even at 10 percent off on credit—would sit in their rooms like so much cold metal. What they need they can't get here at the mall. In fact, none of us—even if we're in good health and still have most of our wits about us—can find what we really need for Christmas at this or any other mall.

What we need is each other. What we need is to be enveloped by the solicitous love of family and friends, to be reassured that we are not alone, to be reminded that whether we are old and confused and sick or young and bright and healthy someone else cares about us.

One of my three sisters organized just such envelopment, such reassurance, such remembrance for my aunt. She asked our aunt's nine nieces and nephews and their families for family pictures and notes. (My aunt and her late husband had no children.) Then my sister arranged them all in a scrapbook (with a wonderful photo of our aunt on the cover) and sent it to her from North Carolina. It was a nine-voice shout against loneliness and neglect.

For much of my aunt's adult life, she has given enormous time and energy to the Veterans of Foreign Wars. In recognition of that commitment, my sister found a red poppy—an important VFW symbol—and pasted it as a brooch on the scrapbook's black-and-white cover picture of my aunt.

Oh, how that poppy struck a nerve. For my aunt, it honored what she held dear. She declared my sister—for that and other reasons—"the fairest of the world." It will be hard to put up with any sibling thus designated, but I suppose the other eight of us first cousins and our families will manage.

Three of my aunt's nieces and one of her nephews live in this area of central Illinois, and their visits—along with visits from her nearby brother and his wife and other family and friends—have become important ways of connecting to the idea that the most important gift we can ever give anyone is ourselves. And to receive that gift it really doesn't matter what shape people in nursing homes are in.

Indeed, the day my daughter and I arrived, my aunt was feeling terrible and, frankly, wasn't always making lots of sense. Worse, she knew it and it frustrated her. Still, she was obviously thrilled we had made the trip.

But by the next day she had made a remarkable recovery and was so lucid and feisty that, without any warning, she burst into a few lines of "Oh, What a Beautiful Morning."

In either condition, she needed visitors who cared about her. And so do countless people in her situation—many of whom have no one.

They would, of course, have someone to care for and about them if a few people in the malls would quit thinking they'll find the perfect Christmas gift there.

The message of Christmas is that God decided the best gift for needy people was God's own self. That is a model for us. We are the perfect gift for others, and the world is full of people waiting in hope to receive it.

The Right Way to Have a Funeral
July 12, 1998

READING, VERMONT—The shovel to dig the grave for my mother-in-law's ashes was in the back seat of my rental car as I drove here to the cemetery.

With world enough and time we could have dug the hole with our hands, probably, but it wouldn't have been as neat. And, naturally, the digging would have been much slower.

The shovel made the work simple, which, in character, differed rather radically from the life of the remarkable, complicated, and lovely woman whose remains we would inter here on a sweet, nearly eighty-degree day when an occasional cloud offered relief from what passes for summer heat in Vermont.

The cemetery, which contains graves of people who died nearly two hundred years ago, would have charged forty dollars to dig a small hole in which to place an urn full of ashes of recently alive skin and bones and love.

The Vermont branch of my family is not cheap. But when a cemetery employee said even he considered forty dollars too much, my mother-in-law's best friend in the universe said no one would pay forty dollars—not when we could, and should, do the job ourselves. So we came here with a plain garden shovel, the type you might use to transplant hostas. I leaned the shovel against a tree and waited until Russell—my wife's oldest brother, Elizabeth's oldest son—arrived.

"This is my job," he said quietly.

"I know," I said. "I know."

A small, selfish part of me wished for a chance to dig the hole, place the urn in it and say the closing prayer to tie together this amazing day. But I have learned, I hope, when to disappear into the background. So I handed the shovel to Russell, and he slammed it into the moist earth.

He was purposeful, full of clarity and grace. He split the ground on four sides and peeled off a chunk of green Vermont turf that spoke of recent rains and monarch butterflies and the kind of sugary skies, overhead just then, that give atheists lapses of disbelief.

"Two feet," I told him. That's how deep the hole had to be.

As I say, I understood what a privilege it was for Russell to dig the hole. And even as he shoveled he said, "It feels like an honor."

Elizabeth's grandson and I watched as Russell leaned to his work with persistence and dug coffee-colored earth out of Betty's final home. (Some called her Elizabeth, some Betty, and some—in touch with her special vision and direction—called her simply Bet.)

People who knew Betty thought it awkward that she could be confined to a granitelike box no more than eight inches high. Betty Locke had never been close to suffering such constraint her whole long and intriguing life. She tended to move about with the beauty—but unpredictability—of a butterfly.

The way we said goodbye to Betty is how funerals should be. Doing it this way acknowledges the reality of our death, our earth to earth, our dust to dust.

We do so many unwise things at graveside services to shelter us from the finality of death. We set up a tent to protect us from the sun. We use Astroturf to hide the earth dug out to create the grave. We leave before the body is lowered into the ground.

Wrong. Wrong. All dead wrong.

This is how we did it: When it was time, Russell picked up the urn and, arms quaking, set it into the bottom of the hole—where, by coincidence or providence—he had struck the flat side of a boulder in this stony soil.

Then we came by, most of us, and threw dirt in the hole as a final reminder that the ball of dust on which we live eventually reclaims us all.

Later, after champagne and potato salad at the nearby church, the love of Bet's life and I came back to the grave and filled in the dirt. Each of us stomped down the earth.

Just as we finished, that very instant, a monarch butterfly—as if having someplace else to go, someplace eternal—flitted over our shoulders and was gone.

Rituals Celebrate the Mysteries of Life
September 1, 1991

ROCHESTER, NEW YORK—Repeating a ritual two thousand years old, the priest held naked baby Julia and three times immersed her in water up to her neck. She didn't even cry.

Around the baptismal font were her parents, grandparents, godparents (my wife and I), cousins, and so forth, collected here from as far away as Utah and Connecticut, for no other reason than to witness this moment, of which Julia will remember nothing.

When I was younger and knew more, I considered such rituals silly crutches for shallow people. But I was wrong. Rituals are important if for no other reason than that they help us remember what we simply must not forget.

Our lives, in fact, are filled with rituals. Some, like baptism, are highly structured and underpinned by centuries of analysis and practice. Others—how we put our little children to bed at night, say, or the way a high school football team gathers around the coach for a pregame cheer—are improvised, fluid. They tend more toward habit than ceremony.

But most have developed for a good reason—to let us pause long enough to notice that what we are doing is somehow important, somehow out of the ordinary. Or at least to let us focus on the meaning of the event at hand in a more concentrated way than simply letting it happen.

Think back over the past few months and you'll probably count dozens of rituals or ceremonies you have observed or in which you participated. Besides Julia's baptism, I can think of a funeral service, a wedding, and many worship services, each a ritual that contained within it subsets of rituals.

But by no means are all rituals religious in nature.

The president's annual State of the Union Address is nothing less than a civic ritual. The same is true of inaugurations and even ribbon-cuttings.

Similarly, many of the drills, movements, procedures, and parades of the military—so fresh in mind because of the Gulf War—are rituals. At the end of each softball game I play in, we stage a ritual. The teams line up for a quick handshake.

Other rituals: We light birthday candles and blow them out.

Statesmen lay wreaths on the tombs of soldiers. We sing the national anthem before baseball games. And on and on.

Not all rituals, of course, are permeated with deep meaning. Some are silly (and sometimes are meant to be). Some are created to manipulate and control. But most rituals are a civilizing, humanizing influence.

They are inventions—sometimes extravagantly designed—to keep us from having to devise appropriate behavior again and again. We say words—wedding vows are a good example—that long years of refinement and repetition have infused with an almost mystical level of meaning.

There may be both mystery and meaning to our rituals, but the ceremonies themselves simply provide an occasion for recognizing mystery and meaning that were already there. Rituals are not—indeed, they cannot be—meaningful if they are separated from the larger truths to which they are designed to point.

A pregame cheer, for instance, does not create a football team. Rather, it reminds players that they are already members of a team and now they must play like it. The water used in Julia's baptism, for another example, does not stay on her forever, marking her as a visible member of what the Apostles' Creed calls the "holy catholic Church." Rather, it was a sign, pointing to the fact that, in a special way, she has been sealed as belonging to that church.

I'm glad I got to watch Julia's wide-eyed response to her baptism. It was a reminder of the importance of rituals—and of the need to study their content so as not to miss the sometimes profound truths to which they merely provide directions.

Take Care, Lest We Leave No Memories to Cherish
March 29, 1998

I have just learned that a month after my great-uncle Fabian's wife died in October 1945, he wrote a letter to his niece describing that terrible day. In his imperfect English he said:

"Anna got up on the morning of Sunday Oct the 14th 8 oclock and went in the kitchen dropped rigth down on the floor; of course I got to her in a secund or two.

"She was onconscos but was breathing hard. As I could not verry well handle her alone, I put tree [that's also the way my Swedish grandmother, Fabian's sister, pronounced "three"] pillows under her head and run in to the next door neabors to get some help.

"And the lady come with me. I was only gone about 2 minutes. And then she [Anna] was sitting up trying to lace her shoes. She said What is the matter I am alright. But we got her to her bed and I went for an ambulanse to take her to the Hospital. Being Sunday and did not have a telephone it took me about 20 minutes to get back, but life was gone than. The woman that was with her said she died in five minutes after I left."

I have read and reread the words "life was gone." Fabian, who himself would die in 1951 five days after my sixth birthday, was eloquent in his adopted language as he expressed both his loss and his acceptance of it. In the gentle but direct Swedish way, he told the truth and came to the point. Life was gone. In their simple completeness, the words are remarkable.

If I ever met Fabian, I have no memory of it. Not only did he die when I was so young, but he lived in Yakima, Washington, and as far as I know was never at my grandparents' farm home in Illinois to visit his sister when I was there.

But recently a young member of that side of my family has taken an interest in things genealogical, and he's been sharing some of his finds with me—finds like Fabian's colorful letter.

I am grateful for these treasures but troubled because I'm afraid fewer and fewer of us appreciate how essential and fascinating these original documents are. Worse, we may have lost years of such historical material because we weren't creating it. Instead of letters, we were using the telephone—the very device I now know Fabian did not have in his house when Anna died.

Now that e-mail is becoming a widely used substitute for regular mail, we again have the means to save some of our personal correspondence (and, thus, vital parts of our histories) so our descendants can better understand us—and, ultimately, better understand themselves.

As I was reading Fabian's three-page letter, I kept wondering if he would reveal how Anna's death affected him, what it meant to him. Or would he keep it all inside the way other stoic Swedes in my family do?

Toward the end of the third page came this answer: "I am feeling as good as I did 10 years ago exept my nerves went Haywire at this last experience but am getting better. Could hardly write my name for a while. Am still shaky, but hope it will leve altogether soon."

"My nerves went Haywire," he discloses. "Could hardly write my name," he confesses. Imagine the anxiety and pain to unpack in those remarks.

Fabian was seventy-two years old when Anna, a year younger, died. And he was not afraid to tell his niece about his own frailties and grief.

Although much of our personal histories is mundane and unremarkable, we're fools if we fail to preserve whatever will let coming generations know that they are connected to the whole of our past, that someone was here before them, someone who, in tasting death, felt his nerves go haywire.

Without that perspective we might imagine ourselves to be alone on the journey. But we are not alone. We are surrounded by what the New Testament book of Hebrews calls a "great cloud of witnesses." And that is the comfort we need to leave our descendants through our records.

Storm Sheds New Light on a Familiar Place
June 21, 1998

DELAVAN, ILLINOIS—By the time we got to church, the early morning wind and rain had bullied its way through fields of my uncle's knee-high corn and pushed into town, unplugging electrical power in the whole building.

The preacher said the lights went out in the middle of the 8 A.M. service in the chapel, so they lit a few candles and carried on. (As far as I know, Christian worship has never actually required electricity.)

By the 9:30 service there still was no power, so we sat in the sanctuary in a kind of sacred twilight, two small candles on the altar offering the only light not strained through stained glass windows. The effect was altogether remarkable and engaging. And I gave thanks for an unexpected reminder that our alleged necessities often are no more than conveniences that insulate and distract us from reality.

The most stunning aspect of the dimly lit sanctuary was the depth of color that almost sang to us from the large round window above the altar. The occluded outside light made the window's blues especially profound in their richness, and I tried to remember ever seeing that window on any of the several times I came to this church as a boy.

There was the day in 1953 when we gathered here to bid Godspeed to my grandmother—dead of cancer at barely sixty-five. But my only vivid memory from that sad day is watching my other grandmother—herself already seventy-one—pat the neatly folded hands of Grandma Tammeus as we passed by her open casket.

I'm sure that as an eight-year-old boy it struck me as an odd and even gross thing for the living to touch the dead. But today that gesture seems to me to have been a loving and fearless act from a spontaneously gracious woman.

I cannot, however, bring to mind the lovely stained glass window from that day or even from the day seven years later when we collected here again to eulogize Grandpa Tammeus after his heart ran out of beats. The reason, I'm sure, is that on those and other occasions the electric lights in the sanctuary provided light pollution, dimming the window's thick colors.

I'm no Luddite. In fact, I am attached to much of the technology that makes the way most of us live possible. So do not hear my praise of church services without electricity as naive advocacy of some long-gone time of supposed innocence. Rather, what I mean to praise are interruptions of our increasingly unexamined expectations.

Those of us who live in cities and suburbs expect, at night, to hear auto traffic and neighborhood dogs and even low-flying aircraft as we slide away to sleep. I certainly do.

But the central Illinois farmhouse of my aunt and uncle is surrounded not by a grid of busy streets but by nothing more than fields of noiselessly growing corn and soybeans. The silence at night is breathtaking. Indeed, when I lie in bed and draw breath I hear nothing but the rhythmic seesawing of air in and out of me. It's almost eerie.

If the windows are open and I listen long enough, I may, eventually, hear a cricket, say, but the overwhelming sensation is immersion in gentle but insistent waves of silence, like shimmering heat rising from cornfields on a torrid day.

It's a reminder to me that not everyone lives—or needs to live—at my normal pace or decibel level. There are alternatives. And my strong, healthy, still-farming uncle in his middle seventies may be proof that such an alternative life can have benefits we ignore at our own peril.

At church, with the power gone, the organ was out of commission. Because of this interruption in our expectations, we listened to— and sang along with—a lively piano. I love organ music (my oldest sister is a Juilliard pipe organ graduate, so I'd better), but there's something refreshingly direct and simple about a happily percussive piano in a church sanctuary, and I was glad for the change.

On all counts, in fact, I was glad on this trip to have insights break in through overturned expectations. I just hope I can remember to look for them in other times and places.

How We Find and Define the Meaning of Life
October 24, 1999

BENNINGTON, VERMONT—The van in which I'm riding is moving down Route 7 just north of town. I'm staring out the passenger's side window at maples and oaks and birches (along with some green tamaracks) flaming up the hills with the colors of biodeath—reds, oranges, yellows, browns.

And I'm feeling entirely dispensable.

The annual leaf-changing miracle, which attracts huge crowds to Vermont, would happen without me, I realize. Indeed, in fifty-four years I have witnessed this show only twice—this year and last. Apparently it got along fine without me.

Not only am I a tourist here in Vermont, I'm a tourist everywhere, it turns out, and the natural processes of the world don't require my attendance.

Without me, all the rivers would run into the sea, breezes would corrugate surfaces of ponds, rain would soak fecund valleys.

Without me, the planets would circle the sun, the sun would burn, and the mysterious force of gravity would help to hold the solar system in place and cause tides to run in and out from this shore and that.

Without me, leaves would fall ahead of winter and decompose into the soil. Earthworms would help make that soil porous and the roots of forsythia bushes would plunge into the soil to suck up nourishment.

It is humbling to realize how unnecessary I am in this way, how completely independent of me nature can operate. Annie Dillard, in her new book, *For the Time Being*, ruminates about our usefulness:

"One death is a tragedy; a million deaths are a statistic." Joseph Stalin, that gourmandizer, gave words to this disquieting and possibly universal sentiment.

How can an individual count? Do individuals count only to other suckers, who love and grieve like elephants, bless their hearts? Of Allah, the Qur'an says, "not so much as the weight of an ant in heaven and earth escapes him." That is touching, that Allah, God, and their ilk care when one ant dismembers another, or note when a sparrow falls, but I strain to see the use of it.

No, she doesn't. Annie Dillard, clear-eyed, clear-hearted observer of both physical and spiritual chiaroscuro, understands well that God's caring about one sparrow is the model for us, calling us to care about each fallen human being. Proof that Dillard grasps this is in her very next sentence: "One small town's soup kitchen, St. Mary's, serves about 115 men a night."

Nature may lope along unhindered without us, but we would not. We need each other—desperately.

I don't want you to imagine that I am saying we have no connection with nature or that we can't derail it, at least temporarily. If the environmental movement has taught us anything, it is that everything we do can and does affect the ground and air (something Native Americans have long known). My point, rather, is that we are, at least individually, unnecessary to the working out of nature's laws. The profound implication of this truth is that our purpose must be found elsewhere.

We approach Bennington; the driver of the van is my father-in-law, a remarkably sturdy man who, on the very day we are riding, is turning eighty years of age. My wife and I have made the long trip from the heartland to honor his decades of service to his community, attachment to friends, faithfulness to eternal values, and love of family.

This is where and how people are necessary. This is how we find and define our meaning. We are there for one another. We are essential to one another.

The trees may blaze into fall color without us, the rivers may tumble toward level ground without us, but no one will be honored, comforted, nurtured, cared for, or loved without us—all of us, individually and collectively.

When we get to Bennington, we pick up my wife's brother at the hardware store he helps to manage and, with a full van now, go to eat lunch, laugh, and take note of eighty years of a man's life.

While we share a meal, the trees on the comely hills here continue changing, readying themselves for the fiercely cold nights and snowy days we can even now sense on the edge of the air each morning here. Let them change, those trees. They don't need us. Rather, we need us.

Let Life Conclude Like the Captivating Tone of a Bell
March 31, 2001

PORT CHARLOTTE, FLORIDA—I want to die smoothly, the way the sound of a struck bell slowly vanishes into the absorbent air.

Not now, of course. Not even soon. But when it does happen— decades from now, I hope—that's how I want to go. Like a struck bell.

I've been thinking a lot about death, oddly enough, on this pleasure trip only because death seems to insist on bringing itself to my attention. In fact, it has been relentless.

I have driven by small-town cemeteries in Missouri, Georgia, and Kentucky, noticing that the bodies are buried in rows much more orderly, no doubt, than the lives of those resting there now.

I've passed by the site of the Chickamauga Civil War battlefield near Chattanooga, Tennessee, where sixteen hundred Union and eighteen hundred Confederate troops became casualties. The deaths were bloody, cruel, and—at a Confederate strategic level—pointless.

I have seen a man in a small fishing boat on the Myakka River here on Florida's Gulf Coast gathering crab traps. Pelicans and seagulls followed him, squawking raucously as he'd toss to them the crabs he didn't want. How glad I was not to be dying like a rejected crab, fast food for hungry birds.

Even when I checked my answering machine at home, I found a message from one of my daughters that she was heading to the funeral of a young father of two of her dance students. Later she called to say how sad the day was and that she loved me and that two little girls don't have a daddy to say that to anymore.

Another answering machine check revealed that one of my wife's good friends had died of cancer sooner than we ever imagined she would.

There was all this and more. So I have given into death's relentless presence, its stammering refusal to go away. And I've been thinking about how I want to die. It is the inevitable conversation we all must have with ourselves. In some ways, it is the most important conversation, too, because it reveals not just whether we understand death but whether we understand life.

My desire to go out like a struck bell is precise. I don't want to go out like wind chimes, the street gangs of bells. Nor like assertive brass dinner bells, such as the one our cook in India rang to call us to meals when I was a boy.

No, just a lovely metal bell, metal struck on metal once, the tone slowly dying in the otherwise silent, conductive air. After I'm gone, people who knew me might remember me when they hear that bell tone, as if it were calling monks to vespers. Death like this would be pure, focused, sanctified.

I don't want to die like those little crabs, caught unaware and then simply heaved to noisy predators. Where is the beauty in that? Where the art? That's all instinct, all mindless appetite.

Nor do I have any interest in exploding against hot lead on some battlefield, even fighting for a good cause. There is too much about such a death that's given over to the decisions of others. I know that good people sometimes must die in this way. But I don't wish to volunteer for the job.

Nor do I want to go with no warning—shot as an innocent by-stander, run over by a careening truck, struck on the head by a falling brick, felled by an unanticipated heart attack, some blown-up aneurysm, some unspeakable surprise that snuffs me out like a half-burned candle.

No, there is no process in that, no drama, no time to get my affairs in order, whatever that means, no opportunity to do the proper choreography of death, the goodbyes, the thank-yous, the regrets, the conversations with God.

And what of simply dying of old age? What of my parts simply quitting, rusting to a halt? I could go quietly in my bed that way, in my easy chair.

This death has advantages over the gunshot, the brick on the head, the soldier's explosion. But it's too quiet for me, too unassuming. My ego would find it dissatisfying.

Let me ring out like a bell, a captivating tone that will linger like hope, like gratitude in the breeze, carried away like the body of a

Cheshire cat. I want that charming tone to resonate deeply in the hearts of those I leave behind.

And what I most want them to remember when they hear that soft chime is that how one dies doesn't matter a bit compared with how one lives. That's the part they must get right.

In an Uncertain World, a Source of Constancy
January 9, 2000

PARIS—The chill winter mist enveloping the Cathedral of Notre Dame tonight creates the same brooding atmosphere outside that's found inside the astounding old temple.

I am sitting in a small area near the main altar toward the front of the great sanctuary. The few dozen seats here are designated for people who wish to pray and are not just for tourists who have come to gawk at this twelfth-century monument to the divine.

So I pray, no doubt in a way that the faithful have prayed here for hundreds of years and the way they've prayed around the world throughout the two thousand years since Christianity branched itself off decisively from Judaism.

But I do not only pray. I also observe. And I think about the way in which the practice of this faith connects people across miles and centuries—people of incredible variety but all rooted in a Middle Eastern peasant by whose life our very calendar is figured.

This evening two men in dark suits, ties, and sweater vests are preparing the cloth for the altar and making other arrangements for a later worship service. Like chambermaids changing sheets, they flap and float the white cloth in the dark, candled air, before letting it settle on its holy place for the Mass.

Then, while one places candles in tall holders, the other checks the connection on the electrical cord to a microphone attached to a lectern. The cord, some awkward accommodation to modernity, is taped to the floor with what looks for all the world like duct tape.

Maybe that's part of what it takes to hold together a world religion—duct tape and what it represents: a willingness to adapt to the times to spread the steady word of hope that faith would speak to a troubled, skeptical, and distracted people.

On a pillar behind me is a plaque in French recording evidence that the faith represented by this huge stone cathedral is directly connected to the branch of the religion with world headquarters in

Rome. The May 30, 1980, visit to Notre Dame by Pope John Paul II (Jean-Paul, in French) is commemorated on the sign. This pope, now near the end of his long and important reign, took time nearly two decades ago to pay homage to the French people and to this famous symbol of the Roman Catholic vision of Christianity and those who pledge allegiance to it.

No doubt part of his reason for coming was that Notre Dame represents the faith that has survived these two millennia and that now claims one-third of the world's population as adherents.

I do not mean that its beginning was similar to the start of the faith. No, Notre Dame, though built in stages (beginning with a foundation stone laid by Pope Alexander III in 1163), was, even at its start, an architectural dream of huge proportions. That very size makes Notre Dame unlike the faith, which began with a tiny band of Jewish people in the backwaters of the Roman Empire—people who, whatever their hopes, could not have envisioned a French cathedral or a worldwide (if lamentably divided) fellowship of the faithful.

But just as there is a core to the religion—the life, death, and resurrection of Jesus Christ—so there is a core to Notre Dame. That centrality, at least viewed from the outside, is the big-boned, imposing presence that has stood for the faith's core, even as the city around the cathedral changed in breathtaking ways in response to history's often cruel, bruising, though sometimes celebratory evolution.

In the evenings now, the streets of Paris around Notre Dame are filled with small Peugeots and Renaults and Citroens and large tour buses. The lighted sidewalks are packed with tourists who seem to get drawn into the front entrance of the cathedral the way iron filings are attracted to a magnet. And the River Seine, along the edge of the grand edifice, provides a way for tourist boats to shine spotlights on Notre Dame as they pass.

So the building, like the faith, has survived. Inside now there is electricity, and you can buy postcards from small gift shops and souvenir medallions from vending machines. But the essence of Notre Dame is the same as it has been for centuries, just as the essence of the faith is the same two thousand years after the birth of its founder.

And in a world that seems to uproot nearly everything every two weeks, the constancy is enough to steal my breath.

When Religion and Culture Are at Odds
June 11, 2000

People of faith, imagining they're defending some divinely mandated position, sometimes circle the wagons around ground the culture has long since abandoned.

Often this leads religious people to wonder why others don't understand them. This is especially true of Christians, who are under biblical edict to share their beliefs and help draw others into the faith.

A matter now in the news—a move by Southern Baptist leaders to have their church declare that the Bible allows only men to be pastors—illustrates what I mean. That's because what's at play in this case is the ancient tension between a desire to uphold strongly held theological positions and a desire to speak a word of welcome and explanation to outsiders.

Sometimes when one religion or another takes a stand that goes against the grain of widely accepted movements in the culture—in this case, equal opportunity for women—it's the culture that's wrong. And nearly all religions are called to be countercultural in some way, challenging conventional wisdom because it's not wisdom at all.

But history shows us that sometimes religions are wrong, no matter how loudly they appeal to authority to prove their case.

Galileo, for instance, did not spend the last years of his life in house arrest for jaywalking. Rather, the pope refused to accept Galileo's (and Copernicus's) idea that Ptolemaic cosmology was wrong. The church, in fact, found all kinds of theological reasons for defending a system that Galileo's telescope called into question.

But what many people even today—especially critics of the church—miss in the Galileo case is that it was much more complex than anyone then imagined.

As long ago as 1925, the English mathematician and philosopher Alfred North Whitehead pointed to this complexity in *Science and the Modern World:* "Galileo said that the Earth moves and the sun is fixed; the Inquisition said that the earth is fixed and the sun moves; and Newtonian astronomers . . . said that both the sun and the earth move. But now we say that any one of these three statements is equally true, provided that you have fixed your sense of 'rest' and 'motion' in the way required by the statement adopted."

In other words, Albert Einstein's theories of relativity (proposed long after Galileo) described the universe in a way that opened a whole new dimension to both Galileo's and the church's arguments—though, as Whitehead notes, Galileo's position was much more useful than the church's for scientific investigation at the time. Indeed, the church's arrogant refusal to affirm any truth in Galilean cosmology was one more futile attempt to imprison a truth it couldn't control.

Another example: Parts of the nineteenth-century American church declared slavery biblically defensible. This kind of thinking—rooted in a reverence for power and wealth, not in respect for human worth—also was reflected in our era in the now-abandoned Dutch Reformed Church's pro-apartheid position in South Africa.

At times, of course, religion's countercultural ways can help correct a run-amok culture. In the midst of the chaos of our time, think of Buddhism's wise call to be mindful and meditative. In a time of anarchistic spirituality, think of Islam's call to be faithful about such disciplines as prayer. Or think of the civil rights leadership that Martin Luther King Jr. and others offered out of a belief that oppressing people violates God's will.

But religion is most vulnerable to criticism when its positions seem reactionary, exclusive, and regressive, not liberating, inclusive, and open to the future.

When patriarchal systems are under attack throughout the culture, it's hard for many Americans to imagine what's worth defending in the statement on women scheduled for a vote at the Southern Baptist Convention's annual meeting this week in Florida.

Don't misunderstand. I'm not saying Baptists don't have a right to believe whatever they want. But when any religious body finds itself so remarkably out of step with the culture around it, it must ask whether, on that matter, the culture possesses more truth than it does. The answer may well be no, but the history of ecclesial abuse of authority in protection of discredited beliefs is long and painful. That history should make religions modest, though it rarely seems to.

Women Take Their Place as Senior Pastors
January 23, 2000

As the calendar slipped from the 1900s to the 2000s, we got all kinds of lists of the greatest people of the past one hundred years. For many publications, it was a cheap, easy, and natural feature.

One such list was produced by *Preaching*, a bimonthly magazine, and it was striking in that none of the century's top ten preachers (or even top twenty) was female. It was a reflection of an androcentrism in Christianity that is showing signs of dissolving, though the road ahead for women in the church is pocked with troubles.

Just for the record, here are the top ten preachers of the 1900s, according to *Preaching* magazine's board of contributing editors: James S. Stewart, Billy Graham, George Buttrick, Martin Luther King Jr., Harry Emerson Fosdick, G. Campbell Morgan, William Edwin Sangster, John R. W. Stott, D. Martyn Loyd-Jones, and Clarence Macartney. The next ten included Norman Vincent Peale, Peter Marshall, Leslie Weatherhead, and E. Stanley Jones.

Many of those names are unfamiliar to most Americans. Why? It's a measure of at least two things: How local the art and craft of good preaching has become and the insufferability of the sermons most of the more famous televangelists deliver.

I have served on a committee that oversees Presbyterian seminary students as well as a committee that helped my church select a new pastor. These experiences, which required reading and listening to countless sermons, convinced me that for some reason God is extraordinarily stingy with the gift of great preaching.

And yet the *Preaching* list raises the offensive question of whether great preaching is somehow beyond the exegetical and homiletic skills of women. The clear answer is no. Even if church history is limited just to this country, in fact, many examples can be found of fascinating women preachers. An unrepresentative list of some of the more spectacular would include Jemima Wilkinson, Sojourner Truth, Julia Foote, Amanda Berry Smith, and Aimee Semple McPherson.

But *Preaching*'s all-male list of great preachers does point to the church's difficulty of finding agreement on what role scripture and tradition allow women to play in the faith. In parts of Christendom it is a white-hot argument, and too often the debate is carried on with no evidence that anyone recalls the commandment of the faith's founder that his followers love one another.

Partly because some branches of the church—most notably Roman Catholicism—do not allow women to be ordained as clergy, the voices of some women have been heard in ways other than from the pulpit.

A good Catholic example in our time would be Joan Chittister, a

Benedictine nun who has become an international author and lec-
turer. With a directness rooted in confidence, she has said this to her
church: "The woman question is not going to go away no matter how
clearly the church says it must." Women, she has written, "are intent
on bringing their own piece of wisdom . . . to the reinterpretation of
a faith that once taught racism, anti-Semitism and slavery with as
much confidence as it does sexism today."

In many Protestant churches, ordaining women as members of the
clergy has been a relatively recent practice. In my own Presbyterian
denomination, for instance, the ordination of the first woman minister occurred in 1956, the same year in which United Methodists began ordaining females. The Episcopal Church in this country didn't
approve of ordaining women until 1976.

The practical effect of this misogynistic history is that only now
are some women becoming senior pastors at multistaff churches. It
has been relatively easy for women fresh out of seminary to find
jobs as associate pastors at large churches or as solo pastors of small
churches. But they've had difficulty breaking through the stained-
glass ceiling to become preachers at the most visible large churches.
Which, in turn, helps to account for why a list of top preachers of the
1900s includes no women.

I have long supported a policy of ordaining women to all church
offices, though I certainly recognize the right of denominations to
come to different conclusions based on their own understanding of
scripture and tradition. But I bet that if, in 2100, *Preaching* magazine
compiles a list of the top preachers of the last one hundred years,
more than half will be women.

Flashes of Light Illuminating the Deep Past
May 7, 2000

CHICAGO—What moved me most profoundly when I saw the
Field Museum's Dead Sea Scrolls exhibit here recently was the realization that scholars around the world have worked for decades
to reconstruct writing that's two thousand years old.

Imagine what that says about how much we value words. (And
imagine how humbling that is for a writer today. Will anyone care
about my own words even two thousand minutes after I'm gone?)

The effort to piece together and understand the Hebrew, Greek,
and Aramaic words found on these hundred-thousand-plus scroll

fragments has been international in scope and has required hands as steady and delicate as those of clockmakers.

Many of the scrolls—the first of which were discovered serendipitously by young Bedouin shepherds in the Judean desert in 1947—are torn or decayed. They must be carefully puzzled back together, and even then scholars sometimes must fill in blanks that time's relentless entropy has created. The wonder is that so much has been preserved.

And yet what has been saved is a marvelous treasure. The scrolls are what John McCarter, president of the Field Museum, calls "one of the greatest manuscript discoveries in the history of archaeology." It's one of the few "greatest" claims you're likely to hear that may actually be understated.

The scrolls contain books from the Hebrew Scriptures (the Old Testament), apocryphal books found in some Christian Bibles, and documents about the people who lived in the Qumran community, near where the scrolls were found in storage jars in eleven different caves.

(It's worth a trip to Chicago to see, but the Kansas City area is something of a center for Dead Sea Scrolls research, thanks mostly to Fred E. Young, emeritus academic dean of Central Baptist Theological Seminary. Young has compiled thousands of works about the scrolls that now are available to researchers on the seminary's Kansas City, Kansas, campus.)

Fragments on display at the Field Museum, which is presenting this exhibit in cooperation with the Israel Antiquities Authority, include parts of (or commentary on) the books of Leviticus, Psalms, Hosea, and Deuteronomy; a prayer for King Jonathan dating to about 100 B.C., and a calendar document listing special nights over a six-year period.

Scholars pore over these and nearly eight hundred other individuals' compositions that make up the Dead Sea Scrolls, looking for clues about who wrote them, how the authors and their contemporaries lived, and why the documents got saved.

It's sobering to imagine how much our written words reveal, but we all know—especially those of us who do this for a living—that words also can conceal, mislead, misrepresent, and propagandize. We also know that we can never say all about anything—all of which should infuse us with caution as we try to draw conclusions from written words, especially those by people long dead. Still, ancient words are small flashes of light into a mysterious time that has helped to shape us, and we ignore them at our peril.

There has always been a special connection between words and religious faith. How, after all, does Genesis say God created the world? Through words. The biblical witness is that God simply spoke the world into existence: "Then God said, 'Let there be light'; and there was light," is the way Genesis 1:3 reports it in the New Revised Standard Version.

Later in Genesis, God turns the power of naming things over to the people he created. In other words, God allowed people to use words to be God's partners in creation. Naming things was understood as a way of bringing something into being or at least affirming that being.

And when the author of the gospel of John wanted to tap into this profound respect for the creative power of words, he echoed Genesis by equating God incarnate, whom Christians call Jesus Christ, with what he calls "the Word." John begins his gospel this way: "In the beginning was the Word, and the Word was with God and the Word was God."

The revelatory power of words (in Christian theology, the Word, Jesus, is the full revelation of God) is found in many cultures and faiths, and at the Dead Sea Scrolls exhibit in Chicago, there is clear evidence that, despite the cacophonous noise of our culture, we continue to value important words. As we should.

A Scholar Who Helped Clarify God's Word
August 30, 1998

It's not unreasonable to ask what—after all these centuries—is left to learn about the Bible.

The simple answer is a lot, despite all the books, commentaries, sermons, concordances, criticisms, and meditations. Indeed, careful scholarship is essential to help followers of both Christianity and Judaism understand holy writ and its meaning for today.

That's why the recent death of the Reverend Raymond E. Brown is such a loss. Brown, seventy, was a Roman Catholic scholar who taught at a Protestant institution, Union Theological Seminary in New York, for nearly two decades. He was perhaps our era's most respected modern Christian student of the Bible.

His passion was understanding what writers of the Bible meant and how their first readers would have understood the words. Among his nearly forty books are definitive works on the biblical narratives about the birth and death of Jesus Christ. His next-to-last book, *An Introduction to the New Testament,* tries to tell people in the pews why all the minutiae of scholarship—the footnotes, the long arguments over precise meanings of Greek and Hebrew words—are so important.

And, more to the point, in this book Brown tried to help Christians, many of whom are abysmally ignorant about the Bible, grasp the meaning of the primary witness to the man they revere as Savior and Lord.

I had a rare chance last fall to hear Brown speak to an almost full gymnasium at Rockhurst University in Kansas City. It was heartening to see several hundred people spend a weeknight sitting quietly at the feet of a modest but clear pastor as he spoke about the Bible.

"It really has been an extraordinary century," he said. That, of course, applies to nearly all aspects of our lives, but certainly also to biblical scholarship, especially in the Catholic world, which, as Brown pointed out, entered into the modern study of the Scriptures in 1893 with encouragement from an encyclical by Pope Leo XIII. Scientific investigation of biblical claims, Brown said, had influenced the pope to set scholars loose.

Since then Bible scholarship has had ups and downs. In both Catholic and Protestant circles early in this century, Brown said, there were moves toward authoritarian decrees full of "utter rigor." These were about such issues as authorship and dating of the books of the Bible. The Catholic tendency in this was (over)matched in Protestantism by the rise of fundamentalism, which, as Brown said, "took the route of Biblical literalism."

By the 1930s, the world of biblical studies was divided into three:

Professional scholars in universities and some Protestant seminaries who were largely unconnected to Catholic scholars. These Protestants were engaged in the kind of historical criticism of texts the fundamentalists abhorred.

The fundamentalists themselves, who were defining and defending biblical literalism.

Catholic scholars, most of whom were engaged in technical areas of study, such as word meanings.

All this began to change by midcentury, Brown said, with the discovery of earlier and earlier manuscripts of biblical books and with a 1943 encyclical from Pope Pius XII that moved the Catholic Church to give more professional training to Bible translators and allowed those translators to use modern methods of critical study.

Indeed, this tended to narrow differences between Catholic and Protestant scholars. In 1949 Brown himself went to study in Rome, where he began his long, remarkably productive journey as a Bible scholar.

Several decades ago, Brown noted, so much intriguing ecumenical biblical scholarship was going on that "there was a brief moment when we thought Camelot had arrived. But Camelots don't last."

Indeed, late in his life Brown worried that the media ignore scholarly work by theological centrists. Worse, he said, such work doesn't get communicated well by the church to people in the pews. Instead, most attention goes to such fringe scholarship as that being done by the so-called Jesus Seminar, a group of scholars who seem most interested in what they don't believe.

And yet Brown was no pessimist. He understood the inherently explosive power of the book he spent his life studying.

"The gospel," he said, "will have its word even after this century passes by." And that word will be clearer because of Brown's vital work.

Violating Any Sacred Space Offends All
August 18, 1996

ABIQUIU, NEW MEXICO—The monks are in their holy place. Let all the earth keep silence before them.

Or, if not all the earth, at least the half dozen of us who have come here to the Monastery of Christ in the Desert for the vespers service, in which fifteen Benedictine monks pray ancient words from the Psalms and, in their well-ordered cycle, prepare for day's end.

The chapel here in the stunning Chama Canyon wilderness—I had to drive thirteen miles on a narrow, crooked dirt road to find the monastery's sanctuary-in-the-round—is sacred space for these men. Huge windows let in slants of late afternoon light and let us look out on the craggy hills, unto which, with the psalmist, we lift up our eyes.

My heart lately has been attached to the idea of sacred space, especially in response to the burning this year of many predominantly black churches in the South. Indeed, I had thought we'd finally run out the string on those awful fires, but then I picked up the *Albuquerque Journal* recently and saw the picture on page A3.

This one was in Kentucky. An FBI agent was shown coming out of a church door, above which scorch marks were clearly visible.

What pains me so much about this evil is something beyond the apparent racism that has put so many black churches in hatred's bull's-eye. My pain has more to do with how much sacred space means to me and how violated I would feel if my own church, say, were to be attacked. I know the monks here at Christ in the Desert would feel similarly wounded.

That's because sacred space is home. It's where the heart and soul go to rest, to be accepted for who and what they are, to be loved. It's one of the places to encounter the divine. It's a place to go and, as author Kurt Vonnegut once said, to daydream about God.

I know the corners and spaces of my own church in Kansas City. I know the stunning colors—especially the blues—of the sanctuary's stained glass. I know the high, sloped ceiling, the clerestory windows above our heads. I know how it feels to stand in the pulpit there and to sit in the pews. I can be there alone and remember the majestic tones of Handel's *Messiah* and Verdi's *Requiem,* both of which I've heard there, or the seductively simple Sunday school song, "Jesus Loves Me."

I know many of the people who—faithful as Abraham, as Job, as Mary—show up on Sunday mornings to lift their voices in worship. When we sing a favorite hymn, a friend and I smile at each other as a way of recalling the stories we've shared about what that song means to us.

I have said farewell to countless friends in that room, as we gathered as a community of faith for funeral services. I have seen babies baptized—babies now fully grown—and have heard us all promise to help guide those children as a church family. I have seen one of my own daughters married in that sanctuary.

I have cried tears of personal pain there and sung songs of eternal joy there. I have listened to comforting words from the pulpit and deeply disturbing words of challenge, too. I have heard scripture read and have felt scripture read me.

I have gathered around the communion table with my family of faith to share the sacred meal, the Lord's Supper. And I've prayed there for miracles, both simple and elaborate.

Is my experience unique? Not at all. Different religious traditions share something similar.

The book of Exodus, for instance, in the Hebrew scriptures, says the people of Israel felt God's presence in the tabernacle, or Tent of Meeting, which Moses set up according to instructions from the Lord. "The glory of the Lord filled the tabernacle," Exodus 40:35 tells us in the New International Version. Which helps explain the sacredness of such space.

This same sense of God's presence in a community of faith is present in a Jewish temple I sometimes visit. There, as part of the service, a rabbi reads the names of each member of the congregation who has ever died in that particular week over the life of the temple. History rings through that sacred space.

The monastery I'm visiting this evening certainly isn't the only sacred space near Abiquiu, here in northern New Mexico. Just outside of town, in fact, is a lovely mosque, which has become sacred space for an Islamic community that has settled here amid the red rock hills of the high desert country.

And on this trip I also was able to visit sacred Mormon space in Salt Lake City's Temple Square, where the Mormon Tabernacle Choir's amazing sounds ring forth almost daily.

People of many faiths, in short, have a deep attachment to sacred places. To violate that space, to desecrate it, to attack it for vile and manipulative reasons is nothing less than evil.

I don't know anyone personally in the congregations whose churches have been torched this year. But my heart grieves for them because sacred space is precious to me. And a violation of it anywhere is a violation of mine.

Clinton's Experience Shows Christianity's Rifts
April 12, 1998

The only conclusion to be drawn from the theological explosions detonated when Bill Clinton received the sacrament of communion in a Roman Catholic Church on his trip to Africa is that, this side of heaven, Christendom will never be united.

To those of us who imagine the benefits of reconciliation under the broad umbrella that is Christianity, Clinton's experience is painful evidence that the theological distance between (and often within) various branches of the faith will keep it divided until history's end.

The president, a Southern Baptist who attends a Methodist church, knows that, as a rule, the Catholic Church forbids serving Protestants the Lord's Supper. But he appeared to act in good faith when he received the sacrament in South Africa from the Reverend Mohlomi Makobane. Father Makobane, in fact, had given a White House advance team a fact sheet that said: "Due to recent rulings from the South African Conference of Bishops, non-Catholics may take Catholic Communion." So Clinton did.

Those same South African bishops later said no such policy exists, and Cardinal John O'Connor of New York said it was "legally and doctrinally wrong in the eyes of the Catholic Church" to serve Clinton the bread and wine.

Also, His Righteousness Himself, the Reverend Jerry Falwell, pronounced Clinton "could not take communion in most, or certainly many, Baptist churches. Certainly not in the one where I've been pastor for 42 years because of the fact that he's not willing to come forward, confess his sins and seek help."

It would be hard to write a brief statement containing more snotty judgmental assumptions than that, but Falwell often has been capable of it.

It must be difficult for non-Christians to understand how this reenactment of the Last Supper—meant to be an affirmation of God's forgiveness and grace—can cause so much dissension. Indeed, it's also difficult for many of us who bear the name of Christ to comprehend it.

The crucial theological nuance here (and, to be fair, many people consider it much more than a nuance) is how to view the bread and wine (or, as most of us Protestants call it because we don't use wine, "fruit of the vine").

The Catholic tradition says those elements become the substance of the body and blood of Jesus Christ. It's a doctrine referred to as transubstantiation, which says that only the appearance of bread and wine remain. There are many shades of understanding among Protestants, but generally they view the bread and wine less literally, though many affirm Christ's real presence in the sacrament.

In some traditions—the Anglican, for instance—communion, also known as the Eucharist, is the center of worship. As such, it helps people understand that, like their neighbors, they need forgiveness and can receive a sign of that gift at what's called the Lord's Table. In most—but not all—Protestant denominations, any baptized Christian is welcome to participate.

As a Protestant, I know both the joy of receiving the sacrament in a Catholic church and the pain of being told I'm not welcome. Several years ago I attended a Catholic service in Rochester, New York, and, though I did not expect to be offered communion, I heard the priest issue a broad invitation that clearly included me. I found it deeply moving to be connected to my broader family of faith in that way.

Likewise, I also found it hurtful to know I was not welcome to receive the sacrament at a Catholic Ash Wednesday service this year in Kansas City. I knew that beforehand, but the ache of exclusion surprised me. After that service, a Catholic friend said to me, "We have to change this. This has to end."

And yet Bill Clinton's experience shows that despite Jesus' own prayer (in John 17:21, New Revised Standard Version) that his followers "may all be one," such unity is illusory. Sadly, other faiths are badly divided, too. And all this division offers the world a lamentable and shameful witness.

Chapter and Verse on Jerry Falwell's Gaffe
January 31, 1999

Give the Reverend Jerry Falwell this: He gets people talking about religion, no matter how silly, arrogant, or misleading he may be. And often he's all three.

Most recently he stirred the waters by preaching a sermon in which he said the Antichrist probably is alive today and is a male Jew.

Naturally, Jews were outraged. One of the more articulate responses to Falwell came from Rabbi James Rudin of the American Jewish Committee: "This is part of what I call millennial madness. To single out any one man and particularly to identify him as Jewish plays into some latent and historical anti-Semitism from the past."

In later trying to explain himself, Falwell not only compounded the affront to Judaism but also managed—as is his occasional wont—to offend people of his own faith by distorting traditional Christian doctrine. Falwell said the belief that the Antichrist "will, by necessity, be a Jewish male" is "2,000 years old and has no anti-Semitic roots. This is simply historic and prophetic orthodox Christian doctrine that most theologians, Christian and non-Christian, have understood for two millennia."

How was Falwell wrong? I hesitate to count the ways for fear of losing track, but let me at least start to point.

Falwell's problem is that he has pledged allegiance to but one interpretation of the enigmatic idea of Antichrist and declared that view the truth. Christian history, however, is replete with many ideas on the subject.

That said, it is true that in one strain of Christian thinking—represented by the sixteenth-century Catholic prelate and scholar Robert Bellarmine—the Antichrist is a Jew who arises from the biblical tribe of Dan. This notion is based on such Bible passages as Genesis 49:17 and John 5:43. But to describe this thinking as orthodox Christian doctrine understood by everyone for two thousand years is simply to ignore huge chunks of church history.

One can draw legitimately different ideas of Antichrist by looking at different passages of the Bible itself, from the book of Daniel in the Hebrew scriptures to the New Testament books of John, the letters of John, Revelation, and II Thessalonians. Indeed, I John 2:18, in the New Revised Standard Version, says "many antichrists" already have come.

Among the many questions end-times theologians must wrestle with when they step into the Antichrist minefield are whether he (if one can even assign sex to Antichrist) is one or many, whether Antichrist is an individual or some kind of powerful institution, and whether he is a civil or a religious power.

In contrast to Falwell's certainty that Antichrist is a Jewish male among us today, many of the sixteenth-century leaders of the Protestant Reformation declared the Roman Catholic papacy itself to be Antichrist. (In most places, that offensiveness has yielded, and it wasn't unusual to find public Protestant prayers for the pope's recent visit to Mexico and St. Louis.)

But listen to these brutal remarks expressing this view from none other than John Calvin, father of the Reformed Tradition: "Whoever will duly examine and weigh the whole form of ecclesiastical government as now existing in the Papacy, will find that there is no kind of spoliation [it means plunder] in which robbers act more licentiously, without law or measure. . . . We maintain that their kingdom is the tyranny of Antichrist."

And in the twelfth century, long before the Reformers, Joachim of Flora, a medieval inventor of prophetic systems, also wrote that Antichrist would arise from inside the church and hold high office.

But, in fact, the list of people and institutions identified as Antichrist candidates over the years is long and remarkable. It includes the Emperor Nero, Napoleon, Franklin D. Roosevelt, Hitler, Stalin, Henry Kissinger, Ronald Reagan, Sun Myung Moon, Saddam Hussein, Yasser Arafat, Louis Farrakhan, Bill Gates, Bill Clinton, and Barney the Dinosaur.

It is, of course, impossible in an essay of this length to do justice to centuries of serious biblical scholarship on the end of the world, the Second Coming of Christ, and the identity of Antichrist. But it's possible at least to hint at the rich and varied interpretations available and to say that many parts of mainline Christianity, unlike Falwell, pay precious little attention to any of this. They prefer, instead, to focus on the call to share good news with the world now and to minister to people in need.

But if Falwell still wants to say something useful about Jewish males, he at least could apologize for Christianity's historic anti-Semitism.

Why Other Nations Fear Our Public Theology
May 9, 1999

The long list of our politicians who have imagined America is God's chosen land now includes Vice President Al Gore, who very much wants to be president.

But as we count him among the prophets of God's unique blessing of our nation, we also would do well to remind ourselves that Gore's pronouncement on this subject carries with it the potential for great mischief and arrogance.

Gore's place among our many public theologians was secured by a recent speech he made to the Detroit Metro Chapter of the National Association for the Advancement of Colored People in which he said:

> I believe that God's hand has touched the United States of America—not by accident but on purpose. He has given us not just a chance but a

mission to prove to men and women throughout this world that people of different racial and ethnic backgrounds, of all faiths and creeds, can not only work and live together but can enrich and ennoble both themselves and our common purpose.

I have no problem with the notion that America can—indeed should—be a model for racial, ethnic, and religious harmony. It's important work on a planet aflame with the deadly results of hatred rooted in our differences.

But is it wise for elected officials to be announcing what our national purpose is based on their particular belief in God? No. It's dangerous and arrogant, and it contributes to the oppressive image of America others in the world sometimes hold. Indeed, citizens of other countries have long had reason to be suspect of our public theology. Listen to a sample of the cloying strain of chosenness some of our presidents have professed:

- "My God! How little do my countrymen know what precious blessings they are in possession of, and which no other people on earth enjoy!"—Thomas Jefferson
- "This generation of Americans has a rendezvous with destiny."—Franklin Delano Roosevelt
- "Our nation was created to help strike away the chains of ignorance and misery and tyranny wherever they keep man less than God wants him to be."—Lyndon B. Johnson
- "I've always believed that this land was set aside in an uncommon way, that a divine plan placed this great continent between the oceans to be found by a people from every corner of the earth who had a special love of faith, freedom and peace."—Ronald Reagan

I am not suggesting America isn't unique. Nor am I downplaying the way, at our best, we have given hope to a world whose people have fled to our shores to escape the poverty, oppression, and rape of their own lands.

But I am saying that when we entangle the historical role we've often played—promoter of liberty, advocate of human dignity—with a theology declaring America God's designated hitter, we risk the sin of misplaced pride. Beyond that we are likely to attract the kind of mistrust of our actions that we regularly see in people around the world.

In the ultimate scheme of things, God may have a special role for America. But that idea is impossible to prove to a world with thousands of different ideas about who, if anyone, God is. Beyond that, it's foolish to leave the discernment and announcement of any such role to our civic leaders.

Al Gore may or may not be a good Southern Baptist and may or may not be in daily prayerful contact with the sovereign of the universe. But as citizens of this country we are under no obligation to cede to him (or to Pat Buchanan or Jesse Helms or any other public figure) the task of announcing to us what our role as a nation might be in the divine scheme of things. Indeed, we would be balmy to do so.

The author Sinclair Lewis once accurately described the tug and pull most of us feel about being Americans and wrestling with our national role: "Intellectually I know that America is no better than any other country; emotionally I know she is better than every other country."

America, in fact, does have advantages over many other lands—in resources, in its history of defending high values, in the freedom it cherishes. But if we insist to the world these advantages accrue to us because we live in God's chosen land, we do so at great peril.

Maybe we should pray for (the back of) God's hand to touch Al Gore—and all candidates for public office—as a gentle reminder not to exploit divine things for political gain.

Settling a Religious Dispute after Five Hundred Years
June 13, 1999

The key dispute in a Christian family feud so profound it has shaped the very world in which we live has been resolved—after nearly five hundred years.

The Roman Catholic Church and the Lutheran World Federation have reached final agreement on a doctrinal debate that grew into the sixteenth-century Protestant Reformation in which a key dispute was over how humans are saved, or "justified," to use an oft-employed theological term.

Is salvation, which is to say being made fit for eternal relationship with God, a gift of God's grace or must people earn their way into

God's favor by good works? This core question, which has become entangled with many complexities, split Western Christianity when Martin Luther addressed it in the early 1500s.

Luther, until then an obscure German monk teaching at a small university, insisted the church was wrong to teach that good works somehow were necessary to salvation. It was one of many complaints he had against the church.

The church had fallen into the indefensible habit of raising money by selling "indulgences," instruments used in the granting of forgiveness of sins. Sinners who wanted to repent were to show contrition, confess to a priest, and do penitential work to atone for their waywardness. But that work could be avoided by purchasing indulgences.

Luther correctly concluded that the system was abusive and unbiblical. With that as a kindling point, the Protestant Reformation began, and the church has remained divided, over salvation and other issues, for nearly five hundred years. (In the eleventh century the church had split into the Eastern Orthodox and Roman Catholic branches.)

Although many other schisms have divided the faith since then, those three divisions—Catholic, Orthodox, and Protestant—remain today.

But now Lutherans (including the Evangelical Lutheran Church in America but not Missouri Synod or Wisconsin Synod Lutherans) and Catholics have agreed on final wording of a "Joint Declaration on the Doctrine of Justification." Years in the making, it sets forth a mutual understanding of salvation and says both sides now should quit condemning the doctrinal stances of the other on this matter.

Although this is oversimplified, the agreement essentially concludes that Luther was right that humans are saved solely by God's grace and that good works are done in response to that gift as a way of showing gratitude.

The declaration, which runs some thirteen single-spaced pages, is an important achievement and may be useful as a model for resolving divisions in other religions, such as Judaism and Islam, and for settling countless other disputes among Christians.

Does the new accord mean Christendom is soon to achieve reunification? Unfortunately, no. There simply are too many divisions in the faith to imagine such a result—barring a miracle—within the next century.

But the Lutheran-Catholic agreement does show that openheart-ed discussions based on mutual trust can lead to discovery of common ground, and it may behoove the church to pursue just such an approach on other doctrines that divide it, such as the sacraments, ordination to ministry, and interpretation of the Bible.

It's important, however, that the church, in pursuing unity, not confuse it with rigid uniformity. That is, the church would do well to identify what author Rex Koivisto, in his book *One Lord, One Faith*, calls its "core orthodoxy," by which he means the irreducible center to which all Christians must remain tethered.

But in finding that center, the church must not discourage a variety of expressions of the faith. In other words, it must be willing to allow for—and even encourage—differences on secondary matters because those differences represent the church's richness by reflecting various perspectives and traditions of the faithful.

The Lutheran-Catholic accord is good news for the whole religious world. But nothing will be gained if the goal now becomes an institution that speaks with one voice on every matter.

Indeed, rather than seeking a false unity, Christianity might do well to consider unity on core orthodoxy only and then simply agree to respect different approaches to secondary matters. That approach might be so liberating it could allow more time for feeding the hungry, clothing the naked, bearing one another's burdens . . .

We Don't Read the Bible; We Assimilate It
July 4, 1999

BALDWIN CITY, KANSAS—What we love, we collect. And that gives me something in common with the late Bishop William A. Quayle, president of Baker University here in the 1890s. Like Quayle, I collect Bibles.

But that's where the resemblance ends. The ones I collect are not rare and valuable. Rather, I'm interested in different translations to compare and contrast ways the original Hebrew, Greek, and Aramaic has been rendered into English.

The internationally known Quayle Rare Bible Collection at Baker is to my collection what the Hope Diamond is to a rhinestone. And yet, in an important sense, each collection is, for people of faith, equally priceless. That's because Christians and Jews believe scripture contains God's authoritative word, though to be sure there are endless intrafaith arguments about how to read and interpret the book.

In determining the eternal worth of our respective collections, it's finally irrelevant that in the Quayle assembly you can find a Bible published in 1611, the year the King James Version first was printed, while my batch includes some paperback Bibles that today would fetch up to fourteen cents at a garage sale—if a buyer made a particularly generous offer.

I mean no disrespect to the thousand-plus Quayle Bibles. I mean only that for people of faith what's important is the books' content. Indeed, the Quayle volumes are a true treasure that can be appreciated on many levels. Not only is this an important gathering of sacred texts, but also it contains countless examples of the art of making books, the skill of early printers, and the beauty created by careful artisans.

From writings on clay tablets thousands of years old, to an ancient synagogue scroll, to handwritten Bibles on parchment from fourteenth-century Spain, the Quayle collection is worth a careful look. And this examination is greatly enhanced by the curator, John M. Forbes, with his well-researched stories about both Quayle and the Bibles.

When Quayle (a great Methodist preacher and distant relative of former Vice President Dan Quayle) died in 1925, he left several hundred Bibles to Baker, a Methodist school that in 1996 dedicated a wonderfully attractive nineteenth-century Methodist English chapel that had been moved to Baldwin City from the village of Sproxton about a hundred miles north of London. (The Quayle collection and that chapel are a two-minute walk from each other on Baker's lovely campus.) Since Quayle's death, many other rare Bibles have been added to the collection.

What is it about the Bible that leads me to collect dozens of translations or that caused Quayle to acquire a first edition of the lyrical King James Version?

The place of sacred texts in history is long, central, and complex. Almost every religion has writings it considers hallowed, though naturally those faiths understand the origin, meaning, and purposes of them in different ways.

In Judaism and Christianity, the scriptures have always held a central and formative role. For Jews, not only do the Hebrew scriptures contain a history of the people, but also, more to the point, they tell the story of their relationship to God, and they present to the people God's requirements for living in relationship with each other, with others, and with their creator.

Those books were and are crucial to the identity of Jews. Indeed, the Jewish founder of Christianity, Jesus of Nazareth, almost certainly grew up memorizing scripture at the feet of a rabbi, probably starting with the book of Leviticus. However, the canon of the Christian New Testament, which offers the gospel (or good news) of Jesus, was not finally set for several hundred years after the life of Christ. Perhaps Athanasius, the bishop of Alexandria in the late fourth century, was most influential in determining which twenty-seven books to include.

For me, no one has said more lucidly than the Reverend Eugene Peterson (whose own popular paraphrase of the New Testament is called *The Message*) why people of faith are so attached to Bibles: They form us, he says. We ingest them and they make us who we are.

"Christians," he writes, "do not simply learn or study or use scripture; we assimilate it, take it into our lives in such a way that it gets metabolized into acts of love, cups of cold water, missions into all the world, healing and evangelism and justice in Jesus' name, hands raised in adoration of the father."

How could we not want to read such a book?

Hell Has Gotten Lousy Press Over the Years
October 31, 1999

Some weeks ago, Pope John Paul II stirred the theologically illiterate mainstream media from their self-imposed lethargy by describing hell as not so much "a place" but "the state of those who freely and definitively separate themselves from God." This raised eyebrows and actually created religious discussion about something other than whether Y2K will usher in the end of the world.

Halloween, that great Christian holiday, offers everyone, through culturally approved rites of fright and extortion (trick-or-treat), the chance to inspect beliefs about hell (and maybe heaven), including some of the ways the place (or "state," to use the pope's construct) has been described.

Friends, hell hasn't gotten very good press. Nor has the depiction of hell over the centuries been rigidly consistent. It's certainly true that the New Testament offers stark pictures of hell, and people who believe that the Bible should be taken literally are attached to descriptions of hell as eternal fire where there's weeping and gnashing of teeth and so on. (The Hebrew Scriptures, or Old Testament, talk about a dark and decidedly unpleasant place named "Sheol," where the dead are amassed.)

In his remarks about all this, the pope revealed again that he is not a biblical literalist when he said that to describe hell, the Bible "uses a symbolical language." It uses "images," he said, and "figuratively portrays" hell.

So, scary images of hell are not new. But they grew increasingly graphic in medieval and later times, especially in the seventeenth century, when John Locke's reward-and-punishment philosophy helped underpin both emergent capitalism and Christianity.

In *A History of Christianity,* Paul Johnson notes that the three "most influential medieval teachers, Augustine, Peter Lombard and Aquinas, all insisted that the pains of hell were physical as well as mental and spiritual, and that real fire played a part in them.

"The general theory was that hell included any horrible pain that the human imagination could conceive of, plus an infinite variety of others. Hence writers felt at liberty to impress their public by inventing torments. Jerome said that hell was like a huge wine press. Augustine said it was peopled by ferocious flesh-eating animals, which tore humans to bits slowly and painfully, and were themselves undamaged by the fires."

Other fierce pictures of hell that Johnson describes include people (well, bankers, really) being boiled in molten gold and members of other professions being beaten with red-hot hammers. In one vision, each square mile of hell is occupied by a hundred million souls and "would thus be treated 'like grapes in a press, bricks in a furnace, salt sediment in a barrel of pickled fish, and sheep in a slaughterhouse,'" Johnson writes.

It's worth noting that in recent times the emphasis of Christian theology has moved away from a description of hell as a place of punishment for people who failed to reach heaven. This shift, at least in part, reflects the Protestant Reformation's emphasis on salvation by grace, which holds that God would prefer to spend eternity with everyone he created. But, according to this stance, people exercise free will and are free to say yes or no to God's gift of eternal life.

The pope's comments reflected this same approach. Eternal damnation, he said, "is not attributed to God's initiative because in his merciful love he can only desire the salvation of the beings he created." Rather, John Paul II said, "damnation consists precisely in definitive separation from God, freely chosen by the human person and confirmed with death that seals his choice forever."

Halloween, as an American cultural phenomenon, tends to devalue the reality of death and questions about eternity by turning all that into a gaudy commercial enterprise. The idea is that if we can laugh at death and hell they can't be very frightening. This approach is not surprising, for nearly the whole of American culture is terrified of questions about death and does its best to deny death's reality. But this is a foolish stance, for if the unexamined life is not worth living, the unexamined death may not be not worth dying.

Music Opens a Window to a Spiritual Reality
September 26, 1999

It was when the choir of which I was a part sang the gently moving phrase "In the desert ways I sing" that the poignant music resonated with some deep place in my spirit and filled my eyes with unbidden tears.

My voice caught and I had to let the rest of the bass section carry on for a bar or two without me. Somehow I regrouped for the second part of the repeated last phrase: "Spring, O Living Water, spring!"

And I wondered anew just how music is able to touch us and change us, reveal us and shape us. Music, indeed, is one of the best arguments I know that humans are not just physical beings but also have an equally real spiritual dimension.

Music quickens our passive souls, offering testimony that we are not merely corporeal products of evolving cells. Rather, in some mysterious way, we are receivers of divine messages mediated to us through many means. None of those means is more persuasive than music, which the essayist and poet Joseph Addison, three hundred years ago, described as "the greatest good that mortals know / And all of heaven we have below."

I am not in any meaningful sense a musician. Most of the musical talent in my family went to my oldest sister, a Juilliard School of Music pipe organ graduate. When I was younger, I sang a little and, for several years, played the oboe badly. I can still carry a tune and read music, but the instrument in my throat is untrained.

Still, when our church music director asked my wife and me to be part of a special performance to celebrate his twenty-five years with our congregation, I was glad for the chance. Accompanied by the Kansas City Chamber Orchestra, we did two stunning pieces one recent Sunday afternoon, the brooding *Requiem* by John Rutter and *Te Deum*, a rhythmically challenging, often soaring, new Andrew Carter work that also features the charming high voices of a children's choir.

Music is both a team and an individual art. The single notes that, together, form a chord find their parallel in the individual voices and instruments that, together, form an orchestra or choir. The whole, however, is greater than the sum of its parts.

If it all works right, what the audience hears is a coordinated, unified totality in which all the singularities are subsumed by an organizing vision that sculpts the electric air in something like the way the composer imagined it when the work took form. And yet within that whole there is space for recognizing and even honoring the individual parts.

In our performance, for instance, there were several brief solos. In the Carter piece these almost plaintive but confessional words are offered with humility (but without accompaniment) by a soprano voice: "We believe that thou shalt come to be our Judge." And in the Rutter work a soprano solo, over the low humming of the orchestra, says, "Blessed are the dead who die in the Lord, for they rest, for they rest, for they rest from their labors."

With these solos, there is no sense that someone has broken away from the whole of the chorus to freelance. Rather, the audience is given to understand that the soloist comes forward with the choir's permission to speak a word on behalf of the unit. It is, I think, this feeling of integration, this fully realized fabric emerging from warp and woof that gives music some of its power.

And yet, in some ways, all art works that way. In great writing, not only is there content of thought to be grasped, but content mediated by the singularities of grammar and syntax and spelling and style and tone and on and on. And in painting we are given the entirety of a scene, but it comes through individual brush strokes and color and light and texture and fixative.

This kind of wholly consummated music finds the cycles humming deep inside our naked vulnerability and resonates with the essence of our beings. It can give us new spiritual eyes and let us see new possibilities or, at least, renew old, moribund possibilities.

The nineteenth-century essayist and critic Walter Pater understood the holistic nature of music (though he may have underrated other arts) when he wrote: "All art constantly aspires towards the condition of music."

That fully woven condition gives music the awesome ability to make our spirits both soar and weep.

The Haunting Eyes of the Boy at Auschwitz
June 25, 2000

WASHINGTON—It's the specificity that finally jackhammers through the cliches about historic evil and shatters your heart here at the U.S. Holocaust Museum.

It's not the unfathomable number of 6 million dead Jews; it's an oboe, now forever silent, that once belonged to Kurt Michaelis of Berlin's Jewish Cultural Society. It's not the stark photos of the nameless human skulls and bones that confronted Allied liberators of the World War II concentration camps—though surely those pictures offend the soul unspeakably. Rather, it's the thousands of photos of real people, now murdered, whose very existence violated Adolf Hitler's twisted sense of who deserved to live. It's those pictures, yes, but also the hairbrushes, the toothbrushes, the countless shoes of the dead.

Until this trip to Washington, I'd not had a chance to visit the Holocaust Museum. To say that it's a must-see destination for the world is to state the obvious. What was not immediately obvious to me when I entered the museum was that I would spend much of my time here wrestling with my own Germanness.

I'm half German, half Swedish. My paternal great-grandparents came to the United States from Germany near the end of our Civil War. They were farmers. Nothing I know about them or their many children and grandchildren (who included my father) suggests anything but people devoted to hard work, religious faith, and family.

And yet it was precisely such people who followed Hitler into the heartless darkness of Nazism. So the ultimate question about the Holocaust is not just how it happened but also whether something like it can happen again.

Part of this question requires us to study Hitler himself. But the distressing thing about that task is that different scholars have drawn for us conflicting pictures.

Ron Rosenbaum, in his 1998 book, *Explaining Hitler*, has it right when he says, "A sure sense of Hitler's mind has escaped us." Indeed, as Rosenbaum writes, "The search for Hitler has apprehended not one coherent, consensus image of Hitler but rather many different Hitlers, competing Hitlers, conflicting embodiments of competing visions."

One of those visions was expressed a few years ago by President Clinton in his remarks at the dedication of the Holocaust Museum. Clinton described how German "culture, which produced Goethe, Schiller and Beethoven, then brought forth Hitler and Himmler," as if Hitler were an inevitable or maybe aberrant product of his culture and not an individually responsible agent. (How Clintonesque.)

I'm not sure there is now or ever was an exhaustive explanation for Hitler. There is much that we know about this cruel man, but there is also much we will never know or never know for sure.

And human beings are simply too complex, too illusive to nail down with final certainty. Werner Heisenberg's famous Uncertainty Principle applies to subatomic reality, but something very like it also seems to be at play in the world of human psychology.

So we wind up knowing not who Hitler was, exactly, but who he wasn't. Who he wasn't, it turns out, is who we must be if we are to stand against the devaluation of life that made the Holocaust possible.

He was a man who encouraged his followers to act out of revenge, fear, and hatred. We, therefore, must advocate—and live—reconciliation, education, and love.

Hitler required followers to pledge allegiance to destructive ideas about race and genetics. We, therefore, must advocate an approach to science that is tentative, modest, and unattached to the notion of final solutions and the efficient evil that accompanies them.

Among the thousands of photos at the Holocaust Museum is one of people arriving at Auschwitz. A small boy, in the arms of someone I take to be his mother, is looking directly into the camera lens. His face is sullen, reflecting some childlike—and therefore pure—sense of betrayal and bewilderment.

That photo, because of its specificity, is a good test. If, when you look at it, your heart doesn't ache, something vital in you has gone dead.

That deadness I associate with Hitler. That deadness allowed the Holocaust to happen. It's that deadness to which we must give no quarter in our hearts, for once it takes root there, any evil is possible—and maybe even inevitable.

Fifty Years of Living Bring Their Own Wisdom
January 15, 1995

The day I was born, FDR was president, the first atomic bomb test was still six months from rocking the New Mexico desert, and the Chicago Cubs were only weeks from the spring training of a season that would find them, at its end, in the World Series, to which they have not returned since.

My journey from January 1945 to January 1995 has been tumultuous and utterly unpredictable, if for no other reason than because I've shared the timeline with a world that seems to run as fast as it can downhill simply to keep from falling on its face.

I think of my fiftieth birthday as a good time to stop running with that world long enough to take a look behind me to see what I've learned and ahead of me to see if what I've learned can do me any good in a future both unknown and unknowable.

I have learned, first, to acknowledge some regrets. Given it to do over, I would eat more peanut butter but less fat. Which is the way with regrets, isn't it? They force impossible choices.

I would sleep more but go to bed later. I would read more but also write more. I would learn to laugh out loud more instead of just smiling and smirking when I'm amused. I would spend more time with my children but also more time alone. I would take up golf earlier and stay with the oboe, which I once played (badly), longer.

I would not quit growing at 6 feet, 3 1/2 inches but would continue to a full 6 feet 4. Or maybe 5. I would be wealthier, so money wouldn't mean as much. I would memorize more poetry. And I would learn to make something beautiful with my hands, something beyond an occasional phrase or sentence that, at least so far, has stood the cruel test of indifferent time.

I would swim better, sing better, and love better. But I would argue more, while being content to lose more of those arguments.

Perhaps the hardest lesson I've learned in fifty years is that humanity—including, for sure, me—is always capable of evil, both breathtaking and banal. It is, in fact, only by the most strenuous of struggles that good wins out in me, when it does. Too often it does not.

There is no use glossing over this. Pop religions and feel-good therapists would wish away evil. But it is real, unimaginably terrifying, and each of us is capable of it. To see evil's possibility in one's self is a great victory, but barely half the battle.

Recently I was reading David Remnick's wonderful book *Lenin's Tomb*, about the collapse of the Soviet Union. And I recognized how my preference for order and calm might have led me to side with the people there—the Stalinists and their clones—who stifled freedom partly because it was simply too messy.

This is not an easy admission. In fact, making it has taken me fifty years, and still I try to delude myself by imagining that—governed by my spit-polished conscience and my rootedness in the ethics of my religious faith—I would always choose good over evil, even assuming that in all cases I knew the difference.

Exactly this kind of illusion made both slavery and Nazi Germany possible. And I say that as one whose bloodline is half German. The other half is Swedish. The Swedes love peace, as a rule, but I'm afraid they often love neutrality, indifference, calm, and isolation more, not always understanding that apart from fairness, from justice, peace is simply not possible. Half Swedish, half German: No wonder my natures war with each other.

I do not know—cannot know—how many more years I have left. The actuarial charts would give me maybe twenty-five, half as long as I've already lived. I would take a guaranteed twenty-five years in a heartbeat if I knew they would be at least as good as the first fifty.

But there are no guarantees, so I have learned that each moment, each day, each year is a gift to be unwrapped carefully but eagerly. In fact, as each day comes now, eager should outweigh careful. I should learn to rip the wrapping paper.

I should, at all costs, avoid the pathetic inaction, the forlorn frozen spirit of T. S. Eliot's character J. Alfred Prufrock, who lamented:

> I grow old . . . I grow old . . .
> I shall wear the bottoms of my trousers rolled.

Shall I part my hair behind? Do I dare to eat a peach?
I shall wear white flannel trousers, and walk upon the beach.
I have heard the mermaids singing, each to each.

I do not think that they will sing to me.

If the mermaids will not sing to me, I—in whatever time I have left—will sing to them. And at the top of my damn lungs, too.

Class of '63 Has Stood Firm
August 29, 1993

WOODSTOCK, ILLINOIS—When 115 of us graduated from high school together here thirty years ago, the coming storms were simply inconceivable. But, dear God, they have come. And come and come.

Seven of us already are dead. The causes range from Vietnam to murder. Even the children of several classmates have died, including some who were also adults by the time of their demise. The pain of this unfair, devastating experience can be seen in the information sheets we filled out before our thirtieth class reunion here this night.

One woman writes: "Son Richard was killed on motorcycle 11–3–91 age 25." Will there ever be a November 3 she won't face with sorrow?

A man writes: "This last year has been very hard, we lost our daughter Jill Oct. 8, 1992 very suddenly." It's the preciseness of the dates that pounds harshly at one's heart, the details of death that scream at us through sentences our old English teachers would correct as not quite up to standard.

Another woman lists three children, the oldest this way: "Todd—Nov. 14, 1968–Dec. 7, 1991." And later she writes: "The grief from losing my son has been such a life altering ordeal, I'm just trying to reclaim it again, if that's possible."

But it's not only these incalculable losses I'm talking about. It's pain of seemingly lesser scope, too.

So many divorces. So many. There are, of course, jokes about them tonight, but the anguish of these failed relationships is not far from the surface.

And not just divorce, either, but other personal crises, too—the children in trouble, the jobs lost, the senile or infirm parents whose parents we have become, the money trouble, the disappointments in love, in career, in dreams.

One man—no doubt speaking for many—summed it up this way on his information sheet: "Spend a lot of time listening to John Bradshaw [the famous popularizer of the notion of our need to heal our inner child] explain what really happened years ago."

And none of this, of course, pays the slightest bit of attention to the social, political, economic, and cultural upheavals that have set our collective teeth on edge for three decades—from Vietnam to Watergate and Iran-Contra, from the Beatles to 2 Live Crew, from the New Frontier to Reaganomics to Bill Clinton's all-Democratic budget, from LSD to AIDS, from Wile E. Coyote to Beavis and Butt-Head, from Martin Luther King and Malcolm X to Jesse Jackson and Clarence Thomas, from Neil Armstrong to Christa McAuliffe, from John, Robert, and Ted Kennedy to Ronald Reagan, from Marilyn Monroe to Madonna and from Mick Jagger to, well, Mick Jagger.

It's been a breathtaking passage, and my small high school class from a little town northwest of Chicago has stood with our faces to the gale, trying to keep our feet beneath us. At times it has felt like the longest, fastest, steepest, scariest roller-coaster ride in the world— running not at normal speed but on fast-forward. Is it possible to charge life with unnecessary use of force?

Well, all I've said here is true. Every word. Which makes all the more remarkable the obvious joy and happiness displayed at our reunion.

Women whose husbands, the jerks, have treated them as if they were chattel, women who have lived pinched, miserable lives, are on the dance floor twisting and doing the stroll and laughing until they nearly cry.

Men whose lives have been chaotic adventures of one small failure after another are telling jokes and dancing their damn feet off.

And men and women who have lived steady, straight-ahead, calm lives—one man has run a barber shop here for nearly twenty-two years; a woman, married nearly twenty-nine years, is "a full-time Grandma taking care of our precious grandson while his mom and dad go off to work"—are dancing, too. Or at least watching and cheering others on.

We have come back to share not only our memories of four years of raging hormones, when we were tossed together by accident of birth and geography, but also what has happened to us since that warm June evening in 1963 when the school finally let us go.

And here is what we have discovered: We are stubborn survivors. It has made a difference that we have lived. We have carved out lives for ourselves or at least are still trying, and we are glad of it.

Life has thrown us curves and spitballs and brushback pitches. It has come at us relentlessly, at times fatiguing us to our marrow. But we are still vertical, still breathing in and out, most of us, and what's more, we are imagining a future that includes us and, beyond that, is better because of us.

One woman says she's just three credit hours from a master's degree in elementary education. Another wrote this: "Recently I began taking classes toward a special ed teaching degree. If all goes as planned, when most smart people from the class of 1963 are retired from their careers I'll be out searching for a classroom that needs me."

So we're serving notice: This unfair, wonderful, mean, beautiful, painful, lovely world hasn't seen the last of the Class of '63. Not by a bunch.

At Least the Sixties Asked the Right Questions
December 11, 1994

Yippie-yuppie Jerry Rubin's recent death sent my head back to the industrial-strength wonky 1960s, when people had world-saving ideas at night but often couldn't remember them the next morning.

I have tried to explain the sixties to my children, young adults who now are about as old as I was in the latter part of that decade. But it's a useless exercise. My kids in this seem like people from China, say, trying to grasp American culture by watching John Wayne movies or *Beverly Hills Cop XXXI.*

There was something so electric, so dangerous, almost, so flat-out weird and wired about the sixties that it's almost impossible to capture the true feel of the time without degenerating into goofy clichés like the mud of Woodstock or the drugs of Timothy Leary.

I did not go to Woodstock nor did I take drugs. Nonetheless, I have been forever marked by the creative zaniness represented by Jerry Rubin, other members of the so-called Chicago Seven, and the folks Newt Gingrich now dismisses as counterculture radicals.

It's not that I always agreed with Rubin or with the late Abbie Hoffman or any of the other edgy voices of my generation. In fact, I usually found those folks indiscriminately disrespectful of everything instead of being disrespectful of just those things that really deserved our disrespect.

Still, having outrageous people like Rubin around meant the rest of us sounded ever so much more sane and safe when we spoke about the parts of our culture and politics that needed fixing. Without the Jerry Rubins, the Abbie Hoffmans, the Tom Haydens, the Bobby Seales, the Eldridge Cleavers, nobody would have paid much attention to the rest of us.

It is possible to stretch this analogy much too far, but in many ways the sixties radicals of Rubin's ilk were entertainers in the way that Jesus was, among many other things, an entertainer. That is, they said and did engaging, puzzling things in the sixties that pointed to truth but that simply could not be taken literally.

For instance, when they said we should kill our parents or should never trust anyone over thirty, only fools thought they were literally serious, just as only fools thought (and in some cases still think) Jesus was literally serious when he suggested that we cut off our hands or pluck out our eyes if those body parts cause us to sin.

There was, however, a profound sense in which we had to unplug from the way our parents and their generation—especially if we were white and middle class—had slept through the Eisenhower years. And there was, similarly, a profound sense in which Jesus meant we must so desire sinlessness (which is to say a whole relationship with God) that we should be willing to sacrifice whatever is blocking such a relationship.

The Rubins of the sixties were splashes of cold water in our faces. "Wake up!" they shouted. "Look at what you are missing!" They helped us ask serious questions: Is the war in Vietnam worth fighting? Why are our schools still racially segregated? Should women really be kept pregnant and barefoot in the kitchen? What is the CIA up to? How can any of us be free if some of us aren't? And on and on.

One of the questions they forced us to ask—though I doubt whether Rubin or anyone else among his sixties associates ever worded it this way—is an old one, indeed.

It goes something like this: Remembering that where your treasure is, there will your heart be also, where is your treasure? To what, in other words, are you committed? What do you love? It's a question for the ages, and I'm glad Jerry Rubin and others, no matter how silly or overwrought they could be, demanded that it be asked.

Dare to Be Immersed in Reality of Life
August 3, 1997

ABIQUIU, NEW MEXICO—I'm sitting on an old Adirondack chair—chipped tan paint on weathered wood—on a veranda of the adobe cottage my wife and I are calling home this week at Ghost Ranch Conference Center.

Amazing red rock mountains flare into a sky sprayed with six dozen kinds of clouds that change every two minutes. What a show.

Just behind me, inside the screen door, two women—Jean from Pittsburgh, Marcia from Denver—are creating music so real and present it both surprises and lullabies my acquiescent, pliable heart.

Jean plays flute, Marcia cello. For an upcoming worship service, they are practicing a lovely and relatively new (1984) hymn by Thomas H. Troeger and Carol Doran called "As a Chalice Cast of Gold."

The reality of this moment—it's as if every nerve ending I own is exposed—has affected me in unexpected ways. I am moved anew by how much better and different music sounds when the musicians are just a few feet away and not separated by the technology of a radio or a CD player.

Better to have recorded music than none at all, to be sure, but when the musicians are present, the layered depths of music's reality are vastly different and touching and, well, uncensored. It's why I prefer live theater to movies or TV.

In an odd way, it's appropriate for me to be struck by the difference between live and recorded art here at Ghost Ranch. For it was here that artist Georgia O'Keeffe spent most of the last forty years of her long and astonishingly productive life as a painter. She had a home both here on the ranch and in town at Abiquiu, several miles away. And it was O'Keeffe's remarkable talent to be able to draw a core reality—some irreducible truth—out of this starkly beautiful high desert country and stroke it onto canvas.

"Nobody sees a flower, really," she once said. "It is so small. We haven't time, and to see it takes time, like to have a friend takes time."

O'Keeffe's unparalleled ability to see flowers, mountains, and more finally has a showplace all its own. The Georgia O'Keeffe Museum opened just a few weeks ago in Santa Fe, an hour south of Ghost Ranch.

No painting, of course—even the originals on display there—can ever be as nuanced and full as the thing painted. But it can offer something reality itself sometimes refuses to give up to casual observers—depth of meaning. O'Keeffe's work, to my untrained eye, manages to speak large and important truths about this enchanted land I have come to love.

Her 1937 pastel *Red Hills with White Flower,* or her 1940 oil painting *Long Pink Hills,* for instance, unmask the way the battered mountains around me fill my consciousness with the context of size even when I fail to imagine that that's what they are doing.

O'Keeffe country causes me to realize again how much I worry that we increasingly seem to settle not for reality but for virtual reality, for reality once, twice, or three times removed, for reality protected by the impersonal distance of cyberspace.

Our culture has become adept at allowing us to remain at arm's length both from nature and each other. We live, many of us, in air-conditioned, centrally heated, single-family homes that make low the hills and valleys of actual climate. Our offices, shopping malls, and cars allow us, in effect, to live indoors, unattached to nature's querulous vicissitudes.

In addition, we build walls, not bridges, between one another. I remember once how a visiting minister in my church stabbed my heart with the truth that week after week we worship with people who nurse hurts we do not know about or suspect because we do not care enough to ask.

And instead of opening our deepest wounds—or, sometimes, our freshest joys—to those around us, we reveal them, if at all, to Dear Abby or Dr. Laura, safely distant.

We e-mail our love. We fax our complaints. We surround ourselves with the moral equivalent of air bags.

This week at Ghost Ranch, I'm walking in sandals on hard red soil and I'm sitting in dry air that slides down the mountains through aspen and pine, cactus and sagebrush, air that carries on its shimmering waves the gentle poetry of well-tempered cello and flute.

And I am reminding myself of what Georgia O'Keeffe's art seemed to reveal so well—that to swim, you must leap into the cold, swift river and feel its reality enter your every pore.

Truths from the Land and the Seasons

The Sea Offers Many Gifts, but Never Silence
October 1, 1995

ISLE OF PALMS, SOUTH CAROLINA—The night has dropped like some insistent wet veil, and here on a beach house veranda, facing the ocean, I am listening to the world.

It's as if all my senses have shut down save hearing. And what I'm hearing is a restless, relentless ocean, so amazing in its breadth, its power, its depth, that it simply leaves me silent.

Being in silence is the only way to listen to the world. You have to become what the Buddhists call mindful. Which is to say you have to set out your nerve endings like so many baited fish lines. And then you must pay attention to what strikes them.

Through the veranda screen I can make out only the dim outline of a palm tree just 15 or so yards toward the ocean, which is itself another 150 or so yards beyond that. Inside the house, the boyfriend of one of my nieces—we're all here for a wedding—is playing his guitar, which, in a muffled sort of way, I can hear through the glass door.

So, then, there's the guitar, a few insects buzzing, and a little drizzle, plop-plopping into small puddles. And over it all, like some cathedral ceiling of endless sound, is the prodigally noisy Atlantic.

The sea is never quiet. It is like some engine plugged into an eternal power supply at the core of the earth.

I am, after several minutes of marinating in this gift of sound, reminded of the astonishing poet Wallace Stevens, who spent a career as an insurance executive in Hartford, but whose piercing mind created some of the century's best—and most challenging—poetry.

I'm remembering a poem that begins,

59

> In that November off Tehuantepec,
> The slopping of the sea grew still one night
> And in the morning summer hued the deck
> And made one think of rosy chocolate
> and gilt umbrellas.

And I remember that the very first time I read those lines—it was at least thirty years ago—I was struck by the gerund *slopping*. It was, I think, exactly the right word and it helped teach me an important lesson for a life of writing, which is that verbs—far more than any other part of speech, especially adjectives—carry the freight. I do not always write as if I know that truth, but my failures do not diminish it.

The other thing that struck me in a vague way then—but sharply tonight—was the idea that the slopping of the sea could ever grow still.

I do not live near an ocean. My experience with the sea is not slim, but neither is it exhaustive. So maybe—at some brief point of delicate equilibrium between the tide coming in and the tide going out, say—it may be accurate to say that the slopping of the sea grows still.

But I must tell you I think Wallace Stevens, when he wrote that, simply winged it for the sake of a line of verse. The sea—at least that part of it I'm hearing so deeply tonight on the South Carolina coast—just does not grow still. Nor does it offer an even, smooth sound. There are rises and falls, crescendos and mezzo fortes, pizzicati and allegros. But never is there nothing. Never is there stillness. There is, instead, a boisterous texture of ceaseless sound. And I can't imagine how it could be any other way.

In fact, the only major sea sound change I know that's even possible happens when nature's angry gods, disguised as a hurricane, attack the coast.

Hurricane Hugo, its voice pitched at a terrible deep scream, bullied its wet and wild way through here in 1989. You still can see palm trees whose tops were simply shorn off in that sickening, fatal noise. Only now have enough new fronds come back to make them look much like palm trees again.

So, terrifying noise from the sea is possible, but not, surely, silence. And whatever the sound that comes from the ocean—whether gentle slopping or breathtaking raucousness—it reminds us, I think, that there is much in this world over which we have no say. We are simply the recipients of nature's gifts or targets of her fury.

That, of course, is what we tell ourselves after each frightening electrical storm, flood, or heat wave. Then, like distracted children, we forget.

But in a place like this, it's hard to forget how weak and powerless we are—here where the ocean is never silent, where it chisels its inexhaustible sound into our very marrow and speaks to us of infinite things.

Promise of Sunrise Can Fill Our Lives
October 29, 1995

For reasons I cannot fully explain, fall sunrises where I live strike my eyes and heart with enough power to leave me silent and filled with a sense of the sacred.

Maybe it's because morning's eastern horizon seems regularly to be dappled with clouds. And these clouds—often long but broken horizontal brushstrokes—serve to focus, shape, and display the amazing light of daybreak. They become a moving canvas.

Or maybe it's because the early light plays off the golds, reds, yellows, and mahoganies of leaves still holding stubbornly to trees.

Whatever the cause, the stunning autumn sunrises this year— pinks and oranges bleeding into peach, reds into purple—have awakened in me a realization of how indelibly the world's natural physical patterns imprint us with understanding, with insight, with deep *aha*s of recognition.

When I was a boy, I saw a sunrise whose meaning it has taken me almost forty years to unpack. In the Bible, forty years sometimes is used symbolically to mean, simply, a hell of a long time. And I have found that sometimes it takes forty years—actual and metaphorical years—to discover what things mean.

The sunrise I'm talking about occurred in the foothills of the Himalayan mountains in northern India. I was a schoolboy there for a time.

On Easter morning of 1956 I went to a sunrise service on the top of a hill. As we looked expectantly toward the east, toward the snow-slicked hills of Tibet, the sun shot rays straight up into the empty, chilly air. Then, at the bottom of a V-shaped spot in the mountains, the sun itself began to appear, slowly but relentlessly filling the air with ineffable light and—as I now understand—affirmation. And maybe even angels.

It has taken me until now to realize what I took away from that morning of grace. Somehow I viscerally grasped the idea of resurrection. I had no meaningful words for that as an eleven-year-old American boy far away from home. I probably didn't even know that some things, to respect their mystery and depth, are better said without words.

But it's clear to me now that ever since that day—despite much outward evidence and many words to the contrary—I have believed in resurrection. And I don't mean that only in the Christian context of Easter, though that certainly has become a core belief in my life.

Rather, I mean resurrection in all aspects of our bruised and difficult lives. I mean a hope—almost an irrational faith—that when parts of our lives go dead, it's possible that they will again know life and health.

We can never know when—or even if—this miracle of resurrection will occur in our lives. But I have discovered that each of us can be agents of resurrection for others. We can be channels of grace. We can be carriers of hope. We can reveal possibilities to others— possibilities they may have thought foreclosed or may never have imagined at all.

For most of us, most of the time, we are the center of our own pre-Copernican universes. So we forget history. We forget others. We lose perspective—especially eternal perspective.

I was taken by surprise the other morning, as I watched the autumn sun pushing its way into the cool air, not only to be reminded of that sunrise forty years ago in India but of sunrises that have happened for hundreds, thousands, millions of years.

We have come to this amazing theater of natural phenomena in the middle of the play—or maybe quite late in the run. We have missed an eternity of sunrises and sunsets, all of which happened without us, without, in fact, any need for us. That they still happen for us is a gift of wonder to cherish, a gift from which to draw deep measures of meaning.

Gift of Grace Bestowed on One and All
December 15, 1996

CAMDENTON, MISSOURI—It was raining when we went to sleep last night, the kind of cold, sharp rain that stings the skin and brings to mind paper cuts and splinters.

We had been out in it earlier for dinner and were glad to get back to our lodge through the mysterious Lake of the Ozarks woods before the rain did something evil in the blackness.

But sometime in the night, while we slept, the rain transfigured itself. It became snow, and the morning broke clear and full of the kind of December beauty you never, ever expect, no matter how often you see it. I am looking across a narrow channel of lake at a hill full of old, tall trees—oaks, mostly. And I'm struck by the soft evenness of the gift of the snow's beauty.

Each branch has been eiderdowned. I have searched for irregularity and—at least from this distance—I have found none. Every one has received the present without any precondition save existence in this time and place.

Theologians speak of this. They call it grace. Or, more specifically, common grace, a term often used to describe the shower of nature's gifts in our temporal lives. It is a concept that grates against the souls of people who live their lives by strict standards of rewards and punishments, by some innate sense that we should get exactly what we deserve and deserve exactly what we get.

The inconvenient, awkward fact, however, is that life rarely works so neatly. Life is unfair not only in its seemingly unjust distribution of trouble but also in its clearly unjust dispensation of grace. Stunning sunsets, after all, are for everyone who can see, even criminals.

I am betting there are people at this lodge who, in the past week, have broken six or eight of the Ten Commandments, and I do not exclude myself from the list of sinners. I also bet there are some who have done their best in the last week to do unto others as they would have others do unto them.

And yet all of us—every one—was given the gift of this beautiful snow this morning. All we had to do to receive it was to rise from our beds and look out the window.

You may, if you like, call that unfair, and no doubt you can make a persuasive case. But I don't call it unfair. I simply call it grace, and

I try not to get so caught up in the astonishing evenhandedness of the event that I miss its loveliness.

Probably each of us can recall times when we've been hit with unfair trouble and, by contrast, with unmerited favor. Both often seem to be connected to our families. For instance, we may be stunned to find a spouse who loves us, then are devastated when that union produces a disabled child. Then, in turn, we are amazed to find that child, instead of causing nothing but grief, is a channel of grace and joy.

Similarly, siblings who seem to cause us endless pain and heartache when we are teenagers turn out, later, to be a bedrock in our support systems.

We are, quite simply, foolish if we expect life to be metered out in fair, equitable, bite-sized chunks that will never choke us.

And we are even more foolish if we cannot see the common grace that floods our lives. We find, for instance, that the rules of physics guarantee that gravity and the coming of the seasons are reasonably predictable. And that sometimes snow upholsters hillsides full of barren trees.

Maybe I'm more attuned to seeing trees that way this crystal day because I am celebrating a gift of grace in my life, the start of a marriage with a woman I cherish, someone who is able to see the uncommon gift of common—but amazing—grace in those same trees. Actually, there's no maybe to it.

Softening the Land's Cold Angles
January 11, 1998

NORTH SPRINGFIELD, VERMONT—The snow falls insistently tonight.

I have turned out the lights inside the house where I'm staying and am watching the amazing show through big picture windows that look out on a knoll lined with fir trees and white-skinned birches.

Oddly, the snow's powerful gentleness speaks in silence to some deep and unnamed part of me. Maybe a wound.

At first tonight I watched the snow through half-open venetian blinds. The effect was strange and, it seemed to me, nearly miraculous. The blinds cut the snow streams into corrugated ribbons that slid down the breeze like small bright stars in some dimly lit eight-millimeter home movie made forty years ago.

With the blinds now pulled up, however, the whole window fills with dappled, falling whiteness. It is hypnotic. I cannot watch it and, at the same time, think about anything else at all.

I think I finally understand these lines from "The Snowman," a Wallace Stevens poem: "the listener, who listens in the snow, / And, nothing himself, beholds / Nothing that is not there and the nothing that is."

This retreat into self that watching snow engenders is what vacation means. It is to vacate—which does not, for me, have to do with becoming empty in the way Buddhists and others sometimes mean when they guide followers toward some mystical detachment from self.

For me, instead, to vacate means to leave behind those irritations and distractions that keep me from knowing my own center, that deep place I might call soul, where I am most I. As I vacate tonight, I am hugely relieved to be in this warm house watching the air fill with snow.

The other night, as I drove south on Interstate 91 from St. Johnsbury, Vermont, a light snow turned heavy and for an endless hour it rushed at my windshield half mad with passion to be on the earth. I had to focus with enormous intensity just to keep track of the edge of the highway and its zippered center line. Three other lives in the car were in my hands.

Snow like that demonizes itself, gives itself a bad name by running amok, becoming destructive and dangerous.

(The snow falling tonight, by the way, will amount to only a few inches, despite its brief intensity, so it will not come close to what the Vermont Weather Book and the Vermont Weather Calendar report happened on October 4, 1804—a "snow hurricane." It started as a tropical storm, but as it worked its way over the higher elevations of the Green Mountains, it dropped thirty-eight to forty-eight inches of snow quite suddenly.)

Once, years ago, I was riding in the backseat of a car on the New York State Thruway near Buffalo when the snow came so hard and quick as to create whiteout conditions. We were swallowed up by frozen blindness. I still marvel that our driver kept us alive. Snows like that harrow the soul.

But snow can be—and often is—much more friend than foe. I

grew up in a small town northwest of Chicago, where, flake by flake, snow built our toboggan runs in our city park, and I would not take any money for the memories of those liberating rides with friends.

And when I was about eleven years old I lived, briefly, in the foothills of the Himalayan mountains in India. From our cabin on clear June mornings we could see the snows of Tibet on mountains that were neighbors of Everest. What mystery, magic, and marvel those white-headed mountains held for me—and, in memory, still do.

And just over a year ago I awoke one morning in the Ozarks to a beautiful powdering of snow on boughs and piers. It was a gift of grace to my wife and me on our honeymoon. So I have come to see snow with realistic eyes. It can be nuisance and killer, but it also can be celebration and gift.

Tonight, as it softens the cold angles of the land that is beautiful Vermont, I sing of snow. And I let it find the jagged places in me that need cover and balm.

Our Wisest Use of Time Should Take Lots of Time
June 29, 1994

LONGBOAT KEY, FLORIDA—Today I am a rich, rich man.

I have my choice of millions of seashells here on a Gulf Coast beach, and I have time to choose. Time and shells. The amazing luxury of it takes my breath away.

My life nearly always finds me watching—and trying to beat—the clock. I face some deadline every day. But here on the beach time moves to a different rhythm, an old, repetitive, easy-gaited motion, hypnotic in its intimations of infinity.

The wind—steady but too hurried today—corrugates the water's surface, while below the waves the endless water responds to some lunar pull, as invisible as heartache, that heaves crumples of ocean into rhythmic but harmless collisions with land's edge. Over and over and over again the waves grasp for land and then, almost as if spent sexually, fall back exhausted.

In my wealth of time this afternoon (to me, two empty hours feel like an eternity), I can choose—or not—to watch this ceaseless cycle.

And it is not all inanimate, either. Just a moment ago in front of me—not ten yards away—a gull hovered a few feet above the water's surface, wing-flapping into the wind, moving neither forward nor back. Its eyes—becoming the calm eye of its struggling body's storm—scanned the blue-greenness just below it. The bird seemed unaware of anything but the possibility of food.

Suddenly it nailed itself into the water, its beak grasping something—I couldn't tell what—and then it fled, sustained again for a time in nature's elaborately organized food chain.

I don't know how long the bird hovered. A full minute? Maybe five? I lost track. I know only that in my treasure of time it didn't matter.

R. P. Dickey, a poet friend of mine—he lives now in New Mexico—wrote some verse thirty years ago that has stayed in my head all this time. It was a celebration of the wise use of time. "I am talking to the man who takes time," he wrote, "nineteen minutes to look at a chrysanthemum."

There are no chrysanthemums on this Florida beach off Sarasota, but some benefactor, as generous as the woman Jesus praised for giving her last coin, has spread the sand with a cacophony of seashells.

Some beaches offer—especially in the morning—fist-sized, unbroken, intricate shells, gifts from the sea. I've found them at dawn on the North Carolina coast. On other beaches, most of the shells are tiny and delicate—a hundred wouldn't fill a fist. I've gathered these miniature gems on the hot sands of Waikiki.

Here on Longboat Key, the shells are, for the most part, of the middle size—half an inch, an inch, two inches.

I am an ignorant shell collector. I gather them but do not know how to name them. I do not know what used to live in them. I cannot tell the cowries from the cones from the volutes. Of the hundred thousand or so kinds of shells, I can correctly identify almost none.

But I can hold in my hand this small white fan-shaped shell with the stunning pinkish flecks, and in it I can sense something beyond me, some gentle, creative force larger than me.

Or I can feel the spiked and bony ridges of another shell—this one almost pure white, the former home of some mollusk that left no forwarding address—and I know that Annie Dillard was right when she wrote that "the Creator loves pizzazz."

Today I am a rich, rich man, with world enough and time. I will spend my wealth here on the wet sand. I will spend it wantonly, prodigally. And in my memory I will own it forever.

The Mountains Have Their Own Truths to Tell
August 23, 1992

ROCKY MOUNTAIN NATIONAL PARK, COLORADO—What moun-
tains offer, finally—besides, of course, the simple and amazing reality of their own bulging presence (which, after all, is enough)—is not
so much perspective as perspective's insights, its "aha" moments, its
clicks of wisdom gained.

From a distance—from Denver, say, or, Loveland—the Rockies are
clearly a looming, magnetic presence on the rim of the western sky.
But they seem, for all that, to be understandable. From the plains,
the flatlands, they are mostly silhouettes, almost smudgy caricatures
of themselves, their sharp, ragged, ripped-on-a-rough-edge peaks
slipping in and out of clouds and haze. And one thing I learned
from living, years ago, in the Himalayas for nearly six months is that
the mountains change shape—and, in a sense, attitude—as we move
about, changing the places from which we see them.

In that fuzzed-over way, they are like people with whom we are
acquainted, but just barely—the guy I see each morning in the back
of my bus, the clerk at the grocery store, say. I can guess about the details of their lives, their personalities, their passions and prejudices,
but from a distance I cannot really know them.

Just as, from miles away, I cannot know the mountains. The distance shows them olive, black, or gray. Or some color-wheel mix of
what the fashion world now calls muted earth tones.

But once you are here, standing on this surfeit of land, this piled-
up, stacked-up, smashed-up Fibber McGee's closet of rock and soil—
its layers layered with more layers' layers—the colors separate into
the greens and browns, the grays and taupes, all the astonishing
shades of what has made the mountains home, including (even in
mid-August) off-white old snow patches like forgotten dabs of shav-
ing cream behind the ear.

Those very colors—and so many, many more—turn out to be
God's own creative flair: ponderosa pines and junipers, Douglas firs
and blue spruces, lodgepole pines and Englemann spruces.

And so far I'm speaking only of trees, which grow up and out and
across and over—a living tableau of all the prepositions and adverbs
of runaway fecundity. I have not even mentioned the wild colors
of the wildflowers. The yellowweed and the alpine sunflower, for
instance, the latter of which can appear to spring from bare rock.

Or the light purple flower of the Canada thistle or the bluish purple, yellow-throated flower of the sky pilot, which also goes by several aliases—Jacob's ladder, Greek valerian, or (no wonder it has aliases) skunkweed, so named because of the relentless smell of its leaves.

Or the deep blue, bell-shaped flower of the mountain gentian or the bright rose-purple of the shooting star, sometimes called the American cowslip or bird bills.

The wildflowers in the Rockies—both subalpine and alpine—are a frenzied, delicious feast for the eyes. But you can't see them from the plains. From way down there you can't see the horsebrush or the Parry townsendia, the western coneflower or the wallflower, the snow alumroot or the dwarf columbine, the alpine sorrel, the wandlily, or the goldbloom saxifrage, a name that means, I have learned, "rock-breaker."

And not just the flowers are invisible from a distance. The birds are, too—the Brewer's blackbird and Cassin's finch; the pine siskin and Savannah sparrow; the western tanager. Even the gray jays jumping about on the stone ledge of a lookout where my wife and I have stopped. They wheel recklessly through the thin air, looking for handouts of bread and crackers from tourists who aren't, of course, supposed to feed them but do. And feed, too, the chunky little chipmunks, like the one just inches from my hand.

Is God, as they say, in these details? I don't know, but for sure the details are in the details.

And the mountains remind us of that—remind us that before we can know about people, about things, about problems, about anything, we must come close and experience with our senses.

We ourselves, in other words, must be in the details. If we hang back, content to look from the plains, we'll never get it.

Imperfection Has a Beauty All Its Own
March 17, 1996

BOCA GRANDE, FLORIDA—I do not, I would guess, collect seashells the way most people do.

Which is to say I don't look for perfection. There is, in fact, probably no such thing as perfection in seashells. And clearly there is none in people.

Even when the Bible says Jesus was perfect, it is making a moral, not a physical, statement. Indeed, the passage in Isaiah that describes the so-called suffering servant, with whom Jesus identified and whom Christians now hold up in hindsight as Messianic prophecy, did not describe a physically perfect being. "He had no beauty or majesty to attract us to him," is the way the New International Version translates Isaiah 53:2.

So we know—despite the airbrushes of *Playboy* magazine and the publicity photos of the Chippendales—that there are no perfectly formed people. What makes people interesting, what makes them different and thus worth noticing at all, are their variations, their oddities, all the funny curves and bulges, the stretched sinews, scarred skin, bruised souls.

It is, at least for me, the same with seashells.

This afternoon, as I stood at the water's edge here on Florida's gulf coast and let the cool waves slap and kiss my imperfect feet, I watched for gifts of shells to be deposited on the sand. One of my favorite finds today was a shiny, nearly black fragment. I am no scholar of shells, but I know this is a piece of a pen shell because I picked up some full pen shells the other day on the beach at Sanibel Island. An elderly man saw those shells—full but oddly scarred— and asked derisively, "Are those your treasures?"

On Sanibel, people come to the beach well before dawn to find the beautiful full shells the sea lifts out overnight. Many of those people probably would not understand my attachment to intriguing imperfection.

But when I look at this dark, mother-of-pearlish shell section, its edges smoothed by the slopping of the sea, I imagine the battles it has fought to get here, how the tides and undertows, over which it had no control, kicked it around, tested its mettle, its tensile strength, its very character.

Sometimes you can look at people and see, especially on their faces, the stunning forces that—like the sea battering this shell— have cuffed them around. Their mouths turn down, their eyelids droop, exhausted by a world they cannot manage.

When I was growing up, I knew a boy named Danny. We were not close friends but his mother was my Cub Scout den mother one year.

Danny used crutches—metal affairs with leather bands that strapped onto his wrists. I think he had had polio. Whatever it was, his legs were nearly useless. But Danny was strong, not only in upper body power but in self-reliance.

I found Danny engaging. I wanted to know why he didn't simply fling away his damnable crutches in frustration and let himself go limp so others would have to care for him. But I was too shy or inarticulate to ask.

Not long ago—more than forty years after I went to Danny's house for Cub Scouts—I was visiting my old hometown, eating in a restaurant with a friend. Who should walk by the front window but Danny, still on crutches, still stocky and muscular, still fascinating to me.

I regret now that I did not run out and greet him. He is the very embodiment of what I mean by imperfections making people interesting, making them who they are as they respond to those flaws.

One of the shells I picked up today has lovely brown imperfect rectangles on its back. But that's not why I saved it.

Rather, I added it to my strange collection because four small white parasitic shells have attached themselves to one side of it. The larger shell—like a ship's hull full of barnacles—had become the vehicle of transport for these smaller shells. I do not think the attached shells have destroyed the larger shell's beauty. I think they have added intrigue to it, creating a story no other shell can tell in exactly that way.

People, too, carry evidence of the burdens that make them real, that test them, that make them whole.

On my right thumb I have a scar from a tin can that sliced me at age three, and on the back of my left hand a scar from a fall on the ice I got doing something for one of my daughters. And on my heart are the scars of disappointment and pain.

These are what, in the end, make us complete. That's because we are like the shells I have gathered today. In some profound way we are the sum of our scarred parts. We should all be stamped "irregular."

Gliding Gulls a Reminder of God's Glory
March 31, 1996

PORT CHARLOTTE, FLORIDA—It is raining. Clouds and fog hang low like prickly dread over the Myakka River, just outside the house where I'm staying.

Out beyond the seawall, across a narrow channel, there's a pier maybe sixty feet long. A small boat is dry-docked at its end. Seagulls arc and dip, float and flap above the pier, somehow tethered to it invisibly in a way that prevents them from circling and circling in a widening gyre until they slip out of range of the pier's inexplicable gravity.

I am sitting in a screened-in room looking at the pier through the rain. And I'm playing a fool's game. I am trying to imagine what is in the minds of these gulls.

This is a foolish enterprise for several reasons. First, there is little evidence that birds have anything in mind at all, as humans understand having something in mind. Birds are, quite simply, wired differently. They do not reason the way we do, when we reason at all—and sometimes I wonder. So what's the point of trying to imagine what's in the heads of swooping, hard-wired seagulls?

Beyond that is the pragmatic question of what I'd do with the information if I actually knew what the gulls were thinking. I have no answer. Nothing comes to mind. But this is vacation time, and thinking about such airy things is what I choose to do. It's how I choose to re-create myself.

I am drawn to what looks to me like mindless ecstasy—or at least pure motion. I am engaged by the strange processes and practices of the world—the world the old reformer John Calvin called the theater of God's glory.

That world's physics—specifically, its meteorology—has caused a downpour today, but the seagulls do not seem even to notice. Or, if they notice, to care. They fly in a rhythmic biodance, the passing air holding them aloft on the amazing structures of their wings—wings they could not have imagined or willed into being on their own.

I have seen gulls off and on all my life. Although I don't live near water, I get to it often enough that I don't gape at gulls slack-jawed with awe as I might a koala, say, or a Thomson's gazelle if I encountered one in my midwestern yard. That said, I confess I do not know much about the habits of seagulls.

About the only thing I remember from reading about gulls is that they open shellfish—reluctant shellfish, to be sure—by carrying them to great heights and dropping them. A species called the laughing gull apparently learns to do this by trial and error, which is to say by dropping shellfish on sand several times before figuring out that results improve if the shells land on hard rock.

Because God or nature (or both, depending on your theology) goes off on amazingly creative binges, there is more than one sort of gull—ring-bill, herring, black-backed—here in Florida.

They are lovely, graceful, raucous creatures that can improve a reach of empty air immeasurably by their very presence, the way a Rembrandt or a Van Gogh adds luster and, well, something amazing to a blank wall.

It strikes me that gulls circling in the rain are true to their natures. They are responding to some inherent pattern that, deep in their genes, tells them to behave as gulls. And almost certainly they have no choice.

We, of course, can choose our behavior. We are created with an inherent goodness. It is stamped on our very souls. Genesis tells us God called "everything" good, us included. But we are free to be evil—and often are.

How lovely life would be if people were always as true to their created natures as these gliding gulls are to theirs. Lovely and amazing.

Children Have It Right; the Action Is Overhead
August 16, 1998

GRAND LAKE, COLORADO—Insistent but rickety clouds the color of old pewter hang over the mountain I can see across the lake here, hiding its peak and spilling an intermittent cool rain that slides down the breeze.

I'm sitting on the wide veranda of Grand Lake Lodge thinking about sky, in which these slowly moving clouds are not trespassers but migrant citizens. Maybe I'm thinking about sky because here in the Rocky Mountains, twelve hundred feet or so below timberline, it feels as if I'm closer to sky than I am on the plains where I live. But that's a foolish notion, unsubstantiated by any science worthy of the name.

Rather, I'm thinking about sky here because it brings the weather like so much imported, unordered clothing. And living here a few days at the foot of tall jack pines spread thick through the mountains, I sense that weather is upon us without much warning. The view of sky is quite limited here, so rain can come from behind a mountain and we don't know until it's nearly overhead.

This differs radically from the skies at home. There on the flat-lands I can watch storms approach for hours sometimes. Rarely do those skies surprise. Only occasional lightning bolts sprung nearly ex nihilo from a hot, hazy sky have the capacity to shock. All else has observable preludes.

Colorado's Rockies have summer skies that can change with rapidity. But, as I say, part of that perception is due to how little of the hemisphere of sky one can see at once.

That aspect is much different from the skies I watched a few weeks ago in the high desert country of northern New Mexico. What an astonishing show the skies there offer. Something amazing—or at least engaging—is nearly always happening in those heavens, which dome over red rock hills and arroyos and dry plains and are rarely hidden by anything.

You can simultaneously see a bright sun in a breathless blue vault of sky in the south, a menacing thunderstorm in the west, fantastically stacked cumulus clouds in the east, and small puffs of innocent white clouds in the north. All at once, mind you. And fifteen minutes later it's all changed.

Whether I'm here in Colorado or in New Mexico or at home on the plains, I almost never think about the atmosphere that surrounds me. And yet it is the very guarantor of my physical life.

Atmosphere means, literally, "sphere of breath," and if I somehow step outside the atmosphere without artificial means of breathing, I'm finished.

How seldom, on the plains, do I consider the crazy idea of running out of air? Yet we are never far from that disaster. In the cosmic scheme of things, the atmosphere is alarmingly thin. You and I dwell in what scientists call the troposphere, or lower layer of atmosphere. Here is where we draw the breath of life. Here is where we see overarching marble-blue skies and rainbows and clouds with shades of gray that range from almost white to almost black.

Here is where we see sheet lightning turn the horizon into what looks like old, badly lit eight-millimeter movies flickering in a far room. And here is where stupendous lightning bolts tear the atmosphere into jagged parts crackling with nature's killing power.

It is through the troposphere that we look—toward, in succession, the stratosphere, mesosphere, thermosphere, and exosphere—to see the eerie northern lights and watch shooting stars flame out like some run-amok rock star blazing to death on drugs and fast times.

We didn't know much about the atmosphere until Evangelista Torricelli invented the barometer in 1643. By then William Shakespeare had been dead nearly thirty years. (Imagine him writing his complete works without even a foundational knowledge of the atmosphere in which he wrote.) But it's been only in the last hundred years or so that we have come to something like a sophisticated understanding of the envelope of air around us.

I suppose I must be out of my usual surroundings to pay prolonged attention to something as common as sky. And I've been so intent on seeing what's above me here that I now notice I've ignored huge yellow and purple pansies in a flower box near my feet. I've paid no attention to motorboats skimming the lake in front of choppy *V*s. I haven't even seen the steam rising from wet wooden lodge steps because the sun has slid through the clouds.

But the real action is overhead. No wonder children lie on their backs and see elephants in clouds. And dragons. They have it right. The atmosphere, which keeps us alive, is itself alive, if only we will attend to its dramas.

Watching Death's Spectacular Show
October 11, 1998

LYNDON, VERMONT—On the other side of the meadow that slants away from the house in which I'm staying, the hillside is well into its annual biodance with death.

When sunlight drills through the big, low-flying clouds, which are sliding to the northeast on a chilly, haphazard wind, it flames the trees to shining oranges and polished coppers and there's no question now that death is ascending these fetching hills. There's no escape from death's insistent presence, though evergreens scattered among the maples, oaks, aspens, and birches will put on a brave show and stand as sacraments of hope that all is not lost.

Vermont—and much of New England—celebrates death in October, though of course no one calls it that. The summer-green hills give way, subtly at first, to the cycles of change that require trees to survive by cutting off the energy of life to their leaves. When the process reaches critical mass, a kind of spontaneous combustion flashes over the countryside and stuns both natives and travelers with colors no one has ever quite reproduced artificially.

This astonishing display draws tourists who, as author Kurt Vonnegut once wrote in another context, come rushing in with the brainless ecstasy of volunteer firemen.

In fact, today, as I drove along Route 2 from the lovely gold-domed capitol building in Montpelier toward St. Johnsbury and neighboring Lyndon here in the Northeast Kingdom, I saw several people along the roadside taking pictures of scenes that have been photographed millions of times in the last fifty years.

Ah, but that's not quite true. No autumn perfectly reproduces any other autumn, so whatever people capture on their 35mm cameras or video cameras has, in fact, never been seen before.

Whole busloads of foliage tourists even now are moving along Vermont's colorful highways just to see the spectacular show death is putting on here.

As I was stopped across the street from the Vermont capitol this morning, I watched two tour buses pull up and disgorge dozens of folks with cameras at the ready. They spread out on the lawn and snapped away, hoping to show the apple-crisp gold of the dome against the turning hillside behind it.

Indeed, before foliage season ends, Vermont expects 6 million "leaf peepers," as some of the locals call them, to come and spend $500 million in the state. The season has become such a draw that it has even attracted academics to study the phenomenon. Kit Anderson, a cultural geographer at the University of Vermont, earlier this year presented a paper on the subject at the American Association of Geographers' annual meeting in Boston. She says people come looking not just for beauty but for stability, security, and harmony.

The Associated Press recently produced a long feature article about fall foliage and quoted Brian Barry, an associate professor of psychology and sociology at the Rochester Institute of Technology in New York, who seemed to understand that tours to see colorful leaves have something to do with death.

"My own sense," he said, "is that as people age they get more aware or more sensitized to life having cycles." As they enter the autumn and winter of their own lives, he said, they come to Vermont to let nature remind them how to cope with final things.

Well, maybe. But my guess is that most people come here in the fall simply because they are drawn by beauty. They rarely imagine how impossible this beauty would be were it not for an annual cycle of death—nor do they think much about what this means about their own deaths, probably.

But death is what's really going on here. And it's a reminder to all of us that when we are brave enough to look even death in the eye, we can see a beauty we are likely to miss if we avoid the subject.

Death minuets its way across Vermont's chameleonic hills, and if we understand what we are seeing we can lose ourselves in the grim spectacle because we know about the greening gift of spring. And, at least so far, spring has always come.

A High-Country Interlude and Reconnection
March 28, 1999

AVON, COLORADO—The house is empty this morning, save for me and the dog, and she's asleep.

My wife (who, in another life, used to teach skiing) and our friends have headed over to nearby Vail to take a few runs down the mountain.

I don't ski. Except for going down a small hill a few times in my great aunt's backyard in Stockholm, Sweden, in 1958, I've never been on skis. I have other athletic vices. Besides, if I want to have my leg broken, I know several people who'd be willing to oblige—and at considerably less than the cost of a ski-lift ticket, too.

So what I am doing this morning is what, in my experience, almost none of us does enough. I am being alone with myself with no mandatory agenda.

I am giving myself this gift of time to become reacquainted with myself, to listen to places in my soul that often get ignored because my life is so busy, noisy, spoken for. This is no complaint. I love my life. I have made choices—most of them good. And I am able, much of the time, to live a life reasonably well centered on the eternal values that give it meaning and purpose.

But now and then I realize that the core of me has simply been along for the ride for too long. I need to acknowledge my central essence and try to listen to how it is doing and what it would tell me.

So in this morning mountain chill, on a bright, azure day, I am sitting on the deck of the house in which we're staying and am trying simply to be and, while I'm at it, to be paying attention.

Across a crooked valley of homes the mountains are dappled with snow and tiny skiers that I have to squint at to see moving.

Mountains always humble me. They tell me I am dust and to dust I will return. They tell me I am a small, dim flash on history's radar screen, and yet even one so insignificant is given the common-grace gift of mountains. Mountains tell me, too, of the human capacity for grandeur. On the way up here last night, we drove through the Eisenhower tunnel, a mile-plus, four-lane part of Interstate 70 lasered through the belly of a mountain. I remarked then to my wife on the astonishing engineering required to carry out so bold and seemingly reckless an idea.

And isn't that the human condition? We are at once transient renters on this planet—"aliens and strangers," I Peter 2:11 calls us in the New International Version of the Bible.

And yet while we are here we imagine and create electrifying things, from mountain tunnels to skyscrapers, from poetry to sculpture, from airplanes to space telescopes to, well, Y2K computer bugs.

Despite the evidence of ageless mountains and stars, somehow we are convinced that a human life's normal span—now seventy-five or eighty years in this country—is a long time, certainly enough to create something lasting.

After dinner last night I stepped out onto the deck to look at the stunning night sky. In crystal air, more than a mile and a half above sea level, the stars—not hidden by the light pollution of the metropolis in which I live—took my breath away. This was, in modern electronic culture terms, the high-definition television version of a nightly show.

And I was reminded of a thought from a book I just read, *Amazing Grace: A Vocabulary of Faith*. In it, the author, Kathleen Norris, reminds us that all the atoms that make up human beings once were part of distant stars.

This morning, alone, listening in silence, I'm grateful to be so physically connected to the cosmos. I'm also glad to be reconnected to the uniqueness of my being and to celebrate the truth that although the soulless mountains and stars cannot think about me, I can think about both them and me. And so I do.

Spring Reveals Nature's Sacramental Beauty
March 17, 2001

As this adamant winter relaxes its indurate hold on the land, the sweet gum tree in my front yard seems deeply conflicted.

Some brown husks of leaves—skeletal remains of last summer—still refuse to let go and ride the air currents to the softening ground. They hang like slabs of dried meat, brittle but glued. But right next to them, buds holding the promise of new leaves swell and begin to crack open, split by the astonishing force of life.

If neighbors were watching me the other day, they could have been excused for concluding that I had gone over the edge. I stood still and silent for several minutes with a small branch in my hand, just staring at the evidence of life and death. The dependability, the inevitability—but also both the fragility and the power—of these annual cycles touched me anew.

We miss so much of the beauty of this aborning time of year because we don't stop and stare, stop and grasp what's really happening. Scott Russell Sanders, in his recent book, *The Force of Spirit*, captures some of what I'm talking about this way:

> This power is larger than life, although it contains life. It's tougher than love, although it contains love. It's akin to the power I sense in lambs nudging the teats of their dams to bring down milk, in the raucous tumult of crows high in trees, in the splendor of leaves gorging on sun. . . . No name is large enough to hold this power, but of all the inadequate names, the one that comes to me now is spirit.

Not noticing spring's amazing display of fecundity is bad enough. Romanticizing it is worse. What is going on under our feet, in trees over our heads, is not some singsongy, sunshiny, insouciant love fest. We are not witnessing a live version of a child's book of garden verses full of syrupy joy, though for sure there is joy in it all for us. I know of no one who sees this more clearly than author Annie Dillard. She looks at a leaf of grass and sees not just one slim green miracle but a meadow full of clones.

"It is not one pine I see," she writes in *Pilgrim at Tinker Creek*, "but a thousand. I myself am not one but legion. And we are all going to die.

> In this repetition of individuals is a mindless stutter, an imbecilic fixedness that must be taken into account. The driving force behind all this fecundity is a terrible pressure I also must consider, the pressure of birth and growth, the pressure that splits the bark of trees and shoots out seeds, that squeezes out the egg and bursts the pupa, that hungers and lusts and drives the creature relentlessly toward its own death.

How strong is this pressure Dillard notices, how rampant the fertility? She points out that in the lower Bronx, people once found an ailanthus tree fifteen feet high growing from the corner of a garage roof. Bamboo, she notes, can grow three feet in twenty-four hours. And once, in an experiment, a single grass plant, winter rye, was allowed to grow in a greenhouse for four months. At the end, the plant had set forth 378 miles of roots—about 3 miles a day. The plant had grown 14 billion root hairs.

"In a single cubic inch of soil," she writes, "the length of the root hairs totaled 6,000 miles." Imagine that. But that's just the point. We usually don't imagine it. We usually ignore it. We usually have no clue about it. We simply see trees budding and grass turning green. Our fancy turns to love and we go blithely on our way, blind witnesses to a power Scott Russell Sanders calls spirit, a power that helps us understand who we really are.

"If," Sanders writes, "we and the creatures who share the earth with us are only bundles of quarks in motion, however intricate or clever the shapes, then our affection for one another, our concern for other species, our devotion to wildness, our longing for union with the Creation are all mere delusions."

But evidence piles on evidence that these are not delusions. When we experience love, concern, devotion, union, we grow to understand that they are even more real than what we can touch and see and verify scientifically.

So in this fertile time of year, we begin to understand that nature is sacramental. That is, it's a visible revelation of the invisible. It points to spirit, to energy, to an inexplicable gift for which our only adequate response is silent gratitude.

Summer's the Time Just to Be
June 18, 1995

As we enter summer—which Robert Louis Stevenson once called "the blue and glowing days"—we arrive at the time of year when we should simply be. And "be" here is a very lively verb indeed.

Summer is for the now. It's when we should immerse ourselves—nerve endings alert, taut, hungry, probing—in the present. It's when our senses should test their powers of observation, of touch, of connection with life's relentless hunger for itself. Summer is, in short, the fullness of life.

"Postpone the anatomy of summer," the poet Wallace Stevens once pleaded. "Let's see the very thing and nothing else." Exactly.

There is an insouciant fatness to summer, and our job—if you can even call it that—is to marinate in it, to run into its warm arms and embrace it with abandon.

Maybe you remember as a small child throwing yourself off the side of a swimming pool and into the saving arms of your mother or father. It's that kind of risky letting go to which summer calls us again and again.

When I was a boy, my idea of a summer's day well spent was to gather up my baseball equipment—glove, ball, bat—and fly out the side door of our house, down the hill, across the corner of our orchard, through our garden, across a neighbor's backyard, and into the street that led me, a block and a half later, to the school playground.

There I would find the "very thing" of summer "and nothing else." There my friends and I would coagulate into ad hoc, jury-rigged teams, and we would play as if the sun had frozen in the sky and tomorrow would never come.

If you don't give yourself over to such pure action, summer at least is where you should crouch hushed—and watch as the very life that spring promised matures.

From the back door of my maternal grandparents' house I could walk in less than two minutes into a cornfield my grandfather planted and prayed over. Sometimes on hot summer days, when the air lay heavy on simmering apple trees, I would go to that field and enter a row of stalks much taller than I was.

It was almost impossible to breathe in there, so still and hot was the Illinois air. But there was something electric about being in that place, something that spoke to me of what I later would learn to call cell divisions and the genetic insistence that life go on.

The poet Hilda Doolittle—better known simply as H. D.—once wrote of the kind of summer heat "that presses up and blunts the points of pears / and rounds the grapes." It's that fertile, thick air I associate with the context of summer, air that tells us to sit in deep grass and spend an hour watching ants, twenty minutes following a ladybug, fifteen tracing the arcing green stretch of a blade of grass. This is when, as Wallace Stevens said, "the mind lays by its trouble." As a place from which to watch the amazing gift of life, summer is,

Stevens wrote, "the natural tower of all the world, / The point of survey, green's green apogee."

The danger in summer is that we'll get so busy with the doing that we won't take time just to be. It's easy to plan trips to the lake, to round up the family for a trek to the beach, for a mountain hike, for an afternoon at the pool.

But the point of doing any of that is not the planning, not the details, not the distractions. The point is to notice the wind corrugating the surface of the lake. The point is to hold a grain of sand on the end of your finger and imagine the amazing journey it took to get there.

The point of summer is to be—with all your nerve endings exposed, longing to touch and be touched.

Autumn Whispers to Us of Final Things
October 9, 1994

I have never had a fascination with death, but autumn, my favorite season, keeps me in touch with its inevitability, its lock-jawed determination to prevail.

And that's not a bad thing. It is wise, as I move through life's middle stages, to remember that the end is coming and, what's more, that it cannot be stopped. Such knowledge leads to wisdom and prevents the arrogance of presumed immortality with which humanity is so often afflicted.

Autumn whispers to us of final things, softly in its early days, louder as winter prepares to take the stage. It is now that the grass slows its growth from the rapacious fecundity of high summer. It is now that the surprising evening air ripples past our bare arms and chills us unexpectedly. It is now that the trees, certain of winter's approach, wisely begin to cut off life to their leaves so as not to spend prodigally what the center of the trees will need to survive.

So we see trees that have been deep green suddenly flame into yellows and reds and golds, as if nature herself were giving us a gift of grace—beauty—to compensate for our loss.

No doubt it could have been arranged for leaves to go directly from lush green to dead brown, with no showing off in between, no flash-dancing, no reckless acts of loveliness. But the Creator seems to love to show off.

Where I live the trees seem to be rushing to yellows and mustards this year, though here and there you can see bright splotches of crimson and deep purple. A tree on the lawn of a synagogue near me has suddenly and thoroughly turned mahogany and is quickly shedding. But less than a mile away I know of a tree turning in a way that makes no sense at all. It has remained green except for one thin patch—perhaps five feet wide—stretching from top to bottom. That patch has gone almost magenta.

That's a wonderful thing about the ways of nature. For the most part, they're not ways you could guess. If humans had constructed nature's rules, they would lack the very surprises and irregularities that give them texture, that give them wonder, that give them life, that make them so believable.

I share this fascination with author Annie Dillard, who once wrote, "I am horribly apt to approach some innocent at a gathering and, like the ancient mariner, fix him with a wild, glitt'ring eye and say, 'Do you know that in the head of the caterpillar of the ordinary goat moth there are two hundred twenty-eight separate muscles?' The poor wretch flees. I am not making chatter; I mean to change his life."

I do not have Dillard's capacity for what even she calls trivia about the oddities of nature, but I do find that my antennae for the ways of the natural world are more finely tuned in the autumn. Perhaps that's because of the sense that time is running out on me, for this year, anyway. And who can ever know if this will be one's last fall, one's last summer? We have no guarantees.

And so, the other morning, I stood not far from a cornfield at the city's edge and tried to take in its death throes. Once green and flexible in summer's warm breezes, it is now going brown and brittle. It is daily, relentlessly, returning to the dust from which it came.

And what autumn is here to teach us, I think, is the hard truth that we all share that destiny. How much better to make peace with it now—while the midday air is still gentle and the nights still soft— rather than waiting until hard-hearted winter speaks to us of death harshly and without remorse. How very much better.

Wait in Stillness as Dark Gives Way to Light
January 16, 1994

Everywhere I've lived—except for warm-hearted India—winter and death have been of one substance.

Both speak of final things. Both have harsh intentions; are uncontrollable, lack manners, subtract instead of add, slow instead of quicken, moan instead of sing. The cold, tedious spaces of winter, like the unmapped canyons of death, are unfathomable. A winter's night can be eternal.

Where I grew up northwest of Chicago, hard by Wisconsin—and where I lived for a few years in the late 1960s, Rochester, New York—winter can bite the soul with ice. It is not Bemidji, Minnesota, or Shungnak, Alaska, but once the ground is tundra-brittle, what else is there to say—or feel?

Winter can work on the heart, can lock down the spirit, can crowd the soul's dark interior plain with isobars of relentless sullenness.

My father died in winter, two Januaries ago now. The whole Midwest that bruised and bruising week was engulfed in a gelatinous mid-thirties vapor, and we buried Dad in earth that wasn't quite frozen, though, of course, it would be soon.

But I was born in winter—forty-nine Januaries ago—so I tell myself winter is not all death, not all endings, not all contractions.

It is, however, a hard lesson to learn, and I cannot imagine our earliest ancestors, without the science of seasons to guide them, trying to understand winter. They must have wondered if it would ever end.

The image of winter as the embodiment of death and finality is, in fact, very old. Two thousand years ago, when Jesus was trying to explain the end of time, he described how people would flee to the mountains to try to escape the turmoil. The thirteenth chapter of Mark, in the New Revised Standard Version, quotes him as telling people to pray that all this won't happen in winter. There will be, Jesus says, "suffering, such as has not been from the beginning of the creation. . . ."

In the Palestinian winter, of course, heavy rains swell streams to impassability for people in flight. Winter, in other words, limits possibilities.

Is there anything more remarkable, more breathtaking, more soul-shriveling than to stand in the evening on frozen ground—brown, brittle grass rigid in death—and watch helplessly as the winter sun slips past the rim of the world, while, from the east, the sky dissolves to black as if eaten by the night's insatiable love for its own darkness?

And yet it is at precisely such a mournful time that we must dream of roses blooming and meadows full of wildflowers grown akimbo, dancing in the air's gentle waltzes. For our minds know what our hearts would deny—that winter, for all its enthusiasm for death, for all its embrace of the soul's black holes, is finally just a passage to spring, when fecundity triumphs and life forces its way back to the top.

We are even given hints. Just before Christmas, the days, minute by grudging minute, begin to stretch out as the long nights reluctantly retreat.

And just now we are passing what meteorologists think of as the depth of winter, the mid-January days in which, on average, the temperatures are the lowest of the year. Now the lengthening days will begin to drag up the thermometer's readings. The lowest part of winter's valley now is behind us, even though spring still is barely a hope.

It is now that winter, if we let it, can give us time and space to let go of what needs to be released. We can settle down, if not for a long winter's nap, at least for a time when we pay homage to the frightful power and reality of death so that we can more realistically—which means more joyfully—celebrate renewed life when it comes with the melting ice.

This is winter. This is where life lies fallow in fields and hearts. This is where—hard as it is to imagine—seed sighs, then germinates, where all that is life begins to imagine itself anew. And that includes us.

We are to be still now. We are to play possum. We are to prepare the soil in which spring may work its miracles of rebirth and wonder.

That is why we have winter.

Making Sense of the News

Cobbled Together from Used Parts
March 24, 2001

The decoding of the human genome is helping us rediscover an ancient truth about ourselves that often gets lost in our culture's myopic, undiscerning proclivity for newness.

We are relearning what the ancient Celts knew; as Benedictine author Esther de Wall put it: There is something in us older than we are.

Once we unravel the long double helix of DNA, once we find our thirty thousand or so genes along those intricate strands, once we listen to what our genome has to tell us, we discover that who we are is in many ways a gift from our ancestors. Our history is deeply embedded in our genetic code, and we carry with us at least part of the story of everyone who preceded us.

We are living genetic libraries. This is both a humbling and a liberating revelation—but one we've known intuitively all along.

When people say a child has her father's nose or his mother's eyes, we mean that there is something in us older than we are. This seems both paradoxical and obvious. Indeed, it is both.

Although we can't escape the fact that we carry bloodlines rooted in the fogs and smokes of antiquity, the fact is that each of us has emerged from this long trail unique, unparalleled.

We know this, as I say, intuitively, but now we see that our uniqueness finds its genetic roots in something called SNPs—single nucleotide polymorphisms.

Humans are, it turns out, 99.9 percent genetically identical. It's that 0.1 percent—those little SNPs—that gives us our physical individuality. So we are humbled to know we aren't really new people and yet liberated by the knowledge that our genetic commonality means we belong to the whole human family.

But the idea that there is something in us older than we are finds support in sciences beyond genetics, too—and even beyond psychology's Jungian notion of our "collective unconscious." For instance, cosmology and biochemistry combine to tell us that the very atoms that make us up—the carbon, the hydrogen, the calcium in us—were not originally ours. They have come to us through time and space. They have journeyed through the explosions of stars, have danced on comet tails, have rained down on the earth in thunderstorms and eventually have coagulated in our sinews, our bones, our hair.

As George Gale, philosophy professor at the University of Missouri–Kansas City, is fond of telling his classes, "The heavy atoms in our bodies used to be part of somebody else's sun."

Our very hearts are a concocted soup of particles that have been pinballing around the universe since there's been a universe—though, of course, in this time and place they serve a function they never served before and never will again.

We are quite literally cobbled together from used parts. Therefore, there is not just something in us that is older than ourselves, there is nothing in us that is not older than ourselves.

It is not yet possible to know exactly how this affects who we are. Do our preexistent parts account for why our deepest spirit sometimes unexpectedly resonates with ancient music we've never heard before?

Is it remnants of bygone civilizations glued into our marrow that causes our souls to long for homelands we've never visited, those points of departure for great-great-great-grandparents who left the Old World or were dragged here in slave ships?

Christians sometimes talk of being "born again" or "born anew," words Jesus spoke to tell Nicodemus how to enter into an eternal relationship with God. The phrase is useful and has an honorable history. But sometimes I fear it lets people imagine they bring nothing with them into such transformations. In fact, when we enter any experience in life we bring with us nearly the whole of human history. Our story began long before us and will continue long after us.

As we unpack our genome, we should do so with reverence, recognizing that we are handling precious historical (even sacred) documents. But we would be foolish to imagine that we are nothing but our genome, nothing but the vast collection of gathered atoms that form us.

The ancient Celts also understood that we are, in fact, mystical new creations, made with the parts at hand.

It's an understanding we would do well to recover in this time when science is racing ahead of us, jangling our nerves.

Deep Scars Etched in Kosovo and Colorado
April 25, 1999

We've all seen photographs and videotape of the bedraggled, bewildered refugees being bulldozed out of Kosovo like toxic waste and the startled Columbine High School students in Littleton fleeing the fierce incoherence of death's booted march through the routine of a Colorado spring morning.

And we have tried to imagine so much pain, heartache, and panic, coagulated like the blood of hunted animals. We have tried to envision how both Kosovars and Coloradans—though facing different disasters—can reclaim uprooted, terrified, untethered lives.

I can't imagine what that will be like. I know only that even the common griefs of lives lived in relative peace never fully go away, that even isolated from war and unpredictable, run-amok violence, we can experience wounds so profound that they change us forever.

I recently rediscovered the breathtaking nature of this truth in the midst of e-mail conversation with my three sisters. We are, except geographically, very close. One sister lives in California, one in Illinois, one in North Carolina. So we talk almost daily through cyberspace.

Recently my oldest sister mentioned that the day before had been the birthday of her first baby. The little girl lasted less than an hour in New York City in 1961 before succumbing to appalling birth defects that later research showed a prescription drug had caused.

I was a high school sophomore then. I have only a foggy remembrance of the birth and death. Somehow it happened outside my physical and (apparently) emotional space, so I have no details in memory from which to reconstruct it. But our recent e-mail suddenly brought back vibrantly hurtful, piercingly clear memories from my two older sisters, one the mother of that dead child, the other now a registered nurse.

I want to share with you some of what they wrote, not because their story is unique or that you should feel any vicarious grief about the loss of my first niece. Rather, I want you to notice how deeply this fairly common kind of bereavement has marked these two women. Then, by contrast, imagine how indelibly the refugees in the Balkans and the students in Littleton will be scarred.

My nurse sister says she "came home for lunch from school and Mom told me that the baby had died. I don't remember Mom crying. I knew that I could not cry. I just didn't understand the message 'the baby was dead.'"

After lunch she walked the half a block back to school and "wished I had somewhere else to go." But she went to her first afternoon class, biology, and "as I sat at the lab table in the back of the room I contemplated the birth and death of the little girl. . . . I began to cry. I had no clue where the tears came from, who they were for, what I was doing in class."

The teacher "came to the back of the class, put his hands on my shoulders and asked me if I were OK. No one in the whole world had ever done that. It mattered to him that I was OK. I told him what was wrong. He rubbed my shoulders a little and asked if I'd like to leave the room for awhile. I said, 'No.' I could not leave the only place on earth that anyone had ever acknowledged my sadness."

The clarity of her memory stuns me. As do the equally distinct memories of our sister: "When I awoke after the breach birth—when I knew several times I was going to die; I could hear them screaming at me—a nurse was sitting beside me. She told me the baby lived for forty-five minutes and it was better that she was gone. I will always remember the eerie purple light and her kindness when she held my hand." When my sister's once-bearded husband appeared in her distressed vision, he had shaved and "I did not know who he was."

Within two weeks, my sister was back at the Juilliard School of Music, where she was a pipe organ major, for final exams and a juried recital. She received a high grade "but I was a zombie and devastated. I could not make the enormous black hole in my heart go away."

If one death can mark two women so irrevocably, what I'm forced to conclude is that the Balkans and Littleton are full of people who can never make the black holes in their hearts vanish. It's not that they can never know joy. It's that even in times of elation they will carry, as permanent legacies, memories of evil, abhorrent days of unrequited bleeding.

Sucked into the Black Hole of Racial Hatred
July 18, 1999

The terrifying story of Benjamin Nathaniel Smith still angers me.

Smith, whose fierce hatred of anyone who isn't white led him on a murder-suicide explosion across central Illinois and Indiana over the Fourth of July weekend, was a member of a repugnant group that misidentifies itself as the World Church of the Creator.

The only words that name doesn't outrageously distort and demean are "of" and "the." The "world" has nothing to do with it. It is in no sense a "church." And identifying itself with the "creator" is unconscionable blasphemy.

What are outfits like the World Church of the Creator about? And how do people get sucked into the vortex of their black hole of hate?

I won't make myself popular with leaders of established religions by saying this, but part of the problem is that far too many people are theologically illiterate—even those who pledge allegiance to a particular religion. They either don't really know what they believe or, if they do, they can't explain why they believe it. They can't, in other words, do what the New Testament book of I Peter calls on Christians to do, which (in the New International Version) is to account for "the hope that is in you."

When people stumble around in a syncretistic fog, untethered to any clear, historically tested set of beliefs, they become gullible enough to buy the boneheaded claims of any bogus "church" that comes along. Unrooted in any set of principles they can describe or justify, they fall for almost anything—even something as absurd as the racist poppycock the World Church of the Creator and similarly evil groups profess.

Now, there's theological illiteracy and there's theological illiteracy. Which is to say that there are good-hearted, well-motivated members of religions who cannot articulate anything like a systematic theology but who grasp what is ethically and morally out of bounds.

By contrast, there are people whose theological lens is either so narrow or so broad that they find it impossible to differentiate morally defensible positions from the kind of destructive rot the World

Church of the Creator, the Ku Klux Klan, and similar fear-based outfits preach.

If their lens is too narrow, they focus so tightly on one matter—race, say—that they fail even to imagine mitigating information. If their lens is too broad, they assume that all ideas are of equal value and, as a result, mistake madness for reason.

Benjamin Smith, it turns out, left clues about what led him into the toxic world of virulent racism.

"What set me into action," he wrote in a hate group's recent newsletter, "was when I was forced to live in the dorms" at the University of Illinois. "I was from a well-to-do, mostly white area (with significant Jewish infestation). I discovered that the vast majority of black, brown and yellow students were here because the government was paying their way. That bothered me. I felt as if what was once our government had begun to turn against white people."

My, oh my. Deconstructing such know-nothingism could fill volumes.

This sheltered lad from a wealthy Chicago suburb (notice his malignant word *infestation* to describe Jewish neighbors) discovered the diversity of the real world and was unprepared to engage it rationally by enjoying and learning from the variety. Instead, he saw everyone as a color. And rather than debating legitimate issues raised by affirmative action and similar efforts to redress past wrongs, he told lies about how the government is paying to educate "the vast majority" of minority students.

Waiting to grab witless people like Smith was the World Church of the Creator, the origin of which can be traced to Ben Klassen, who was state chairman of George Wallace's 1968 American Independent Party's presidential campaign.

Klassen, who committed suicide in 1993, wrote a 1973 book advocating a "Rahowah" (racial holy war) against blacks, Jews, and others. The World Church of the Creator, now based in East Peoria, Illinois, is said to have nearly fifty chapters nationwide. Heaven help us.

We simply must find a way to help people evaluate loony ideas coming from alleged religions. If we don't, more Benjamin Smiths will fill our news columns—and our cemeteries.

A-Bomb: We've Reaped the Whirlwind
July 16, 1995

Fifty years ago today, at 5:29:45 A.M. at Alamogordo, New Mexico, the sky at the Trinity test site ignited, and nothing in the world has been the same since.

That stunning flash was brighter than the sun and ten thousand times hotter. If we follow the shock waves from the first atomic bomb test, we find that the event has left us confused, frightened, and unable even to imagine how to get the profoundly disquieting nuclear genie we set free that morning back into the lamp.

There is, in fact, no turning back. In a successful war effort to preserve our freedom and defeat the forces of darkness, we sowed the wind and have reaped the whirlwind.

When that test bomb lit up the predawn desert on July 16, 1945, Robert Oppenheimer, director of the Los Alamos National Laboratory, which produced "the gadget," remembered a line from the Bhagavad Gita: "I am become death, the shatterer of worlds."

At the same moment, the only newspaper reporter to cover the event, William L. Laurence of the *New York Times*, lying on his belly, thought of God's command from Genesis 1:3, "Let there be light."

And Kenneth Bainbridge, the test director, turned to Oppenheimer and said, "Oppie, now we're all sons of bitches!"

This jarring juxtaposition of sacred writ and profane exclamation set the pattern for how, over these fifty years, we have tried to live on the same fragile planet with the eight-hundred-pound gorilla of nuclear weaponry.

We have prayed to God for wisdom. We have cursed our fates. We have found somber meaning in our unleashing of this elemental force of nature, this shatterer of worlds. We have cowered in terror at the evil such power can represent—and not just represent, but actually be. And we have used atomic power for peaceful purposes as well as to kill.

The initial reaction of the scientists who created the bomb was exultation. But that was coupled almost immediately with dread.

The brilliant physicist I. I. Rabi, on hand to watch the test that morning, described it this way:

> We turned to one another and offered congratulations, for the first few minutes. Then, there was a chill, which was not the morning cold;

it was a chill that came to one when one thought, as for instance when I thought of my wooden house in Cambridge, and my laboratory in New York, and of the millions of people living around there, and this power of nature which we had first understood it to be—well, there it was.

Those scientists soon reported their chilling success to President Harry S. Truman, who was meeting with allied leaders at Potsdam. Truman quickly authorized use of the bomb. Then this rough beast, its hour come round at last, slouched towards Hiroshima to be born in the shape of a mushroom cloud. Indeed, within weeks two bombs were dropped on Japan, collapsing the empire and preventing a costly allied invasion of the island.

Rabi's accurate conclusion: "A new thing had just been born; a new control; a new understanding of man, which man had acquired over nature."

From that day to this we have lived in the shadow of that cloud and the bombs that stir it to terrifying life. We have argued over the uses and potential uses of nuclear weapons. We have protested them. We have given thanks for their role in preventing a third world war. We have analyzed them almost to death. We—and other countries—have spent kings' ransoms to produce them so we wouldn't have to use them. We have devised treaties to prevent their spread. And recently we have even agreed to destroy some of them and not point them at each other.

But the one thing we have not done is outrun them, hide from them, make them go away. We cannot. We have, after all, eaten of the tree of the knowledge of good and evil.

Almost immediately after the bombs were dropped on Japan, the idea of such a stupendous killing machine swept through our culture, our collective conscience. It was, in fact, astonishing how quickly the dark reality of what we had unleashed impressed itself on the nation's psyche.

Some of this reaction is reported in Paul Boyer's book, *By the Bomb's Early Light*. For instance, a New York minister described his thoughts when he heard about Hiroshima: "Everything else seemed suddenly to become insignificant. I seemed to grow cold, as though I had been transported to the waste spaces of the moon. . . . For I knew that the final crisis in human history had come. What that atomic bomb had done to Japan, it could do to us."

Since that day, we have lived with a terrible, palpable sense of vulnerability.

H. V. Kaltenborn, the NBC radio commentator, said when Hiroshima was destroyed: "For all we know, we have created a Frankenstein! We must assume that with the passage of only a little time, an improved form of the new weapon we use today can be turned against us."

What, finally, had we created—or at least uncovered?

There are many ways to answer that, but what it comes down to is high-tech, man-made mass death. Since July 16, 1945, we have faced the deeply traumatizing vision of the instantaneous evaporation of the human race.

It's not, God knows, that before that date humanity hadn't figured out how to kill itself efficiently. Indeed, much of history is simply a recounting of the crimes of death we have visited on our kind.

This is especially true of the twentieth century, beginning with World War I, a profoundly shocking series of mechanized death actions that left the world reeling and the poets mourning that the world had lost the flower of its youth for a world no better than "an old bitch gone in the teeth."

The spiral of violence that grew into the sneak attack on Pearl Harbor, the firestorm bombing of Dresden, the carpet bombing of Japan, and, evil of evils, the Holocaust itself led almost inevitably— as scientists pursued "progress"—to nuclear weapons. The path to Hiroshima was paved with scientific breakthroughs.

But it wasn't until Alamogordo-Hiroshima-Nagasaki that we found a way almost literally to wipe out all human life in a day.

Eventually Americans accommodated themselves to the reality of the bomb's presence, but as the years went by—and nuclear weapons spread via science and treason to the Soviet Union and elsewhere—there was never any forgetting that we had made technologically efficient mass death a serious possibility.

We built bomb shelters and debated whom we'd allow into them. As children, we crawled under our school desks to prepare for attack and for radioactive fallout, even while wearing our "Atomic Bomb Rings" from General Mills. And we kept up the scientific push begun in the Manhattan Project until we had the hydrogen bomb and until, finally, we had outfitted missiles with multiple warheads bristling with threatening energy of unspeakable deadliness.

Science, the very thing the Enlightenment had given us to know our world more certainly, gave us Werner Heisenberg's Uncertainty Principle as a foundational understanding of the subatomic world. That meant, in a sense, that all bets were off.

Then science broke open the atom itself, and the astonishing energy from the resultant explosion tore away our protection, our pre-nuclear intuition that we always had a chance to outrun arrows shot from bows.

The truth that is so striking fifty years after Alamogordo is that high-tech, man-made mass death was made possible by what philosophers and social analysts have come to call "modernity"—that onward and upward post-Enlightenment "progress" in science, technology, politics, and economics.

As President Clinton has become fond of saying about the spread of such good ideas as democracy, those very ideas carry with them a dark underside.

There is great—and maybe, this side of paradise, unresolvable—tension between our naturally curious minds and the sin of pride, which is to say, the bad choice Adam and Eve made in the old Bible story. They wanted—and tried—to know what God knew, just as we, too, demand to know all of life's secrets. Even Stephen Hawking, the superstar of modern physics, has had the stunning arrogance to claim that once we figure out the so-called grand unified theory of the universe, "we will know the mind of God."

The problem in our pursuit of cosmic mysteries is that along with the redemptive things we've managed to learn, we've also discovered how to commit instant global suicide. We proved that at Alamogordo. And though so far we haven't been quite crazy or unlucky enough to pull it off, we can never, ever forget that we know how.

That's the remarkable, breathtaking truth we have lived with for fifty years. But it's a truth that has not made us free. Neither has it made us noticeably humbler or obviously wiser. It has simply made us terribly vulnerable and, in poet William Butler Yeats's apt phrase, it has vexed us to nightmare.

Astonishing Resources Created Such a Weapon
August 20, 1995

LOS ALAMOS, NEW MEXICO—These telling words in a display at the small Los Alamos Historical Museum here describe the first atomic bomb: "Concentrated in that small unimpressive amount of metal was the work of a hundred thousand people, the industrial strength of America, the hope that with it we might even stop the war." They are from Frederick Reines, one of the physicists who, fifty years ago, helped build that stunning weapon.

There were not, of course, a hundred thousand people living here at the secret Los Alamos bomb research facility in the Jemez mountains of northern New Mexico. At the peak of laboratory activities in the 1940s, the population was more like six thousand. The other ninety-four thousand or whatever number were scattered across the country working on bits and pieces of the Manhattan Project.

In Reines's words there is, nonetheless, an important reminder of how—driven by fear and a primal survival instinct—America collected astonishing resources to produce the bombs that ended World War II.

If you wander around Los Alamos today, it's not easy to imagine the crude nature of the encampment that, in 1943, confiscated and moved into the old Los Alamos Ranch School, which had operated since 1917 as a special institution for (mostly wealthy) boys. Official documents describe that scientific enclave as "a ramshackle town of temporary buildings scattered helter-skelter over the landscape, an Army post that looked more like a frontier mining camp."

Today Los Alamos has become simply an attractive small town (though still with a national scientific laboratory) entered by a perfectly modern highway, not the "tortuous, winding dirt road" the first scientists found in 1943.

And in the midst of a town with a Furr's supermarket and a Café Allegro coffee shop selling Red Zinger tea and espresso, it's easy to lose sight of the enormous energy that went into creating a place where scientists could imagine how to set free the atom's awesome power.

Perhaps the most remarkable thing was the secrecy. On August 6, 1945, the day the atomic bomb fell on Hiroshima, the Santa Fe *New Mexican* described how complete that secrecy had been.

"The taboo on the mention of Los Alamos," it reported, "was final, complete and until today, irrevocable and not susceptible to any exceptions whatsoever.

"A whole social world existed in nowhere in which people were married and babies were born nowhere. People died in a vacuum, autos and trucks crashed in a vacuum. . . . Even the graduates of the Los Alamos Ranch School, the institution which preceded Uncle Sam's Atomic Bomb Project Laboratory, ceased to be graduates of Los Alamos; they bounded direct from Public School No. 7 clear into the classrooms of Harvard and Yale."

As I say, I am mostly struck by the size and narrow focus of the project. Since then, our country has seen a similar mobilization of resources from time to time. The drive to reach the moon comes to mind as do the several wars we have fought since World War II—perhaps the Gulf War, in its terrible speed and energy, being the most breathtaking example.

But I'm having trouble remembering many examples of similarly concentrated national crash courses designed to ameliorate social problems. One possible example, given all the money spent on it over the years, is the fight against cancer. But even that has not been pursued with the stark intensity we saw fifty years ago here in Los Alamos. And the War on Poverty wasn't much of a war at all.

Indeed, it raises the question of whether our failure to solve such social problems as poverty and poor education is because we lack resolve or, rather, because someone has decided—maybe even correctly—that such problems, because of their terrible complexity, do not lend themselves to the singularity of effort that drove scientists in Los Alamos.

The atomic pioneers of fifty years ago, after all, were given only one goal—and were spurred toward it by such taskmasters as J. Robert Oppenheimer and General Leslie R. Groves, men who were, quite simply, driven.

I don't know whether it would work to collect six thousand people for two years and set them to the task of, say, fixing public education. Maybe that is asking for a simple answer to a complicated problem.

But Los Alamos, where such an effort worked spectacularly well to find a more efficient way to kill people, makes me wonder what we'd lose by trying.

Misusing Elian's Story for Political Gain
February 13, 2000

Apotheosis, the practice of declaring mortals divine, was a common practice in ancient Rome. Common, at any rate, if you were an emperor.

However, this honor was not accorded Vespasian (who ruled from A.D. 69 to 79) in his lifetime. History records his dying words this way: "Vae, puto deus fio," meaning, "Oh dear, I think I'm becoming a god." He was right. Immediately after his death he was deified.

You may be under the mistaken impression that the highly developed modern mind of humankind—stuffed, as it is, with both the wisdom of the ages and today's leading economic indicators—has thrown off apotheosis as a bad idea and superstitious act. But no.

The modern equivalent of declaring certain mere mortals divine has been happening recently with a six-year-old boy, Elian Gonzalez, whose mother fled Cuba with him late last year.

Elian's mother died at sea, while somehow he survived and was rescued on Thanksgiving. As you know, he now lives with relatives in Miami and has become the center of a stupefying international custody battle in which several members of Congress have competed for the title of Most Abhorrent Demagogue. (I have declared that contest a tie.)

Surprisingly enough, the media (which often employ the ritual of apotheosis for Hollywood starlets and CEOs of profitless Internet start-up companies) have been outperformed by some members of the virulently anti-Castro Cuban community in Florida.

Here, in fact, is what the Associated Press reported recently about Elian: "Some Cuban Americans revere him as a divine messenger, believing it is God's plan for Elian to remain in the United States."

One elderly Cuban American, demonstrating outside the home where Elian recently met with his Cuban grandmothers, declared: "Elian is a prodigy of God. God brought him to this country. I think he should stay here."

A Cuban artist, Alexis Blanco, has produced a painting called "The Boy of the Dolphins," depicting Elian wrapped in a blue blanket inside an inner tube and surrounded by three dolphins as the hand of God pulls puppet strings that lead the boy away from godless communism.

I would be the last to deny God's sovereignty by declaring that God would never use a small boy to accomplish the divine will. In fact, the Christian religion, to which I belong, is rooted in the story of just such a thing happening two thousand years ago.

But the metamorphosis of Elian Gonzalez into a divine child gives us a chance to think about the distressing human tendency to enlist God as a political ally in any cause, both high-minded and ignoble.

For clearly some people have sought to turn Elian into God's anti-communist messiah.

Most of us know, of course, that 150 years ago in this country, various voices in the Christian church pointed to God's word in scripture as a justification for the unholy institution of slavery. And only in recent years has the Dutch Reformed Church in South Africa quit using the Bible to defend apartheid, the evil policy of racial segregation.

The hard lesson is that we attach divine purpose to humans and merely human events at our peril. Was David Koresh the Lord's prophet, as he claimed? Many of his Branch Davidian followers believed so and—due to a run-amok government—paid for that false allegiance with their lives.

Elian himself, of course, being only six years old, is too young to lead anyone astray in that way on purpose. Friends of the Gonzalez family say Elian told about seeing an angel out at sea and about dolphins swimming near him, which may have protected him from sharks. But he cannot and should not be blamed for the imaginings of people who would use his painful story for political gain.

Being cautious about attributing divine intentions to parts of the human drama, however, does not mean that we must close our eyes to the sacred. Indeed, too often people seek God only in what they don't know and not in what they do. They fail to see the mysterious and astonishing workings of God in the mundane aspects of life, from sunrises to the physical laws that allow the cosmos to exist— laws for which, most people of faith would say, God is the guarantor.

What we must cultivate is the ability to discern between where God's hand is really at work and where, instead, our own agendas have led to delusion.

The World Needs Genome Guidance
July 2, 2000

The recent announcement at the White House that the first draft of the human genome has been completed made it seem as if utopia were here. Hear some of those words again:

- " . . . the most important, most wondrous map ever produced by humankind."—President Clinton

- "... an epoch-making triumph of science and reason."—Clinton
- "... an undertaking that can benefit the whole of humankind."—British Prime Minister Tony Blair
- "... a revolution in medical science whose implications far surpass even the discovery of antibiotics ..."—Blair
- "... the most visible and spectacular milestone of all."—Francis S. Collins (one of the leaders of the Human Genome Project)
- "... a happy day for the world."—Collins
- "[This] will have a profound impact on the human condition and the treatments for disease and our view on our place in the biological continuum."—J. Craig Venter (his Celera Genomics Corporation completed its own draft of the human genome at the same time the Human Genome Project did)
- "... a new starting point for science and medicine, with potential impact on every disease."—Venter

To be sure, there also were a few words of caution about the hard work and dangers ahead. But they were nearly drowned in a sea of hyperbolic congratulations at least equal in size to the 3.1 billion subunits of DNA that make up the human genome.

And yet we'd all do well to listen to the warnings about the path ahead. We'd do well, in fact, to become genetically literate. If we don't, we may well lose control of our very lives.

The Human Genome Project has been wise to use part of its funding since the beginning to explore the ethical, social, and legal implications of this research. If nothing else, this work has identified some of the questions we all should be asking.

Here are a few such matters to ponder as we bravely enter this new world:

- Who should have access to your own genetic information? Insurers? Employers? Other family members? Courts? Schools? Adoption agencies? Law enforcement agencies? The military? Is there an easy answer that applies to all these?
- Do you own your genetic code? Or, once it's been sequenced

and identified, can others have a claim on it? If so, under what circumstances?

- Do you want to know what your own genome reveals about your vulnerability to diseases? If you choose to remain ignorant—even though genetic therapy could keep you from getting some of those diseases—are you causing an unfair allocation of health-care resources by requiring treatment after the onset of the disease?
- If no treatment is yet available, should there be any genetic testing?
- Should parents have the right to design their babies by paying for genetic manipulation before conception? If they have such a right, what are the implications for the gene pool?
- Should parents have the right to allow children to be born with genetic defects if prebirth genetic therapy could have prevented it?
- How reliable are genetic testing and genetic therapy?
- Who decides what is "normal" and what is a "disability"?
- The government already has issued lots of patents on genes. Should this continue? What should the rules be?
- How much of our behavior can we blame on genes? Are we free moral agents who should be held accountable for our behavior or are we biologically determined puppets, manipulated by our genetic codes?
- Given finite health-care resources, how much should be devoted to genetic research, how much to treating currently ill patients, and how much to nongenetic prevention strategies, such as fitness education?
- Some disease genes, it turns out, also confer resistance to other diseases. So just because we can disable a disease gene, should we?
- Are we more than our genome? That is, are we, as many religions maintain, also spiritual beings? And, if so, how do we integrate that understanding into what we're learning about genetics?

Well, this is just a bit of what faces us. Scientists have brought us here—but we'll make a serious mistake if we don't bring in ethicists, sociologists, poets, preachers, philosophers, and others to help guide us now.

Tobacco Family Fortune a Mixed Heritage
July 6, 1997

WINSTON-SALEM, NORTH CAROLINA—On a wall at the Southeastern Center for Contemporary Art here hangs a reddish smoky-artsy photo of a bar (well, maybe a bar; it's hard to tell) by Madison, North Carolina, photographer David M. Spear.

A sign in the photo says, "Tobacco—the new 'black-brown' shade that goes with everything."

It's jarring, that sign in that picture, because these days tobacco doesn't go with anything. And as the new tobacco legal settlement sinks in, nowhere is the killer product more of an awkward member of the family than here in Winston-Salem, once (and maybe still) the tobacco capital of the world.

R. J. (for Richard Joshua) Reynolds showed up in these parts in 1875. He came at age twenty-five from a wealthy Virginia family. Like a lot of twenty-somethings, Reynolds had a terrible idea. Hindsight, indeed, shows his idea was worse than those of most young people. He decided to go into the tobacco business.

Another young man with a bad idea, P. H. Hanes, also showed up here, but three years earlier, in 1872, and two years older, at twenty-seven, from North Carolina. His terrible idea was to go into the plug tobacco business.

But in 1900, Hanes made a brilliant move. He sold his tobacco outfit to R. J. Reynolds and went into the textile business. The result, eventually, was world-famous Hanes underwear and hosiery. Proof of Hanes' brilliance is that no one, from what I can tell, has ever filed a suit claiming that Hanes underwear causes cancer.

By contrast, the company R. J. Reynolds founded has been a major target of folks who say smoking cigarettes can kill you. And the recent proposed tobacco settlement is, in effect, a public admission by tobacco interests that the product Reynolds started peddling in 1875, though legal, has done enormous damage to countless customers. What a business.

This is not to say that the Reynolds folks are finished with the dirty business of selling tobacco. Oh, no. You can still take a tour of a Reynolds plant here and watch the company produce eight thousand cigarettes a minute, testimony to the addictive powers of both nicotine and money.

(I didn't take the Reynolds tour when I was here recently. I don't need to see such a ghastly sight to believe the breathtaking truth that the demand for this killer product is high enough to sustain such numbers.)

Nor is it to say that nothing but evil has flowed from the Reynolds's fortune. Not at all. The Reynolds and Hanes clans— plus some other rich families here, especially the Grays—have all been wise enough to share their financial success with their town, which became known as Winston-Salem in 1913, at the merger of Winston and Salem, two fine names now sullied by being cigarette brands.

Indeed, the name Salem comes from the Hebrew word that means, essentially, peace. And Old Salem, a wonderful place to visit, was—and, with modifications for modernity, still is—a Moravian church town.

Imagine naming something as destructive as a cigarette "peace." What gall.

Author Hamilton C. Horton Jr., in his 1992 book, *Living in Winston-Salem*, writes this of wealthy family contributions to the area: "No worthwhile endeavor has been without the generous support of those families." Everywhere you go here, you find evidence of Reynolds and Hanes money, from museums to colleges to churches. The reach of those fortunes makes strangers think of the most dedicated of company towns.

And as just such a stranger to these parts, I have been struggling with the unseemly nature of all this. I have been trying to imagine how a lethal product like cigarettes has woven itself into legitimate and beautiful and healthy aspects of life here. And I've been wondering whether this multibillion-dollar tobacco settlement can, in the end, really purify or redeem anything.

It's hard to know, but it won't happen unless there are people willing to tell the true history of duplicity, greed, and gross moral failure that has characterized the tobacco industry for a very long time.

And yet even if tobacco sellers have been guilty of all that—and I believe they have—it is instructive to imagine how we ourselves might have behaved in 1875 when faced with the opportunity that presented itself to young R. J. Reynolds.

And it is even more revealing to imagine the impurity of motive and action to which we ourselves might have stooped if we had found ourselves, almost by birth, part of the tobacco industry at some point since 1964, when Surgeon General Luther Terry first warned that smoking cigarettes can cause cancer.

(If you, like me, used to smoke, you were, in effect, once part of the tobacco industry. Another small test of this might be whether we allow ourselves to invest in mutual funds with tobacco holdings.)

Please understand I am not defending duplicity, greed, and gross moral failure. I'm simply saying that R. J. Reynolds's original sin—which he would not have understood to be sin at all—has cast a complex net over many people, from tobacco farmers to factory workers to executives to lawyers who seek to protect those tobacco executives from the consequences of behavior they knew was wrong.

The havoc tobacco has wreaked on the world needs to be condemned. But as I look at wonderful art in a home that once was owned by the Hanes family, it is sobering to remember that—like a televangelist who preaches moral purity but hires prostitutes to satisfy his extramarital lusts—sometimes the spotlight of outrage we shine on the sins of others illuminates our own as well.

Honesty a Rare Commodity in Tobacco Saga
May 3, 1998

The debate over tobacco and its use by teenagers has become a School for Scandal.

Enrollment is free. The only thing you have to do to learn about dishonesty, disingenuousness, and profitable deception is to stay up with the news. Imagine how many teens are getting advanced degrees in immorality simply by following this tawdry tobacco saga.

The tobacco industry and the politicians trying to wrestle with it are in a Tar Baby fight. There will be no winners. The losers, however, clearly will include the teenagers who watch this wretched show and imagine that to succeed in the world one must behave like this, bereft of redeeming values.

Heaven help us.

A primary problem is that historically so few people have been willing to call things by their right names when speaking of tobacco and its destructive character. Frankness and honesty in this story have been rare commodities.

Nicotine is a drug. It is harmful and addictive. Is there any doubt about that now? Is there any doubt that smoking tobacco can cause cancer or that it can lead to all kinds of other diseases? That it can, in the end, kill?

Young people who understand the nature of nicotine also know that, with the exceptions of nicotine and alcohol, the government tries to forbid over-the-counter sales of addictive and harmful drugs. So why, they wonder, are nicotine and alcohol not prohibited? Ah, why not indeed.

This is where young people learn about the power of money, of how money can buy politicians, how it can buy slick marketing techniques like Joe Camel to encourage young people to become addicted to nicotine.

This is where they discover that tobacco companies, which no longer can hawk death on TV commercials, publicize their products by sponsoring sporting events and plastering their brand names on all kinds of merchandise.

This is where they learn how tobacco companies suppress damaging research and destroy evidence of the hazards of smoking. This is where they read that when R. J. Reynolds's top scientist was trying to isolate a tobacco carcinogen in the 1950s, the man who was president of the company then, Edward Darr, asked: "Do we really need to be doing that kind of work?"

This is where they see a picture of the president of the United States—the same man calling the tobacco companies bad names and fighting them left and right on teen smoking—dancing around with a cigar in his mouth, celebrating a legal victory in the Paula Jones case.

Boys and girls, can you spell *hypocrisy*?

This is where they learn the sorry history of the Eighteenth Amendment to the Constitution and the failure of Prohibition—a failure rooted in huge public demand for a product that, when abused, causes nothing but trouble.

Do you see what happens here? Do you see how all of this—and much more that I haven't even mentioned—leads to cynicism, to mistrust, to despair?

The result is that when we read this right-on quote from Minnesota's attorney general, Hubert Humphrey III—"This massive fraud and conspiracy [by the tobacco industry] left an unprecedented toll of death and disease in America"—we wonder, on the basis of no evidence whatsoever, how Humphrey might be compromised in all this.

Or when we hear House Commerce Committee Chairman Tom Bliley, a Virginia Republican, say he's "very concerned about teenage smoking and am taking steps to help reduce it," we wonder why he's doing this now after being a loyal ally of the tobacco interests. Again, without knowing anything about it, we ascribe untoward motives to him.

America's history with tobacco has damaged our people beyond imagining. Now it will surprise no one to learn that tobacco is eating away at the trust of the next generation. Life-affirming values are going up in smoke.

Anxiety Grows as 2000 Draws Near
August 31, 1997

The end is nearly here for this breathtaking millennium, which began with Western Europe gripped by almost unimaginable millennial fever as the year 999 became 1000. As a new millennium approaches, it is unleashing a similar angst—both religious and secular in its roots.

Nervousness over whether computer programs can be fixed in time to preserve the records of this century are mixing with frenetic religious speculation that a new millennium may mean the end of the world.

The only certainty is that 2000 is bringing with it an astonishing set of predictions, fears, plans, hopes, and just plain nonsense.

The marketplace of millenarian ideas—which increasingly means the ubiquitous, irresponsible Internet—brims with bargains, from Christian premillennialists to secular postmillennialists, from survivalists to members of Hinduism's Kala Jnana movement, who await the coming (soon, they say) of an avatar of righteousness to establish a heavenly kingdom on Earth.

"Although often depicted as a fringe phenomenon," says millennial scholar Daniel Wojcik of the University of Oregon, "millenarianism is extremely pervasive."

In his thoughtful new book, *The End of the World as We Know It*, Wojcik says these apocalyptic visions reflect "perceptions of overwhelming societal crisis and a pessimistic outlook for a world so corrupt that it can be redeemed only by superhuman forces through a worldly catastrophe."

This maelstrom of wonderful or wacky ideas divides generally into those with religious and those with secular roots. Both camps (they are not neatly separated) believe the end of the world is coming. The only question is whether it will happen in five minutes, in five billion years (when scientists say the sun will burn out), or sometime in between.

Naturally, it's the doomsday-is-almost-here folks, both religious and secular, who get the most attention.

Author and missionary Lester Sumrall, in his book *I Predict 2000 A.D.*, says the end will come by 2000—"Then Jesus Christ shall reign from Jerusalem for 1,000 years." (Sumrall left before he knew if he was right, however. He died in 1996.)

By contrast, Los Angeles psychologist Robert R. Butterworth, who studies social angst caused by dire predictions, says this: "All those folks who are predicting events from waves of transcendence to prophecies of doom as we enter the year 2000 are going to have a rude awakening when nothing happens—apart from some wild parties and computer snafus."

Of course, not everyone with religious explanations is in a panic. Important voices of calm and reason in this fearful wilderness can be heard pointing out that Jesus said only God knows such things. And who can be certain what God intends?

Still, the biblical prophecy business is a bull market. What amounts to an entire apocalyptic industry looks for and interprets signs of the end, debating each detail and nuance of prophecy, especially the "rapture" of the Christian church. Practitioners in this vast enterprise write books (for instance, about what apocalyptic things the Virgin Mary tells people in apparitions), broadcast findings on radio and TV, set up Internet Web pages, and gather huge followings of people who are at once nervous and joyful with anticipation.

In evaluating these faith-based ideas it helps to remember that the click from 1999 to 2000 reflects a calendar based on an erroneous calculation of the birth of Jesus done by a sixth-century Scythian monk named Dionysius Exiguus (often called Dennis the Diminutive). His work led to our modern calendar with its A.D. (for Anno Domini— Year of our Lord) designation. Thus, the two-thousandth anniversary of Jesus' birth probably occurred several years ago. Also, this millennium is a man-made derivative of base-ten thinking that won't really end until December 31, 2000.

Calendars—no matter how calculated—are littered with failed apocalyptic dates. Early speculation said history would end in 6000 A.M. (Anno Mundi), one calculation of which corresponded to 800 A.D. This was based on the idea that the world would last one thousand years for each day Genesis says it took God to create it (plus a thousand-year Christ-led reign of peace).

In our own time, Jehovah's Witnesses and others have specified dates for the end, only to see them pass. The Seventh-Day Adventist Church, in fact, which grew out of a movement that said Christ would return in 1843 or 1844, eventually issued a statement in 1995 opposing date setting.

Indeed, certainty about Christocentric cosmic events on round-number dates may diminish when we recall that this is the Jewish year 5757 and Islamic year 1418.

Although millennialism's forms have mutated to reflect new concerns, people have long worried about how history will end. For instance, as 999 turned to 1000, Western Europe, especially the Carolingian Empire, was at once terrorized and ecstatic. But hysteria and expectation of the Second Coming gave way to disappointment (and relief).

Nearly all religious millennial speculation grows out of the last book of the New Testament, Revelation, especially chapter 20, which speaks of a thousand-year reign of Christ. A core issue for Christians is how they read the Bible. Do they take it literally, as fundamentalists advocate? Do they view the one thousand years as symbolic? Or do they simply construct their own doctrine?

Reference to Revelation by biblical prophecy writers often is accompanied by allusion to such books as Daniel and Ezekiel in the Hebrew Scriptures, or Old Testament. They are said to hold keys to future events, including identity of the so-called Antichrist, a term that has been applied to everyone from popes to Jimmy Carter and Ronald Reagan, from Nero to Napoleon and Mussolini, from Hitler to Stalin, Mikhail Gorbachev, and computers.

Whatever problems scholars have had with Revelation, it's still true that Christianity's view of history is apocalyptic. It believes Christ will return one day to inaugurate history's end.

English author and theologian Stephen Travis explains: "The hope of Christ's coming at the end of history is the logical and necessary outcome of our faith that God has already acted for our salvation in the historical events of Jesus' life, death and resurrection.

To remove the hope of a final consummation of what Jesus Christ began in history is to undermine the whole idea of God acting in history."

As 2000 nears, however, all this religious millennial talk now competes (or mingles) with secular millennialism, which worries about an apocalyptic ending by nuclear holocaust, say, or environmental disaster. Or which postulates salvation arriving via UFOs. Or looks for another fatalistic resolution of the problem of evil. In this view, we need not wait for God to smash the world. We can do it ourselves.

For instance, books such as John Walvoord's *Armageddon, Oil, and the Middle East Crisis* and Hal Lindsey's *Planet Earth—2000 A.D.* take note of potential secular catastrophes and try to fit them into premillennialist interpretations. In addition, visionaries report a growing flow of messages from the Virgin Mary predicting earthly doom.

But many people with no attachment to theology hold deep fears and beliefs about the world ending in some cataclysm (what Wojcik of the University of Oregon calls "a meaningless apocalypse"). And many of those people, too, are astir as we approach 2000.

Some of this fear is unique to this century, especially that related to nuclear weapons. There has always been speculation about another great flood or a plague or disease—or about some asteroid or other cosmic body crashing into Earth and destroying it. But nuclear and environmental anxiety has grown in importance.

Some beliefs may not quite reach apocalyptic levels, but Stjepan Mestrovic, a Texas A&M sociology professor and author of *The Coming Fin de Siecle,* speaks for many when he says: "TV, our fast lifestyle, the decline of tradition, the disappearance of the community—all this has finally killed off our emotional life. I see 2000 as a culmination of this process. The Internet and personal computers won't build bridges. They'll isolate us more into our own private, mental, unemotional lives."

Whatever happens, it's clear that some wise people expect the world to continue.

And just as it's advisable to be wary of a meteorologist who fails to carry an umbrella when forecasting rain or of an economist whose spouse does all the shopping, it's sensible to observe practices of people who study millennial predictions. Thus it's instructive to know that the Center for Millennial Studies, directed by Richard Landes, a Boston University history professor, is planning events that will run well past the new millennium's start. The center, expecting no rain, carries no umbrella.

Similarly, it's worth noting that in his long 1994 apostolic letter, "As the Third Millennium Draws Near," Pope John Paul II says the future of the church belongs to those "who, born in this century, will reach maturity in the next." Doesn't sound like he's expecting the curtain to drop.

And yet the truth is no one knows whether 2000 will usher in the end of history or merely the end of 1999. And even people who tend to dismiss doomsday talk get drawn in because the questions raised by the new millennium are about final things—with all their terrifying and exhilarating possibilities.

But, in the end, the point is that no one knows if the world will end today in fire or ice, a bang or a whimper, or simply continue for five billion more years. And that ignorance makes everyone an expert and allows false prophets—Herff Applewhite, David Koresh, Shoko Asahara, and others—to play on people's fears and convince them of the logic of their twisted visions.

Now, indeed, we see through a glass, darkly. But we are not blind. And although there are no guarantees, the date-setters' consistent failure suggests there will continue to be plenty of problems to solve in the new millennium—and lots of time in which to solve them.

Science and Religion Run on Different Planes
May 30, 1999

The recently renewed debate over creation and evolution shows not only that science and religion don't understand one another well enough but—worse—sometimes neither side understands even its own self-interest. (And, by the way, the "sides" are not neatly separated but overlap.)

The truth is that at times both sides have lost sight of what is crucial to each and are fighting over secondary matters.

The hostility that has grown out of this appalling display hurts all of us. Science and religion have much of value to say to one another and need to be about that task rather than excoriating one another over peripheral issues.

Christians staking so much on the validity of so-called "creationism" seems to have lost sight of what, for followers of the faith, core orthodoxy is. Essential Christian doctrine has nothing to do with a literal interpretation of the Genesis creation. Rather, it has everything to do with who Jesus Christ is and what he did for humanity—with, in other words, the gospel, the irreducible center to which Christians are tethered.

As Robert W. Jenson says in his compelling 1997 book, *Systematic Theology: The Triune God,* when Jews ask who God is, they answer: "Whoever rescued us from Egypt," a reply based on both history and an interpretation of history through the eyes of faith, not science. When Christians ask the same question, they also answer in a historical-faith way: "Whoever raised Jesus from the dead." Both faiths find their centers in that approach.

As for modern science, its center has nothing to do with a final commitment to any theory about how the world began or how life developed. Rather, it is defined by its commitment to open and constant testing of its theories. Indeed, scientific theories—even ones seemingly locked in concrete—fall by the wayside regularly.

Just last month, scientists and theologians met for three days at the Smithsonian Museum of Natural History in Washington to discuss whether new data from the Hubble Space Telescope can shed light on the question of God's existence. They did not settle this, of course. Indeed, it may be impossible to resolve it to the satisfaction of both science and religion.

But a crucial comment emerged that shows the tentativeness required of science. Joel Primack, a physicist at the University of California at Santa Cruz, said: "Today data are flowing in so fast from new telescopes and other scientific instruments that the question is whether a single one of the current [cosmological] theories can survive."

That's how science works. You look at the world and propose a theory to explain what you see. Then you run experiments to test your theory. Then you try to repeat your results. This often leads to modifying the theory and redoing the process. And on and on. Which is not to say that scientists never feel certain about anything. Rather, it means scientists need to be modest about what they think they know because long-held theories can turn out to be fallible or at least more limited than suspected.

Take, for instance, Isaac Newton's laws of physics. They stood for several hundred years as reliable descriptions of how the physical world works. But when we split the atom in this century we found that Newton's laws seem simply not to apply in much of the subatomic world. Something else, something remarkable and even bizarre goes on there. To begin to grasp what that might be, we've turned to such minds as Werner Heisenberg's and Albert Einstein's. But much mystery remains.

Even if science were able to solve not just evolution but also other mysteries, could it then say why humanity exists or who, if anyone, God is or what God has in mind? No. That's the province of religion. In turn, can religion use science's methods to prove what it trusts to be true? No. Much (though not all) of what people of faith believe is based on divine revelation, which simply cannot be tested by the scientific method.

That's not to say science can't help us grasp our place in the cosmos or that faith can't be both rational and reasonable. But it is to say that they operate on different planes and that one cannot answer the deepest questions posed by the other.

In the end, we'd all do well to remember that neither science nor religion rises or falls on the outcome, if any, of the creation-evolution debate.

Seeking the Dubious Comfort of Certainty
August 29, 1999

Ever since the Kansas Board of Education decided not to require that macroevolution be taught in public schools, I've been struggling with why that action and so much of the critical reaction to it have struck me as reprehensible.

I've finally figured it out. Both have been based on an unwarranted and unbecoming sense of certainty. Indeed, certainty is a curse not only of our American culture but also of human society generally.

That's because far too often we have nailed ourselves to some supposedly absolute truth without imagining either the consequences or the likelihood that we haven't seen all the evidence.

In religious terms, such certainty often gets labeled *fundamentalism*. It's a term that must be used, if at all, with care, for it can refer not just to intolerant certainty generally but also, pejoratively, to people of strong religious faith who are not—no matter what they look like from the outside—all alike and without reason.

Fundamentalism of all sorts, in fact, while it may (and should) be criticized for narrowness of vision, is often a reaction to much that really is wrong and discomforting. Fundamentalists, though usually I'm put off by the certainty of their answers, often raise the right questions or correctly identify the evil in our midst.

Use of the term *fundamentalist* to describe a particular segment of Christianity can be traced to 1920, when a Baptist layman and journalist, Curtis Lee Laws, used it to describe those who were defending the theological positions outlined in a series of pamphlets published between 1910 and 1915. The publications—called "The Fundamentals: A Testimony to the Truth"—promoted belief in the infallibility of the Bible, the virgin birth of Jesus, the physical resurrection of Christ, and other tenets. The authors were trying to reclaim sacred traditions as antidotes for a church (and a culture) they said had lost its way.

The reality was that so-called Christian liberalism had strayed rather remarkably from theological positions the church had held for centuries. Beyond that, the culture generally was disillusioned about the human condition because World War I had so starkly revealed humanity's capacity for evil. So the people who became known as fundamentalists were, in fact, reacting to real problems.

But the fundamentalist movement was not the only religious response to what was happening. Another was the 1918 publication of a commentary on the book of Romans by German theologian Karl Barth. That commentary simply exploded the liberal hold on church theology and resulted in a move back toward orthodoxy.

The reason to study movements of fundamentalism (they can be found in many religions and cultures) and simultaneous developments is to remind ourselves that it's wise to be modest about what we really know.

But in claiming a place to stand, both people of faith and scientists have committed sins of false certainty and arrogance. We have seen countless examples in the Kansas debate over evolution. This is nothing new. When Copernicus suggested that Earth revolved around the sun and not vice versa, Martin Luther and John Calvin denounced this as unbiblical.

The problem is that people seem to have a natural dislike of ambiguity and are irretrievably drawn toward certainty. "Little comfort can be sucked from a perhaps," the seventeenth-century English clergyman Stephen Charnock once noted. So we seek the comfort of certainty.

I'm not arguing that we can't know anything with confidence or that everything is relative and, thus, up for debate. All ideas are not equal. But when we are so certain of our truth that we refuse to entertain additional evidence it leads to destructive conflicts that not only baffle but damage our children, whose curiosity is often a marvel to behold.

Our children should know what we believe and why. But they also should be encouraged to ask hard questions, to follow wherever the evidence leads, to be discerning, and to be wary of incontestability.

And when children reach an answer, they would do well to hold it gently, remembering that others may have reached a different conclusion by different routes.

Religion Shouldn't Be Defined by Science
November 7, 1999

A new scientific study done in Kansas City that says prayer seems to help heal sick people may appear to be a vindication of religious faith and practice. But it's really just one more example of the unthinking, silly way that faith too often gets seduced by science.

Seduced by Science, in fact, is the name of an important new book by a Georgetown University law professor, Steven Goldberg. The subtitle is *How American Religion Has Lost Its Way.*

As it happens, Goldberg devotes an entire chapter to a critique of many previous studies purporting to show prayer has medical benefits. Goldberg doesn't doubt for a minute that prayer can do all kinds of good. But that isn't the point, he says. Rather, the problem is that religion is allowing itself to be defined by the standards of scientific research. (The same is true, of course, in the debate over evolution.)

"It is not science that is threatened by the current infatuation with the medical power of prayer," Goldberg asserts, "it is religion. And it is threatened not by the possibility that science will find that prayer is useless. It is threatened by the possibility that science will find prayer works."

He asks readers to imagine what it would mean to say that prayer "works." The result, he says, would be that "prayer can then be neatly domesticated and categorized. It will be like aspirin or acupuncture—indicated for arthritis, not indicated for pancreatic cancer."

Indeed, he says, this is exactly the way "prayer is currently presented in the bulk of the medical work that touts its effectiveness as medicine." The problem with this, of course, is that it boxes up prayer as a drug and ignores the countless mysteries and spiritual aspects that faith communities associate with prayer.

"There is a real danger," Goldberg correctly notes, "that the scientific and medical perspective will gradually crowd out the distinctive religious values of prayer," which he says include humility, acceptance, and understanding.

The Kansas City study seemed to be of a piece with many previous studies on prayer. It was conducted by researchers at the Mid-America Heart Institute at St. Luke's Hospital and published recently in *The Archives of Internal Medicine.*

Some patients were prayed for regularly by people outside the hospital who didn't know them. And those patients achieved a better recovery based on some thirty-five different medical measurements.

If this is how science must convince itself of the value of prayer, I have no objection, though I would point out that there was absolutely no way of knowing whether other people, unknown to the study leaders, were praying for (or even against) some of the patients. And there was no way of factoring in the potential efficaciousness of more general prayers uttered by Tibetan monks or Bolivian priests, say, seeking healing "for all those who are suffering ill health anywhere in the world," which certainly would have included the Kansas City heart patients.

But all that is beside the point. The point is that, in the end, prayer is not a medical tool. And people of faith should not be silent in the face of efforts to usurp it and make it one.

Prayer may well have some or all of the effects science seems to be finding, but whether science can verify prayer's value by using scientific standards should, in the end, have no effect on the understanding of prayer held by people of faith—even the one type of prayer (petitionary, or intercessory) that is the subject of these medical studies.

Libraries could be filled with books about prayer, so it's useless to try to say anything comprehensive or exhaustive about what it is in just a few sentences.

But at its fullest, prayer is far more than pleading for medical miracles or presenting God with an alphabetized list of our needs.

The late American clergyman Harry Emerson Fosdick had it right in his book on prayer: "God is not a cosmic bellboy for whom we can press a button to get things."

Prayer is multilayered and mysterious. It is simple and elegant. It is faith whispering into the abyss and then listening. It's a way people of faith stay centered on the eternal.

Prayer is not a prescription drug. And when science tries to reduce it to that, religion should offer a second opinion.

The Human Impulse to Seek Tangible Proof
August 15, 1999

In *The Innocents Abroad*, his masterful account of foreign travel, Mark Twain repeatedly satirizes holy relics.

"We find a piece of the true cross in every old church we go into," he writes, "and some of the nails that held it together. . . . I think we have seen as much as a keg of these nails. . . . And as for bones of St. Denis, I feel certain we have seen enough of them to duplicate him if necessary."

It's proof that skepticism about such matters isn't new, probably because it's so often justified and because veneration of relics can be idolatrous. And yet there's something deep within us that wants to believe.

That's why the Shroud of Turin has captivated people's imaginations for so long—and why it continues to be news. I myself have been intrigued by the shroud since I read a book about it twenty years ago.

An insistent tradition says the shroud is the burial cloth of Jesus Christ. This thirteen-feet-long, three-feet-wide piece of linen, which has been kept in Turin, Italy, since 1578, bears a remarkable image of a man's crucified body. Efforts to explain the image, date it, and determine its origin have been numerous but contradictory and unsatisfactory.

Earlier this month researchers reported new evidence that the cloth dates from before the eighth century and comes from the Jerusalem area. This finding contradicts a 1988 carbon dating study that led a group of experts to suggest the cloth was created in the thirteenth or fourteenth century and probably was a medieval forgery— a finding that was itself quickly called into question.

The new analysis of the shroud will not, of course, settle the matter because so far scientists have been unable to state conclusively what the shroud isn't. If ever they can prove, by reasons of age or origin, say, that it could not have been the burial cloth of Jesus, the shroud finally may be relegated to a historical footnote. But until then it remains a magnet for both the curious and the faithful.

Indeed, even if the shroud is proven a medieval forgery, interesting questions about it will remain, including how it was created and whether the body of the man it shows really suffered. Who, then, was he?

Why do such things engage our hearts and minds? Many people would insist that true faith requires no such physical items. After all, both the Hebrew and Christian scriptures call God a spirit. But I say, not so fast.

There's plenty of biblical evidence that humans have always needed and wanted tangible evidence—proof, if you will. And, more to the point, the biblical narrative suggests God understands and even affirms this trait.

For instance, when God first gets the attention of Moses, it's through the starkly physical burning bush. And when God tells Moses there what to do to get Pharaoh to free the Israelites from Egypt, Moses correctly anticipates skepticism.

He says to God (in the New Revised Standard Version of the third chapter of Exodus): "If I come to the Israelites and say to them, 'The God of your ancestors has sent me to you,' and they ask me, 'What is his name?' what shall I say to them?" He wants proof. So God then gives Moses an enigmatic but revealing answer: "I am who I am." Which also can be translated "I am what I am" or "I will be what I will be."

In the New Testament, even one of Jesus' twelve disciples insists (in John 20:25—a gospel full of signs and wonders for skeptical people) he will not believe in the resurrection "unless I see the mark of the nails in his hands and put my finger in the mark of the nails and my hand in his side." A week after Doubting Thomas says this, according to John, Jesus appears and invites him to do exactly that as a way of affirming belief. (Even the incarnation itself can be seen as God's offering tangible proof of his love.)

Our age insists on irrefutable scientific evidence for almost everything (even though science cannot answer everything). As long as science can't prove that the Shroud of Turin couldn't be Jesus' burial cloth, the relic will remain a possible answer to people who—like people throughout history—have said what Missourians often say: "Show me."

And the biblical evidence is that God, though asking us to walk by faith, not by sight, does not belittle the request.

"Frankenfood" Isn't the Real Problem
April 9, 2000

MANHATTAN, KANSAS—The rules at Kansas State University no longer let Professor Barry Flinchbaugh smoke cigars in his campus office, so now he just chews on them.

When discussing genetically engineered crops—and how ignorant most of us are about them—he can degrade a full-length cigar to a stub in half an hour. It's a measure of his passion for the subject.

Flinchbaugh, an agricultural economist, has it right: Crucial biotechnology questions aren't getting asked much. Some public discussion finally has begun on genetic manipulation of humans, but it's long past time for Americans to engage in an informed, rational debate about genetic engineering of crops. And it should be different in tone from the ill-informed food fights that have broken out in Europe (with ripple effects last year in Seattle's streets at a world trade conference).

What's to debate? It may surprise you to know that the primary issue isn't whether genetically modified organisms, or GMOs, are healthful or safe. There may be questions left about health and safety—as indicated last week by a scientific panel—but the frightening charge that we've moved into an era of "Frankenfood" is overblown. Instead, the debate should be about who controls the crop gene pool.

Professor Robert S. Zeigler, director of K-State's Plant Biotechnology Center, points out that in 1975, when genetic manipulation was new, there was "a self-imposed moratorium on genetic engineering" to allow time to "define what the questions were, what the concerns were. We've been able to satisfy those involved that there's not a risk of a Frankenstein being created." But, he says, many people opposed to genetically modified crops "were not even born, or barely so, when the scientific community grappled with many of the issues they are raising today. I guess the answer, 'Well, we explained it to your mom,' doesn't carry a lot of weight."

Agriculture Secretary Dan Glickman puts it this way: "I believe that distrust is scientifically unfounded."

The gene pool control question we should worry about is whether the government can prevent large agribusiness companies from becoming monopolies and controlling our food supply. This gene pool, says Flinchbaugh, has been in the public domain since the U.S. Department of Agriculture was created in 1862. But starting in 1980, courts have allowed genes to be patented. This has raised troubling issues, and Flinchbaugh says the gene pool "is rapidly leaving the public domain."

"I'm just flabbergasted that very few of us are talking about the question," he says, "and it's the question of [gene pool] control."

A genome—plant or human—is a set of instructions that tell the organism how to grow. Changing a plant's genetic blueprint is not a new idea. "We've been genetically engineering since we did the first cross-breeding of cattle ten thousand years ago," he says. Wheat itself is an ancient hybrid of several kinds of plants, and it's humbling to learn its genetic makeup is far more complex than the human genome.

Once scientists learned to manipulate genes, the process of change speeded up remarkably. Biotechnologists now can alter the genetic makeup of plants in a flash, though such changes require generations of testing. Indeed, three federal agencies must thoroughly evaluate genetically modified food.

An example of a change genetically engineered into crops is resistance to pests. Genetically modified corn, for instance, makes itself toxic to European corn borers. This means farmers can use less chemical pesticide.

"It's very much an environmentally friendly set of technologies," says Zeigler, though critics—many quite passionate—worry about genetic changes being inadvertently transferred to other plants, with one possible result being superweeds.

If, in fact, GMOs are safe, and everyone is convinced of it, the upside is large. "Agricultural biotechnology has enormous potential to help combat hunger," says Glickman. And, he adds, "biotechnology can help us solve some of the most vexing environmental problems: It could reduce pesticide use, increase yields, improve nutritional content, and use less water."

Probably few Americans know that most soybeans and more than a third of the corn grown in this country now are genetically modified. Farmers have moved to GMOs in just the past few years because they make economic sense.

"We're down to three hundred thousand commercial farmers in this country that produce 80 to 85 percent of what's produced," Flinchbaugh says. "And what we all forget, including Washington, is that if you're one of those three hundred thousand farmers who've survived, you're pretty damn astute. And you're always analyzing and looking for a way to improve your bottom line."

But the rapid move to GMO crops raises the distressing specter of a lack of competition among seed companies. Increasingly, those companies are big chemical firms. Monsanto, for instance, is agriculture's genetic engineering giant.

"There's no question that chemical companies are getting into this because they see their market for chemicals is going to dry up," says Zeigler.

"Right now," says Flinchbaugh, "we have competition. But the outcome of free enterprise unfettered is always monopoly." He's correct that we need "as many players as possible developing GMOs. Government's role is to foster a competitive economy—either through antitrust or regulation."

Glickman worries about this, too: "One of my biggest concerns is what biotechnology has in store for family farmers. Consolidation, industrialization, and proprietary research can create pitfalls for farmers. It threatens to make them servants to bigger masters rather than masters of their own domains."

It's too bad the economic concentration issue has gotten lost. But it has happened partly because when the public pays attention at all, it's to other GMO concerns.

Consumer worries are high on the list, especially as anti-GMO protests in Europe and Asia spread to the United States. Some American food processors, in fact, have said they won't buy GMO crops or at least won't use them in certain products. Naturally, this worries farmers, who wonder whether there will be a market for their crops—here or abroad.

Other issues include genetic diversity, labeling food products, and use of "terminator" technology to make seeds of GMO plants sterile so farmers can't save seed for the next crop.

A new thirty-eight-member U.S.D.A. biotech advisory committee that gives every indication of being both good and independent will look at all that and more. It's headed by Dennis Eckart, a former

Ohio congressman, who says he's overwhelmed by how little even well-read members of the public know about GMOs. But because the committee's job is to make recommendations to Glickman, educating the public "is probably a task that will escape resolution by this committee," he says.

Eckart hopes the committee can avoid becoming a venue for extremists. "What I'd like to try to do is create a thoughtful process and get it out of the hands of the leafleteers or the two-thousand-dollar suits," he says.

It's crucial that this committee raise the right questions and help everyone understand what's at stake, because Flinchbaugh is right that "now is the time to begin thinking about and debating what kind of policy we want ten years down the road."

If we wait, too many questions may be settled to the public's detriment.

Making New Products One Atom at a Time
March 26, 2000

Scientists say the promise of a remarkably better future for all of humanity lies in smallness.

The name of this glorious savior is nanotechnology. Indeed, its potential is simply staggering, even if most of us so far have almost no grasp of what it may be able to do or even what the term means.

Much of the nanotechnology hype sounds incredible, but, in fact, it appears rooted in reality. And yet because humans are so susceptible to utopian thinking, so ready to believe in big-lie promises, we would be well advised to take a deep breath and pay attention to the few words of caution scattered among the golden promises.

A recent report by the National Science and Technology Council, which President Clinton created in 1993, is full of breathless prose about nanotechnology, but eventually does acknowledge this: "No one knows how much of nanotechnology's promise will prove out. Technology prediction has never been too reliable."

So as we learn about this scientific move to incredible smallness, we should keep such caveats in mind. Even more important, however, will be remembering that no science has ever changed fundamental human nature and its frustrating mixture of generosity and selfishness. Rather, science has simply expanded the arenas in which those good and evil traits are played out. If, however, our world is going to be so radically changed by nanotechnology, we should at least try to grasp the essentials of it.

The word *nano* is derived from the Greek word for "dwarf" and now means one-billionth of something, such as a second of time. *Nanotechnology* refers to the manipulation of individual atoms and molecules to manufacture new materials that may have amazing properties.

For instance, nanotechnology promises data storage methods that go a million or billion times beyond today's computer chips. Another product may be new prosthetic and medical implants that interact with the body and never wear out. There's also the potential for unimaginably strong, tough, and light materials for use in all kinds of vehicles. And on and on.

Even better: Because these products will be made atom-by-atom from the bottom up, experts say they will result in far less pollution than typical manufacturing processes.

Neal Lane, assistant to President Clinton for science and technology, says the administration is convinced "that nanotechnology will have a profound impact on our economy and society in the early 21st century, perhaps comparable to that of information technology or of cellular, genetic and molecular biology."

Indeed, if quantum physics and cosmology were the world-changing sciences of the twentieth century, it seems likely that genetics and nanotechnology will be the premier sciences of the twenty-first.

At the moment, nanotechnology is young and relatively untested. But scientists know they now have the technical ability to manipulate individual atoms and molecules at the level of a nanometer, which is one-billionth of a meter.

As the National Science and Technology Council says, "by creating nanometer-scale structures, it's possible to control the fundamental properties—color, electrical conductivity, melting temperature, hardness, strength—of materials without changing the materials' chemical composition."

This is the way Roald Hoffman, a Nobel laureate chemist at Cornell University, has described that lofty promise: "Nanotechnology is the way of ingeniously controlling the building of small and large structures, with intricate properties. It is the way of the future, a way of precise, controlled building, with, incidentally, environmental benignness built in by design."

The government has been putting millions of research dollars into nanotechnology, and private enterprise is seeking to move the science forward, too. Indeed, both approaches are important. But as we head into this tiny world of massive possibility, we must remember what we've learned from previous scientific breakthroughs: Nothing is guaranteed, and even the most benign technology can be used for evil.

In fact, we'd do well now to try to imagine how nanotechnology will be misused so we can at least stay even with the knaves who will inevitably do just that.

Some Questions Can't Be Answered by Science
January 16, 2000

No doubt many Americans were surprised when *Time* magazine recently named Albert Einstein as "Person of the Century."

That's because many people have failed to grasp where science took us in the twentieth century. It was an astonishing journey, but too many people ignored it by pretending they couldn't understand what the subatomic physicists, the cosmologists, or the geneticists were doing.

Yes, the details are complex and at times baffling (even to scientists). But this is no excuse for ignoring the big picture. For the truth is that the work of the physicists and the cosmologists—much of it built on a foundation laid by Einstein's remarkable brain—has altered the shape of the world in which we thought we lived. The revelations that light bends around large objects, that space is curved, that so much depends on the constancy of the speed of light, that energy and matter are somehow interchangeable, that we cannot simultaneously know the speed and the location of subatomic particles—all that has undone our tidy Newtonian world.

Indeed, the mysterious and unimaginably tiny world of particle physics and the enigmatic and unimaginably large world of astronomy have affected everything we think we know, including conventional wisdom about God and our lives as spiritual beings.

The science has been fascinating. But in the midst of news about black holes and muons, Big Bangs and cosmological constants, religion too often has fallen silent. Or, as Georgetown law professor Steven Goldberg argues convincingly in his new book *Seduced by Science: How American Religion Has Lost Its Way*, religion has tried to make its point by appealing to scientific truth instead of religious truth—and often there's a difference.

Thus we get foolish, overdrawn arguments about evolution versus creation or over whether the Bible's account of Noah's flood describes a historical event. Goldberg is right to complain that religion too often allows itself to be painted into a defensive corner and thus argues its case on science's terms.

To understand how this has happened, it's important to grasp how radically different the world is because of Einstein and the science of the twentieth century (to say nothing of how Charles Darwin's ideas have moved the culture).

A good way to come to terms with some of that is through a new book by Amir D. Aczel, *God's Equation: Einstein, Relativity, and the Expanding Universe.* In language accessible to nonscientists, Aczel describes how Einstein's lucid thinking unraveled foundational secrets of the universe. Although Einstein made it clear he did not believe in a personal God, Aczel is on target when he writes: "to him science was the process of discovering God's creation."

More than four decades after Einstein's death, his theories and thinking—and even what he called his mistakes—continue to guide scientists who also are trying to understand the universe, whether they call it God's creation or not. Indeed, the surprising revelation two years ago that not only is the universe expanding, but it's doing so at an accelerating rate, has reinforced the usefulness of Einstein's work.

And it's clear that science's goal—a Grand Unified Theory of Everything, if such a thing is possible—must find a way to relate what happens on a cosmic scale with what happens inside the atom. Physicist Stephen Hawking says once we have this final "everything" formula we will "know the mind of God."

It's that kind of astounding arrogance that religious voices must confront. Religion must counter science's assumption that the world is only materialistic and that all its mysteries one day can be fathomed by the human mind. Religion must remind us that we are finite creatures whose reach can never be infinite.

In recent years some scientists and others have sought to integrate science and religion more fully by proposing a concept called "intelligent design." It would not try to prove, say, that the God of the Bible exists but, rather, suggest that scientific evidence points to a cosmic designer. (Intelligent design, too, has many critics.)

Will science in the twenty-first century top the Einstein-led marvels of the 1900s? Almost certainly. But science can never answer some questions. And the job of people of faith is to speak that liberating word of truth.

Ignorance Confounds the EgyptAir Inquiry
November 28, 1999

The great prayer investigation that grew out of the recent crash of EgyptAir flight 990 revealed again how abysmally ignorant most of us are about the practices of religions not our own.

Beyond that, of course, people often can't articulate even what their own religion professes. Many members of the Jewish and Christian clergy, for instance, will say, with sadness and exasperation, that some members of their flocks are as biblically illiterate and theologically clueless as the 10 percent of respondents in a recent poll who thought Joan of Arc was Noah's wife.

One of the consistent (and, to some, surprising) messages of the EgyptAir case, for instance, was how thoroughly Islamic life is grounded in prayer and in various traditional formulations of the prayers that help form the fabric of that life.

No doubt most of us have seen photos or film of large groups of Muslims kneeling for prayer, and, indeed, daily prayer is a vital part of Islam. But the language of prayer simply permeates life for Muslims.

The Council on American-Islamic Relations, for instance, says *al-hamdulillah* is a one-word prayer (in Arabic) meaning "praise be to God" and is used to express acceptance of God's will. Indeed, a common response when a Muslim is asked the everyday question of how he or she is feeling would be the alhamdulillah prayer.

This practice of integrating prayer into daily conversation is not, of course, unique to Islam. Christians and Jews often end sentences of intention with the phrase, "God willing." At its core this is a prayer that God will grant the wish. Even offering a simple "God bless you" to someone who sneezes is an example of how prayer language often pervades our most common activity. So, of course, do our profane requests for God to damn this or that. (It's no doubt a blessing that God seems not to grant these countless curse-prayers immediately.)

I know an Episcopal priest who, scared half witless on a roller coaster once, was surprised to find herself singing the Lord's Prayer, which had become part of the fabric of her life.

Likewise, early in the EgyptAir investigation, Islamic experts pointed out that a phrase heard uttered—possibly multiple times—on the flight voice recorder, *tawakaltu ala Allah* (translated as "I put my trust in God" or "I put my faith in God's hands"), is one of many prayerful phrases of supplication, known as *duaa*, that Muslims use daily.

All this talk of prayer in the media, however, has failed to shed much light on the way various religions understand and use the practice.

Journalists reporting the EgyptAir story left me with the impression that they—like many Americans—think of prayer as being almost exclusively of one type, petitionary. That's prayer in which people ask (or, in case of emergency, plead, similar to a 911 call) that God grant some request.

But prayer is much more than that. *The Handbook for Today's Catholic*, for instance, reflects this understanding of prayer common to the Judeo-Christian tradition: "Prayer is you relating to God in the deepest recesses of your personality. It is you seeking and communing with the living God."

This Catholic guide, interestingly enough, says something about prayer that brings to mind the prayer heard on the EgyptAir tape: "At its most personal, private prayer is spontaneous or impromptu—and sometimes even wordless. Nonetheless, formulas are practical helps for breaking into prayer and expressing faith."

The cockpit prayer seemed to be an Islamic-style spontaneous "formula" prayer.

Christian prayer inevitably reflects Trinitarian theology, which Lutheran theologian Robert W. Jensen, in his recent book *Systematic Theology: The Triune God*, calls the church's "first deliberately defined dogma."

But prayer need not simply be words. Indeed, the fourteenth-century German Dominican and mystic, Meister Eckehart, insisted that prayers include charitable works, giving, and fasting.

If there's a religious lesson in the EgyptAir disaster, it is to be cautious about focusing on one aspect of anyone's faith as a clear window into either individual behavior or a whole religion.

Many of us blithely invoke the divine for specious, greedy, or silly purposes, giving us little room to criticize or even analyze the prayers of others.

The Enduring Mystery of Religious Conflict
December 5, 1999

Religious disharmony, which has plagued humanity for thousands of years, is with us as we near the end of a millennium. It's enough to destroy forever the bogus Enlightenment idea that humanity is perfectible.

In fact, the phrase "religious disharmony" is a gross understatement. In many places around the world people are being oppressed and killed for their religious beliefs.

When he spoke to American troops in Kosovo recently, President Clinton included this aberration of religious values in what he called "the number one problem in this whole world today." That problem, he said, is "racial and ethnic and religious hatred and dehumanization."

The "dishonor roll" of religious violence in this century (to say nothing of the whole millennium now nearly gone) is simply stupefying, and no doubt the Holocaust of World War II tops the list with 6 million dead Jews. But just in the past few years our planet has flowed with blood in Rwanda, Bosnia, Kosovo, Northern Ireland, Sudan, and elsewhere from conflicts that in one way or another stem from the inability of humans to tolerate, much less love, people who seem to differ from them racially, ethnically, or religiously.

Not all of this astonishing carnage has its roots in religious differences, but much of it does. And recent news stories continue the pattern of division, as Christians and Muslims have fought over construction of a mosque next to a major Christian shrine in Nazareth, the hometown of Jesus, and as Christians have fought amongst themselves over a matter so small as a proposed new door to the Church of the Holy Sepulcher in Jerusalem.

But one's focus need not be global to see dispiriting examples of people of faith fighting amongst themselves, fighting people of other faiths, or being oppressed by secular forces.

In fact, I would be shocked to discover a Christian, Jewish, or Muslim congregation anywhere that has not experienced some kind of internal turmoil. Each of those faiths, of course, is divided in sometimes painful ways, but, as I say, even within congregations that, from the outside, seem to be homogeneous and harmonious, there often is division and even hatred.

It has been true in my own Protestant congregation, which has been split asunder more than once since its founding in 1865. Indeed, as an antislavery church, it grew out of discord. But it has survived and today is strong and growing. Still, when we wonder why people of faith argue with and even kill people of other faiths, it's humbling to look at strife within the community of faith we know best.

Some of this tension, of course, is healthy. Some has its source in people who rightly challenge an aspect of theology or practice that has gotten out of balance. In fact, I sometimes thank God for heretics, and on at least one matter I myself hold a view I believe is right but that the majority of my denomination considers beyond the pale of orthodoxy.

The question, however, is why religious dissension often leads to hatred and even violence. What sort of prideful arrogance causes people to take up arms against those who differ from them?

I don't know. But I suspect it has to do with our need for certainty, our desperation to be right, our fear that we may be wrong about the truth to which we may have committed our lives. "Often wrong but never in doubt" is an epitaph that could apply to all kinds of people who hold strong religious beliefs. And yet it must be said—indeed, I would shout it—that without a commitment to ultimate truth, without faith in something transcendent, life wouldn't be worth much.

And for all the bloody messes religious dissension has scattered across the globe in this century and millennium, it's also true that religious faith has given billions of people better lives—and hope—through promotion of healthy and eternal values, love being at the top of the list.

It would be lovely to imagine that a new millennium will bring with it a new era of religious peace and harmony. And though this is something all of humanity should work for, we would be naive to expect it just because the calendar is changing.

The sad truth is that people of faith will continue to fight and be fought against after Y2K arrives. And faith itself will continue to be wounded and discounted because of it.

Out of Control, Yes, but Maybe Not Helpless
April 27, 1991

Without quite realizing what I was seeing, I watched something amazing Thursday—a small, burning airplane falling out of an indifferent sky.

Under its straining single engine I could see an odd golden glow. Was it some kind of special light? I wondered at first. Was the sun—all but enveloped in April-gray clouds—darting rays through a break and lighting up some piece of polished metal under the nose of the craft? The idea of fire came to me, too, but I could make no sense of it.

I heard the desperate feathering or churning of the doomed engine as the pilot—the only person with even a pretense of control—maneuvered the plane to an open space, no doubt hoping to save both himself and others. He found such a space—a grassy lot—in our crowded city, but could save only others. He died in an anarchy of flame.

I did not see the plane hit the ground. I had lost sight of it below treetops before that happened. (In fact, I didn't know for sure it had crashed until twenty minutes later when the TV told me.)

But in those twenty uncertain minutes I was struck anew by a sense of limits. Even had I clearly understood that I was watching a plane going down, even had I known the pilot, even had I been a pilot, I could have done nothing to save the man or his plane.

Some people—closer to the disaster than I—saw the pilot's horrified face as he wrestled to control the Cessna 210 Centurion. "His face was just in terror," a witness said.

But those people, too, were helpless. All they could do was try to stay out of his way, try to save themselves.

It's easy to forget our limits, our occasional helplessness—probably because we want to forget. Are, in fact, encouraged to forget.

A few years ago Richard Bach, author of *Jonathan Livingston Seagull*, wrote an utterly fatuous little book called *Illusions: The Adventures of a Reluctant Messiah*. The main character—a pompous twit—was the pilot of a small plane.

In one part he brings that plane in for a dangerous landing that should have required all of a 1,320-foot-long pasture. He casually lands it in half that space and at half the speed required just to keep the plane afloat. Another pilot, amazed, asks how he did it.

"Listen!" the pilot-messiah says. "This world? And everything in it? Illusions! . . . Every bit of it illusions!"

The mindless new-age message of Bach's book is that we can control almost everything about the world. We can land planes on a dime, make wrenches from our toolboxes float to us through the air. We need merely to take control, to visualize the reality we want to occur. We need only to make ourselves divine.

But, of course, we are not gods. We are creatures. It's true that Psalm 8:5, in the Revised English Bible translation, says God has made mankind "a little less than a god, crowning his head with glory and honour." But even that exalted position does not let us snatch falling planes from the sky, calm stormy seas, or quell earthquakes.

The words God spoke to poor put-upon Job out of the whirlwind always remind us how we fit in the scheme of things: "Where were you when I laid the earth's foundations? Tell me, if you know and understand." Job's answer was wise. He said such things are "too wonderful for me to know."

My heart aches today for the man who tried to land the airplane I saw staggering through the sky. And I wish I had clearly understood what I was seeing when it appeared before me. But I know such discernment would have availed me nothing. Some things we simply cannot affect. Simply watching, I was doing all I could.

The pilot, however, seemed never to stop trying to avert disaster. Even if, in those moments of terror, he sensed his limits, he also did what he could. Which is all we can ever ask.

So Much Suffering in Such a Small Place
May 1, 1994

DALLAS—The surprise here on the sixth floor of the Texas School Book Depository (now sanitized as the Dallas County Administration Building) is not the carefully restored sniper's nest.

It's not the fact that the whole floor from which Lee Harvey Oswald allegedly fired shots that killed President John F. Kennedy on November 22, 1963, has become a tourist exhibit, with videos, photos, and maps.

No, the surprise on my first visit ever here, my immediate and overwhelming impression, is how small Dealey Plaza is. You can walk the length of the grassy knoll in less than two minutes, even at a leisurely pace. The blocks are short, the triple underpass low. And on the sixth floor I feel close enough to the ground to believe I could hang from a ledge and drop to the sidewalk without hurting myself badly. Surely so small an arena could not have contained something as momentous as the JFK murder.

For me and my generation—late World War II babies and the first Boomers—Kennedy's death was a seminal, watershed event. I was a freshman in college then, imagining my future—was, in fact, listening to a physics lecture about transistors—when someone walked in to say the president had been shot.

Within the hour, we learned Kennedy was dead, and something in people my age died, too. Call it naïveté or innocence, if you must name it. Say that eventually we'd have lost it anyway as we learned of the evil in the world, of the unfairness, of what we used to call sin before we became too sophisticated to use the term.

No doubt you'd be right. But somehow it seemed all wrong to have it happen in the click of a trigger on a Friday afternoon.

I suppose it's happened to other generations. I think of Fort Sumter. Of Pearl Harbor. Hiroshima. But I also know some generations had the luxury of losing innocence gradually. That was the case after World War I, for instance, when people slowly began to realize that—no matter what Woodrow Wilson said—we had not made the world safe for democracy. Still, the loss was equally profound, and eventually it fueled the anger in poet Ezra Pound's words that young lives had been sacrificed "for an old bitch gone in the teeth, for a botched civilization."

Maybe because of a similarly deep loss for people my age, I've been irresistibly drawn to Dealey Plaza ever since that bloody day in 1963. But for one reason or another, until now I've never come here to touch it, see it, let it mark itself on my psyche.

Being here jars me. These historic places are always different from the pictures in one's mind. That's been my experience at the Taj Mahal, at Big Ben, at the Coliseum in Rome, at the Church of the Nativity in Bethlehem, at the Alamo, and, on this trip, at the Branch Davidians' burned Mount Carmel home east of Waco.

Here, as I say, there is for me a sense of disappointment in scale. But I'm also feeling irrational anger that somehow the world has carried on business on these mean streets, that they haven't been frozen in history, as has the corner of the sixth floor above them.

It's foolish, I know. But I can't deny my desire to stop cars passing along the very path JFK rode and shout something crazy at people like, "Take off your shoes! This is sacred ground!"

Sacred? Come on. An important, but flawed, man lost his life here. That's all. Let's not deify people.

And so, oddly dissatisfied by the experience of being here, I walk away, get in my rented car, and leave.

To get on the highway to the airport, I have to drive down Elm Street, right where JFK's car traveled. As I go under the triple underpass, I sigh in ambivalent disappointment at myself for further sullying this ground.

But I forgive myself for intruding, for my morbid curiosity, as I hurry to catch a plane, live a life, sort through new memories in search of meaning.

In his poem "Musée des Beaux Arts," W. H. Auden writes,

> About suffering they were never wrong,
> The Old Masters: how well they understood
> Its human position; how it takes place
> While someone else is eating or opening a window or just walking
>   dully along . . .

Suffering—whether random and absurd or great and redemptive—happens in unremarkable locations, sometimes in places where the blocks are short, the space cramped, the sixth-floor windows eerily closer to the ground than seems possible.

After Dallas, I know more fully what Auden meant about the banality of evil and our response to it.

Hope's Resilience in the Face of Silent Ruin
March 15, 1998

Trudy Calabrese's noble life of generosity led, not long ago, directly to her grotesquely evil death.

The stark malevolence of what happened to her raises the question of how people committed to morality, to living for others, to the inevitable struggle between righteousness and iniquity, can find the will to carry on.

Elizabeth (Trudy) Calabrese, forty-one, of suburban Phoenix, was married to Rosario, a cabinetmaker. They had two children: Lisa, ten, and Francesco, six. Trudy also was a church volunteer who delivered food to people in need.

Just a few weeks ago Trudy took a box of food to a Phoenix family. Police say the couple receiving the food tied Trudy up and—maybe in the presence of some of the couple's four children—sexually assaulted her, then killed her with a knife and wooden club. Police have charged John E. and Kara Sansing with first-degree murder, kidnapping, and armed robbery. The *Arizona Republic* quoted police as saying John Sansing told his sister he was high on crack cocaine at the time of the attack.

A few days after Trudy's battered body was found in the Sansings' backyard, over three hundred people jammed the Calabreses' church for her funeral.

"She was very caring and compassionate and always smiling and cheerful," they heard her pastor say.

I did not know Trudy Calabrese. But some acts—even those perpetrated on strangers—take our breath away and force us to reexamine the nature and consequences of evil in our midst as well as our own response to it.

There were, of course, the expected postmurder stories in the Phoenix papers about rules that volunteers should follow in delivering food to strangers. And food pantries there were, predictably, reviewing their procedures. But there also were determined words about continuing to do good works despite the reality of evil.

"Based on what we know about Trudy Calabrese," said the executive director of the Association of Arizona Food Banks, "she wouldn't want us to stop because of what happened to her." And the community relations director for a Phoenix food bank said bravely that if others were kept from volunteering because of Trudy's death, "that would be to let evil win."

In an odd way, it may be easier to confront evil when there is no mistaking it (though surely much of the twentieth century argues otherwise). A case like Trudy Calabrese's, after all, makes good people rise up almost instinctively, despite legitimate fears that they may be the next victims.

But what of more subtle evil? How do we find the courage to keep going when wrestling with malevolence less spectacular than what killed Trudy Calabrese?

I think of Karen Ann Quinlan, the young woman who, in 1975, suffered irreversible brain damage from a combination of tranquilizers and alcohol ingested at a party. Though her family got legal approval to take her off a respirator, she lived comatose for nine more years. Some member of her family—usually a parent—came every single day to be with her through that. Every day. They responded to a call to be faithful in the face of silent ruin.

For a recent memorial service, a friend asked me to speak words he had written about his wife. Her mind and body had withered to nearly nothing because of a degenerative disease. Yet somehow her family—my friend, three children, others—stood with her during two harsh decades of decline.

What gives people such courage? Hope, I think, the kind of hope the Apostle Paul means when (in the New Revised Standard Version) he writes in Romans 5 that "suffering produces endurance, and endurance produces character, and character produces hope, and hope does not disappoint us."

This kind of hope isn't crushed by evil but is kept alive by people with an eternal perspective, people who commit to doing right no matter the cost. They, thank God, will not let Trudy Calabrese's killers have the final word.

"Soul to Soul," We Share a Common Bond
May 16, 1999

I've opposed the death penalty for as long as I can recall.

But I've tried to learn from those who agree with me and those who don't because people of good will differ on this. For a time I based much of my opposition on the Decalogue's prohibition against killing, but I know now that the biblical witness on this—and most issues—is more complicated.

My latest chance to confront the question came from a priest who was with Roy Ramsey when the state of Missouri executed him last month at a prison in Potosi. Ramsey was convicted of killing a retired Grandview couple, Garnett and Betty Ledford, in 1988. (But he consistently denied his guilt.) The priest, W. Paul Jones, who's also a Trappist monk, is my friend.

But we don't always agree. Indeed, this summer, at a Presbyterian conference center in New Mexico, he and I will coteach a seminar on the theological divisions within Christianity. The class will focus especially on Holy Communion. Protestants (I am one) have different views of the sacrament than do Roman Catholics (Paul is one, though most of his life he was a Protestant).

I mention our friendship and willingness to disagree as background to my asking him to tell me about being a death row priest. Paul opposes capital punishment passionately.

He wrote in an e-mail message that after he arrived at the prison for the execution, he asked if he could hear Ramsey's confession.

"That would require that I be alone with him in order to preserve confidentiality," he recalled. "I expected a prompt no. But instead the 'execution arranger' took my request seriously.

"The head of the education department was also a Catholic deacon. So he could come in and be a representative of the prison, and, at the same time, as a deacon, he would be under the same canon law dictum as I—to hold everything that was heard in absolute confidentiality."

Paul stepped beyond a red do-not-cross line and knelt at the perforated metal bars.

"There was no protest. So I put the end of my fingers through the holes. Roy poured out his soul. About half an hour later, he was exhausted—and finished. I asked him to touch the end of my fingers with his. He is a huge man, the envy of any professional football team looking for a fullback. His touch was gentle. I gave him absolution and blessed him. . . . And I will never forget it—soul with soul."

Something remarkable happens when you recognize you share a common humanity even with people convicted—or guilty—of murder. It's humbling to know we are all flawed and need forgiveness and grace. This doesn't mean you minimize crimes. Rather, it forces you to understand that all of us deserve punishment for something and that as long as we are unrepentant and unforgiven, we, too, are in a prison of our own making.

Paul: "As he left, the education supervisor told me that over 80 percent of the prisoners there were illiterate. So it almost was with Roy, whose large capital letters in his letters looked like those of a kindergarten child."

I know evil is real; too many people love darkness more than light. But something in our national values is mocked when so many prisoners are illiterate and when the racial proportion of death row inmates is so skewed.

Paul was taken to a small room from which to watch Ramsey die.

"I sat in the front row. . . . The [death] room was totally white—antiseptic. . . . [Roy] quickly looked around until he saw me—and smiled. I gave him a thumbs-up sign—and he nodded. Then I mouthed the words: 'Roy, I love you.' Immediately he mouthed back, 'Paul, I love you, too.' Then he closed his eyes and died. . . . I was escorted out through the back way, where the garbage is taken out. And as I drove away into the dark, rainy night, a hearse passed me. It was coming to take away the final 'garbage'—my friend Roy. In my heart was a deep, silent rage. This was all wrong, totally and completely wrong. It was now beyond debate for me."

Our hearts rightly ache for the Ledfords and their survivors, but I, too, find nothing redemptive in Ramsey's death. Rather, I find in it another example of the evil humans first began to spread when they imagined they possessed divine wisdom and its awesome prerogatives.

No Such Thing as "Exclusively Religious"
August 22, 1999

Pope John Paul II is planning what he considers the most important of all his foreign trips—to the Holy Land later this year to celebrate the birth of Jesus Christ two thousand years ago.

He states his desire for the journey plainly in a recent letter: "It would be an exclusively religious pilgrimage in its nature and purpose, and I would be saddened if anyone were to attach other meanings to this plan of mine."

It's a false hope. And surely this politically potent pope knows it. Indeed, it's hard to imagine how he can conceive of a way to separate religion from other aspects of life.

It is, after all, a foundational position of Roman Catholic—and, more broadly, Christian—theology that the sacred and secular are, finally, indivisible. That's because Christianity views all of life as a gift from God. According to this understanding, life is to be lived in gratitude to the Giver, and just as no part of life can be viewed as exclusively secular, so no part—even pilgrimages by popes—can be "exclusively religious." There's no such category.

In fact, months before the trip begins it's clear that John Paul's "Great Jubilee" pilgrimage is simply dripping with global political implications and is fraught with potentially explosive consequences.

The man who, quite rightly, can take considerable credit for the fall of communism in his native Poland and then in eastern Europe cannot pretend any of his trips will be understood as only religious. The very geography of this trip—to which the pope pays so much attention in explaining his hopes for it—guarantees that anything he does will have consequences far beyond the "exclusively religious."

His desire is to visit places that have been crucial in biblical history, beginning with the city of Ur, where God called Abram (later Abraham) to become the patriarch of the Jewish people. The ruins of Ur, it turns out, today are known as Tell el-Muqayyar and are in southern Iraq. And Iraq, of course, is led by Saddam Hussein, the pariah with whom most other heads of state will have nothing to do.

If, as is his wont nearly everywhere he goes, the pope spends time in Iraq with the head of state, imagine the world's reaction to seeing the leader of more than one billion Catholics carrying on with a murderous despot who uses biological weapons on his own people. Even if John Paul's hope for that visit is to call attention to the plight of the Iraqi people under Hussein, that message may get lost in criticism of him hobnobbing with a dictator.

And that's just the start of the trip. Everywhere the pope plans to go, in fact, there is political and social turmoil. It can be argued that the very existence of such trouble is a good reason for a representative of the Prince of Peace to make the trip. I buy that argument. But it's misleading at best for him to claim his trip will be exclusively religious.

The pope says that both his stop at Ur and his visit to Jerusalem can "express the church's awareness of her irrevocable links with the ancient people of the Covenant" and he says his pilgrimage "seeks to honor the deep bond which Christians continue to have with the Jewish people." These are not idle words, for John Paul II, preeminently among popes, has worked hard and with sincerity to improve Jewish-Christian relations.

But because the Middle East remains a flash point as the Jewish state of Israel tries to work out peaceful relations with Arab neighbors and with Palestinians who want Jerusalem to be the capital of their nation, anything the pope does there will have political ramifications.

Jerusalem is sacred not only to Christians but also to Jews and Muslims. Whether it wants to be or not, it is an international city. And almost anything a global figure like the pope says or does there has the potential to stir the embers of distrust and to delay a peace settlement if it is said or done without imagining the repercussions.

This is an important trip for John Paul II. He will remind the world why—besides computer bugs—Y2K is significant. But his commitment to peace should be measured by how sensitive he is to the political consequences his journey of faith inevitably will have, because "exclusively religious" is the one thing this trip cannot be.

Public Figures, Policies, and Events

We Owe a Great Deal to Harry Truman
April 9, 1995

Judged now by the unforgiving light of history, Harry S. Truman was a gift America gave itself.

When he became president fifty years ago this week, on April 12, 1945, he did not, of course, seem like a gift at all. He seemed more like one of history's occasional practical jokes.

Even Truman himself, at least at first, was overwhelmed by the notion that he had become leader of the free (and dangerously unstable) world. When he heard about Franklin Delano Roosevelt's death, he told reporters, "I felt like the moon, the stars, and all the planets had fallen on me."

Almost nothing about Harry Truman reminded people of FDR, the giant father figure who had led them through both the Great Depression and World War II with Brahmanic assurance and style.

Truman was a nasally midwesterner who'd never even graduated from college. He appeared to be the untrustworthy product of Kansas City's corrupt political machine. He was a compromise vice presidential candidate who, by the unlikeliest turns of events, had slipped onto the 1944 ticket with FDR (whose previous running mates had been John Nance Garner and Henry Wallace, of all people). And it was clear to almost everyone that as president he would be in way over his head.

"The country and the world," said David Lilienthal, head of the Tennessee Valley Authority, "don't deserve to be left this way. . . ."

But first impressions are often wrong—and in this case they were dead wrong. Truman's values, it turned out, were old-fashioned and decent. His moral compass was true. Why, the man was even unshakably in love with his wife.

And fifty years after the trauma of the Roosevelt-to-Truman transition, it is abundantly plain that Harry S. Truman was the right man at the right time. The sad reality, however, is that it has taken most of those fifty years for the country to realize that.

As Robert H. Ferrell says in his recent biography, *Harry S. Truman: A Life*, "For a generation or more after 1945, Americans underestimated Truman, and only in the 1970s, after several more presidents, did they recognize his virtues."

Truman, it's now clear, was decisive, honest, direct, and, after he found his sea legs, not the least bit intimidated by the phonies who inhabited the world of politics and diplomacy. His values— rooted deep in midwestern farm soil and a Baptist upbringing— were America's values, or at least its ideals. His allegiance to national goodness and destiny matched the model of the great nation Americans kept in their hearts.

Only America could have produced a Harry Truman. And only America could have placed him in a position to do what Clark Clifford and others said he did: save the free world.

To accomplish such a feat, Truman had to be educated, and, in the end, he taught himself. It was true he had acquired a public high school diploma in Independence and had tried a few courses at Spalding's Commercial College in Kansas City. But Truman's real education came more directly from the people he met, the jobs he held, and the books he borrowed from the public library.

Taking advantage of Ben Franklin's and Andrew Carnegie's notion that everyone should be able to read books from a public supply, Truman was a voracious reader. He devoured biographies and history, especially, and discussed what he was learning in letters he wrote to his fiancée, Bess Wallace, when—for eleven long years—he was a farmer in Grandview while Bess lived the life of high society in Independence.

"From the time I was ten years old," Truman wrote in a memo when he was a senator from Missouri, "I had spent all my idle hours reading, particularly biography and history." In that memo he compiled a simply extraordinary reading list that began: "Read the Bible from cover to cover four or five times before I was fourteen, the *Encyclopaedia Britannica, Abbot's Lives, Plutarch's Lives*, Gibbon's *The Decline and Fall of the Roman Empire*," and on and on.

Truman's mind was quick, curious, and spongelike. Those qualities served him well in the Oval Office, where he faced an almost impossible deluge of complex information and advice through which he had to pick his way to make one crucial decision after another—often at top speed.

Truman carried with him this important lesson from American history: There is a real difference between whoever happens to be president and the office of president.

"He knew," writes Ferrell, "that when people came to see him, they came to see the president, not Harry Truman. He strove mightily to keep the two people apart."

This profound understanding—which, to our detriment, has escaped some other presidents—was clearly the product of his own peculiarly American self-education. And his 1953 return to Independence to become simply "Mr. Citizen" shows it was a lesson he never forgot.

Truman's quiet resumption of private life—and his successful campaign to create a library where scholars could study not only him but also the presidency—allowed time for Americans to begin to realize that postwar America is very much created in Harry Truman's insightful image.

It is no exaggeration to say that the shape of late-twentieth-century America—and in many ways the shape of the world—is due in no small part to Truman.

Truman—as a young man nothing less than a racial bigot—issued the order that integrated the armed services and thus helped set the nation on the rough road to modern racial justice.

He helped move the country from a wartime to a peacetime economy, and though it was a bumpy trip, that transition created the foundation for the incredible rise of living standards and economic expansion that has marked the last fifty years.

After bringing World War II to a close, he helped create the international mechanisms that have kept an uneasy peace through two terrifyingly dangerous generations. His adoption and promotion of the Marshall Plan brought compassion—permeated by wisdom—to bear on postwar Europe, thus avoiding the costly mistakes of isolationism and revenge that characterized the response of the so-called winners to World War I.

NATO and the U.N. have Harry Truman's fingerprints all over them. His Point Four program reached America's helping hand across the globe. And his help establishing Israel gave long-deferred substance to the hope of a people who had been crushed by Hitler's evil vision of humanity.

Truman, the only person ever to order use of the atomic bomb in war, understood the world-threatening nature of nuclear proliferation, and he worked hard to prevent the cruel Soviet empire from expanding its territory and becoming a nuclear bully. The Berlin airlift—ordered against much advice and nearly all odds—was his way of saying no to the brutal ideologues who ran Moscow.

Without the firm anticommunist policies Truman put in place, the Berlin Wall never would have fallen in 1989. And however frustrating the stalemate of the Korean War was, it helped to create an atmosphere in which powerful market-driven economies in Asia could rise.

We are today, quite literally, the children of Harry Truman's decisiveness and vision.

Not everyone applauds that result, of course. For instance, in a recent essay, Lewis Lapham, editor of *Harper's* magazine, says:

> Our [postwar] generosity achieved its most impressive effects among those nations previously endowed with a tradition of wealth, trade, industry and education. Western Europe prospered, and so did Japan. But the countries that in 1945 were poor, agricultural and illiterate remain as they were before the advent of American idealism—still illiterate and poor, still dependent on foreign bank loans, and the distinction between the haves and the have-nots begins to take on the aspect of a terrible permanence.

But that complaint seems like blaming the preacher for the intractability of sin or the teacher for the hold of ignorance. No president can ever deserve all the credit or blame for what a nation or the world becomes after him. But just as we are today one republic, undivided, thanks to Abraham Lincoln's refusal to see the union split, so, too, are we today an economic powerhouse and the world's only major superpower because we have traveled the path on which Harry S. Truman set us.

He was not a man without flaws, of course. He was loyal to a fault to fools and charlatans. He was impulsive and, at times, crude and profane. He created the constitutionally loathsome loyalty program in the face of an internal communist threat that existed largely in the manipulative mind of the blithering Joseph McCarthy. But despite all those—and more—faults, he was a gift we gave ourselves.

"He was the kind of president the founding fathers had in mind for the country," David McCullough concluded in his recent biography, *Truman*. "He came directly from the people. He was America."

And fifty years after receiving such a gift is a good time to celebrate it.

The Complicated Nature of Trust
February 8, 1998

Trust is a complicated act of will and experience. But it is worth exploring its complexities because the Monica Lewinsky–Bill Clinton matter, at its most fundamental level, has been about trust.

Do we citizens trust the president? Does Hillary Rodham Clinton trust her husband? Did the president foolishly trust a young woman to keep silent? Do we trust the justice system? Do we trust the words of lawyers or spokespersons? (I ask this in light of these words from former White House spokesman Ron Nessen: "Nobody believes the official spokesman . . . but everybody trusts an unidentified source.")

These and similar questions inevitably lead us to ask about matters that affect us more personally. Do we trust the people we know? And especially the people we love? Is even so-called "unconditional love" contingent on the ability to trust?

More than 2,300 years ago, when political correctness no doubt meant something very different, the Greek comic dramatist Antiphanes wrote: "I trust only one thing in a woman: that she will not come to life again after she is dead. In all other things I distrust her."

Perhaps Bill Clinton would be in better shape today had he lived by Antiphanes' outrageous words. But what sort of man would he be then?

The awkward thing about trust is not just that it is essential in a long-term committed relationship like marriage but also that it is both complex and fragile. And once it has been broken, it is extraordinarily difficult to resurrect. The relationship, in many ways, is crippled.

And yet putting it that way is too categorical, too quick to preclude redemptive acts. There simply are too many levels of trust for anyone to say that breaking it is always fatal. Beyond that, acts of forgiveness and true repentance sometimes heal broken trust in ways that can last.

Trust, as I say, is measured at many levels. Do you trust your spouse to call you when he or she promises to? If the call comes five minutes late, has your trust—and the marriage—been shattered irrevocably? Of course not.

Can your family trust you to pay the bills and not spend money foolishly? Do you stretch the truth about these matters? If you do, are you just forgetful and irresponsible and, thus, not to be trusted with financial matters? If so, does that mean you are untrustworthy in all aspects of a marriage?

Any marriage requires wide measures of mutual tolerance and understanding. We are human. We mess up and will again, despite pledges to do better. If annoying but small failures destroy a marriage, it was built on sand in the first place.

But there is a qualitative difference between breaking trust in insignificant ways and marital infidelity, in which one makes a decision to give one's body and/or heart to another. The daily question is whether we still believe and live by the marriage vows we spoke at our wedding.

If trust at that level has been broken—and Clinton has acknowledged it was at least once in his marriage—the work required to restore it is colossal. It is nothing short of a willed miracle each time a marriage wounded in that way is put back together. And no one outside the marriage—no one—is in a position to know fully how it fell apart or how it was restored.

The kind of trust required in a successful marriage must be taught—and it's best if it's taught by example, not through high-toned sermons. I have decided, on the basis of long experience, that children lie naturally and must be taught to speak and live truthfully. (Rearing children makes one believe in Original Sin—as well as in redemption.)

Based just on what I now know about Monica Lewinsky, she strikes me as someone who never has understood the crucial nature of trust. If she has a moral compass, it seems to spin untethered to any North Star of truth or principle. Too often, Bill Clinton strikes me the same way.

That does not mean Clinton's policy positions are wrong or that he is not an effective politician. And it does not mean Lewinsky is damned.

But if the untrustworthiness we find in high places (meaning a disconnect between private and public morality) reveals a moral vacuum that we then tolerate, we as a nation have fallen into ruinous, if understandable, cynicism. And if we don't find our way back, our future is bleak.

What Chelsea Clinton Must Teach Her Father
August 23, 1998

Dear Chelsea: The question you face is what to do now that your famous father has failed you.

At age eighteen, you almost certainly have learned a good deal more about life's squalid corners than I had at your age.

If, before the last week or two, you hadn't already discovered that parents can betray your trust and behave in destructive, repugnant ways, you know that now. I'm sorry for any child who learns such stark lessons, but to some extent it happens to everyone. And there is, in the end, no way to protect children from it. All parents fail—some much more spectacularly than others, but no parents make it through life without embarrassing and disappointing the very children they love.

Your case, of course, is special because not just you and your mother but the whole country—indeed, the whole world—has been treated to the awful spectacle of imagining your reckless father committing tawdry acts of lust in or near the Oval Office.

No doubt you, like most children, can barely imagine your parents doing anything sexual within the boundaries of marriage. Most kids find it disgusting to think of their parents in that way. But to learn that one of your parents engaged in such acts outside marriage surely vaporizes any illusions you may have had about what some supposedly rational adults do.

You strike me as a bright young woman, capable of surviving a great deal. So I tell you what you may know already: You have choices about what to do.

You can disown your father. Indeed, this would be an understandable reaction, given the way he has heaped embarrassment and shame on his family. But, in the end, it would be self-destructive.

There certainly are times and circumstances in which the most helpful thing is distance between parent and child. But it's no long-term solution because it leaves a relationship asunder that is clearly meant to exist.

Another choice is for you to ignore what your father has done and how it has made you feel. I cannot, of course, know your feelings. Although I have met your father in the past, I know you only from your limited public appearances and from infrequent media stories.

But I do know that ignoring feelings, avoiding conflict, and pretending things are all right is no solution. I have used that approach too often in my own family and can testify that it finally does more harm than good. I don't mean to suggest that you confront your parents about every little grievance or that you see a professional therapist to work out anger over trivial matters. However, if you try to paper over real pain, it will come back and wound you in possibly permanent ways.

What is left, then, is the only alternative that makes sense. You first must name your pain. This requires you to be honest with yourself about the ways you feel violated by what has happened and then to express that clearly within the confines of your family.

You may feel that your job is the same as that of your father's political supporters—to rally around him and help save his presidency. No. Your job is to be sure that you and your parents understand what you are feeling and that you grasp your own vital role in helping to heal the needless wounds your father has inflicted on you, your mother, and himself.

Confronting this pain may be the hardest thing you've ever done. I will never forget the bruising agony I felt several years ago when I had to inform my own children that their mother and I, after almost twenty-seven years together, had failed to hold our marriage together. But, in the end, there was nothing to do but acknowledge the failure. They survived as whole and healthy young women who love both their parents, and so can you.

But you and your family can be healed only by walking intentionally through the white hotness of the pain. Your father seems remarkably adept at avoiding that. But you aren't responsible for his behavior, only for yours.

And if he won't name this evil plainly to you, you will have to name it to him. Your father is forever talking about doing the right things for our children. And he's right. But if he doesn't understand that such truths begin with his own child, you will be forced to teach him.

I know of no sane adult in the country who wishes you ill. And I know of no one who wouldn't offer whatever help you ask for. But we cannot go through this for you. We can simply wish for you the best. And we do.

In an Old-Growth Forest's Majestic Presence
July 11, 1993

MOUNT HOOD NATIONAL FOREST, OREGON—I am standing on a downed Douglas fir trunk that began its life long before the first pioneers arrived 150 years ago at the nearby end of the Oregon Trail. Even, in fact, before the birth of David Douglas, the early-nineteenth-century botanist after whom it got its name.

If this mansion-length, moss-covered, squishy corpse were upright, I could not get my arms around it—even if it were half its diameter.

The trunk is one of several similar dead soldiers on the forest floor within my eyesight. But my eyes aren't focused on the ground of this small clearing, where oxalis, salal, and sword fern have claimed voracious squatters' rights.

Rather, I am looking toward the tops of dozens of Douglas firs that have arrowed up at least 150 feet. The wind streams through them and they softly wave it on its way.

This is what's called an old-growth forest. It's nothing less than a chaos of fecundity, and it's what environmentalists and their backers say must be saved.

It is an ancient theater of life in which new trees shoot out of dead trunks. Fungus and moss upholster spreading branches. Ferns and wildflowers quilt the ground. Fallen trees lean at crazy angles amid the pounding, powerful force at work here, the force of life. Sunlight squeaks through the canopy, creating a living chiaroscuro—light and shadow in a strobelike biodance, chasing each other's essence.

Environmentalists decry the loss to logging of 90 percent of the old-growth forests in America. And they are trying to convince the White House and the public that the remaining forests here in the Northwest must not be logged to death.

"The way the last great old-growth forest in America is going to be saved," says Jonathan Nicholas, a columnist for nearby Portland's daily newspaper, the *Oregonian,* "is if people in New York, Chicago, Kansas City, and elsewhere rise up and say, 'Hey, you can't cut down our trees in Oregon.'"

And my own heart tends to lean toward people who love the forest for what it is, not merely for what it can provide as a source of livelihood.

For instance, Regna Merritt, Northwest field coordinator for the Oregon Natural Resources Council (ONRC), a coalition of environmental groups, is with us in the forest today, mostly talking in calm scientific terms about the multilayered forest canopy, clear-cutting of forest areas, biomass on the forest floor, and so forth.

But her eyes flash a little fire after all that and this is what she says, finally, with an edge to her voice: "The timber industry has had a heyday here. And we think it's over."

And this: "We need a kick in the butt to fund research and development because the answer is alternative fiber [to wood]. We don't need to use the best wood in the world for two-by-fours and pallets."

Another person whose heart is on fire to save the ancient forest is Andy Kerr, ONRC's director of conservation, who sometimes is called the most hated man in Oregon for his forceful environmental stands. "Our problem," he says, "is not that we're running out of trees. We're running out of forests."

If that seems a hard concept to grasp, consider the difference between what's called old-growth forest, where I've come today, an hour or so from Portland, and a forest that's been replanted after having been leveled for lumber. The old-growth forest is made up of a diversity of trees—not only Douglas fir but also Pacific yew, cedar, spruce, ponderosa pine, western hemlock, and others.

Its multilayered canopy—which is to say a combination of ground-level plants, trees 15 to 20 feet high, and trees more than 150 feet tall—provides a protective cover for such rare species as the spotted owl as it seeks to survive. (Kerr says studies show that at least 667 species of animals are more or less dependent on the ecosystem of old-growth forests.)

So-called second-growth forests, by contrast, are quite different, though from a distance they may look to the untrained eye very much like an ancient forest. For instance, they are mostly full of same-size, same-age, same-species trees—all thirty-year-old Douglas firs, say. And these trees are, essentially, a cash crop. They will be harvested forty to eighty years after planting. They are, thus, impermanent. Such forests do not—indeed cannot—contain a wide and wild range of growth and vegetation, the fecund chaos that makes up old-growth forests, the very living-dying, growing-decaying biomass needed to support populations of not only spotted owls but also, among others, of marbled murrelet seabirds and northern goshawks, which also have been losing the species survival battle.

Kerr speaks for other environmentalists when he declares: "The future of Oregon's timber industry is second-growth, not old-growth forests. It's time the forest industry lived off the 90 percent of land they've already cut in the nation."

This passion to save the forests versus the effort to save logging jobs is the thicket the Clinton administration has entered. The dispute brought both President Clinton and Vice President Gore to Portland in April to listen to people representing various interests. In the president's new proposal to curtail logging in the Northwest, he seeks something probably impossible—a policy that will satisfy everyone.

The proposal, announced July 1, would reduce logging to about 1.2 billion board feet of timber a year (from more than 4 billion in the 1980s), establish protective reserves for the spotted owl, set up areas for experimental harvesting techniques, create no-logging buffer zones around sensitive streams, protect some entire watersheds, and ask Congress to spend $1.2 billion over five years to help the Northwest's economy as well as eliminate a tax subsidy for timber companies that export raw logs.

It's hard for me not to feel sympathy for everyone in this debate—individual loggers, timber companies that employ them, environmentalists, and a government trying to be both a mediator and a protector of the public interest.

All have legitimate interests, though I won't pretend that each side—even the government—always has the public interest at heart. No, the issue is complicated by politics, egos, tradition, and money.

But I can tell you that I've never before experienced the awe of being in an old-growth forest. And I believe it would be nothing less than a crime against nature to allow these ancient stands of wildness to disappear.

Regna Merritt has just pointed to a tree she estimates is at least five hundred years old.

It is a profoundly humbling thing to stand next to its deeply grooved trunk and look up into its huge, majestic presence. It reminds us of our own impermanence. It speaks of the earth's different, slower rhythms and patterns—cadences with which humanity seems to have lost touch.

Down here on the forest floor, amid the wild columbine, the Oregon grape, the vine maple, the deer fern, the rhododendron, and the huckleberries, here amid the monstrous firs and cedars and pines, through which clouds wander, leaving their precious moisture as fog drip—this is where we can be quiet again and learn that maybe a 250-year-old downed and rotting tree trunk is helping to do something of inestimable value: In its slow dying it is feeding new (and preserving old) life, life full of pizzazz and wonder and, well, maybe even art.

Perhaps we should just watch this show and learn from its primeval pulses. Where else, eventually, could we go to see such ancient fermenting miracles, and to try to imagine what they mean?

At Waco: Religious Freedom under Fire
April 17, 1994

WACO, TEXAS—A worn Bible lies on Amo Roden's makeshift bed.

It's opened to the apocalyptic book of Revelation, which she studies furiously as she waits for the end of the world here on the very land where last year ignorant agencies of our federal government attacked people who share her religious beliefs.

She and friends have built a rough shack that looks like a clubhouse cobbled together by clever youngsters. A sign on an outside wall says: "The Branch Davidian Seventh-Day Adventists Office." Though she has a farm nearby, this is where she lives now.

Within one hundred yards of her hovel are the piled-up ruins of what once was Mount Carmel, where just a year ago David Koresh and about eighty of his followers died in a run-amok fire that ended an utterly unnecessary fifty-one-day standoff between the Branch Davidians and the government.

Today about five acres of the seventy-seven-acre site—the part where people lived and imagined the end of history—is surrounded by a chain-link fence topped with barbed wire. Security guards keep watch inside. "Keep out," says a sign on the fence. "This area is quarantined by order of the Texas Commissioner of Health." Just to the right of a long driveway that leads to the fence from a rural road ten miles east of Waco, Amo Paul Bishop Roden sells souvenirs, makes her claim to the property, and prepares for what she's certain will come, and come soon—the dawning of the reign of Christ on earth.

"I believe that within five years we'll see the establishment of the Kingdom of God, but I can't be positive of the timing," she says.

Several miles away, in a pretty, tree-shaded section of northwest Waco, Sheila Martin, who lost her husband (a Harvard-educated lawyer) and four children in the fire, lives in a small white house and waits for God to gather together a faithful Davidian remnant to usher in the end of time.

"We just think that right now God's going to do whatever he needs to, whatever it takes," she says. "We're waiting. I live now with the faith that God's going to get us through."

Roden and Martin may appear to be simply more religious nuts in a land that seems to grow them in prodigious numbers. And maybe they are. But there's an important lesson to be learned here on this Texas pasture land and killing field—a lesson our government violently failed to grasp: In the United States we protect people with strange religious beliefs, we don't assault them. That, at least, is how the Constitution says it's supposed to work.

At Mount Carmel the government, almost willfully disregarding the sanctity of religious liberty, blundered its way to disaster. Had it taken even fifteen minutes to understand the religious views of Koresh and his followers, the Bureau of Alcohol, Tobacco, and Firearms never would have launched its largest law enforcement effort ever—even if, as seems likely, Koresh was violating firearms laws. It was incredible overkill that, evidence shows, could have been avoided by arresting Koresh alone away from Mount Carmel. Other share that view:

- "Not only was there a lack of awareness concerning the deeply religious nature of this community, but equally tragic was a lack of awareness concerning what kind of religious community it was—what it means to have this apocalyptic view of history. Without that insight, it's very difficult—really impossible—to approach these people in a positive way."—James Breckenridge (professor of religion at Baylor University in Waco)
- "This is Bill Clinton's Bay of Pigs. I'm concerned about the preciousness of American citizenship, and they [federal au-

thorities] cheapened the citizenship of every one of us. This kind of excited eschatology [study of the end of history] has happened again and again in Christian history, and there are better ways to deal with it than burning them to death."— Franklin H. Littell (professor emeritus at Temple University, visiting scholar in religious studies at Baylor and chairman of the board of the American Council on Religious Movements)

- "What happened at Mount Carmel was historically unprecedented. I feel very, very strongly that it was ill-advised and based on ignorance. What they did was not only wrong but we should hold them to account and we ought to say, 'Never again should we have federal agents behaving in such a manner.'"—James E. Wood Jr. (director of the J. M. Dawson Institute of Church-State Studies at Baylor)
- "Incredible as it may seem, religion as an issue was apparently accorded little room in the consideration of policy or action toward the Branch Davidians."—Lawrence E. Sullivan (director of the Center for the Study of World Religions at Harvard University)
- "This was an attack on freedom of religion in a very subtle and perhaps hidden way. From the beginning of the ATF's investigation, they ridiculed the religious beliefs of the Branch Davidians."—Dick DeGuerin (the attorney Koresh's mother hired to represent him in the standoff)

This indicates the depth of outrage among religious scholars and others. What disturbs them is that at Mount Carmel our government seemed blithely unaware that religion in the United States—no matter how out of the mainstream—exists not by the forbearance of the secular state but by constitutional right, to say nothing of basic human right. It is not simply to be tolerated—a very low standard, indeed. Rather, it is to be accorded at least equal footing with—and the same respect as—the right of free speech, the right to assemble peaceably, and the right to petition the government for redress of grievances.

At Waco, our government ignored both its constitutional and its spiritual roots. It unleashed on a deeply religious—if strange and misguided—people the repressive, coercive, violent power of the state. Then its representatives lied about what happened. Then they tried to hide what happened by issuing reports that reeked of deceit.

The government's failure—built on hostility toward religious freedom—was both widespread and deep, finally reaching all the way to the Oval Office, where President Clinton, when informed of the plan to gas the Branch Davidians, first failed to demand the highest standard of constitutional protection for people of faith and then compounded his failure with postfire dismissive rhetoric that stained and cheapened his office.

"The killing of people at prayer is an outrage against faith and humanity," Clinton said earlier this year after Christian worshipers in a Lebanon church were bombed and Muslim worshipers were shot at Hebron in the West Bank. Had he said something similar after the Waco fire, he'd have been equally right.

Much attention has been paid to the tactical failure of the initial ATF raid of February 28. Even by the Treasury Department's own biased account, it was an almost unbelievable series of errors that resulted in the deaths of six Mount Carmel residents and of four brave ATF agents who trusted their incompetent superiors. Attention, too, has been given to errors of law enforcement judgment that led to the fire fifty-one days later. But there's been little public discussion outside religious academia about the government's assault on religious liberty.

This is a reflection of a fairly recent trend in our society—the trivialization of religious belief and the dismissal of faith as little more than a hobby. Yale law professor Stephen Carter, in his book *The Culture of Disbelief*, offers that view. Oddly enough, Clinton has praised that book in public often. But if the president read it, there was no evidence in the Waco disaster that he or most other federal authorities understood its important message: "it is at precisely . . . the moment when the religious tradition most diverges from the mainstream that protection is both most needed and most deserved."

Amo Roden agrees the government made no effort to understand the Branch Davidians before attacking them but says the point is irrelevant. She holds a complex conspiracy theory that the government attacked Mount Carmel to kill Koresh and destroy records that would show he had something (it's unclear what) on the feds.

Her notion is hard to follow and not very credible, but her criticism of Koresh (she thinks he misread Scripture and was not the so-called sinful messiah he claimed to be) is informed by the fact that she's what she calls the "contract wife" of George Roden, the former Branch Davidian leader (now in a mental institution) from whom Koresh wrested control of the sect and the land in 1987.

She's trying to gather money to pay back taxes on the property and reacquire it on behalf of her husband. She says other Branch Davidians will soon come to join her and reestablish a community there.

And she has a warning for authorities who might want to attack the sect again: "When dealing with hard-core Christians, the government should know they don't back down."

Koresh Saw Himself as God's Prophet
April 17, 1994

David Koresh's theological center of gravity was the mysterious book of Revelation, also called the Apocalypse.

Such great minds as Martin Luther and John Calvin found only puzzles in the New Testament's last book. Koresh, however, found answers and himself in the book. Koresh decided he was the messianic figure Revelation calls the Lamb of God, the only one who can open the book's so-called Seven Seals to usher in the end times.

"You have here a group that is apocalyptic to a degree that would make most mainline Christians uncomfortable," says James Breckenridge, professor of religion at Baylor University in Waco. "This small community identifies itself with a kind of faithful remnant. And this scenario is set up where we have the faithful remnant awaiting the imminent end of all things, and the government agents represent really a satanic force.

"So you have the prelude to a kind of Armageddon here. Which means that when the government agents take this kind of aggressive action, they are really seen as the fulfillment of prophetic utterances that they've been hearing for quite some time in their very long, long Bible studies."

Mainline Christianity, thoroughly apocalyptic in its view of history, says Jesus Christ, as risen Lord, not Koresh or anyone else, is that Lamb of God, and someday he will return to inaugurate history's end.

Indeed at Baylor, a Baptist-founded school, a Baptist preacher from Louisiana recently told students, "one day Jesus Christ is going to return," and all creation "will say, 'Jesus is Lord.' " It's a common theme of the faith.

But, as Daniel L. Migliore of Princeton Theological Seminary says in his recent book, *Faith Seeking Understanding,* "Christians make no claim to know either the date or manner" of Christ's second coming. In fact, says Migliore, "they have been told [by Jesus] not to spend their time speculating about the timetable of the last events but simply to keep alert."

Koresh, well outside mainline Christianity, was consumed with "the last events." He claimed to be God's anointed prophet: "God speaks to me; I have a message to present," Koresh said in the midst of the siege.

"He convinced [his followers]," says Gary J. Coker Jr., a Waco lawyer who once represented Koresh, "that he was somewhat more than your average human being, that he was a prophet. The ones I know still believe it."

J. Phillip Arnold of Houston, one of two theologians who tried to show Koresh the siege did not have to end in violence and death, says the longer Koresh "studied the scriptures, the more intimate he became with them. He began to write himself into the story of the Bible. He began to find a role for himself."

Using Revelation this way was not unique. In the late 1950s, Bible translator and scholar William Barclay introduced his own translation and exposition of the book by saying "it has sometimes become the playground of religious eccentrics, who use it to map out celestial timetables of what is to come, or who find in it evidence for their own eccentricities."

That's an excellent description of Koresh.

Other scholars, such as M. Eugene Boring of Texas Christian University, point to centuries of misuse of Revelation: "Although every biblical book is subject to misinterpretation, no other part of the Bible has provided such a happy hunting ground for all sorts of bizarre and dangerous interpretations."

There's widespread obsession with Revelation's metaphors, symbols, and spectacular scenes because the book explores a subject that has long engrossed humanity—how the world will end. Different segments of what's become a Revelation interpretation industry offer different versions of the end.

One view is called premillennial, which generally describes Koresh's position. Breckenridge says a shorthand way to describe that notion about the end of history and the inauguration of a thousand-year reign of Christ on Earth is that "things are going to get a lot worse before they get better."

Scholars disagree about who wrote Revelation. What is clear is that this is wildly imaginative, apocalyptic writing that describes the author's lengthy, detailed vision. It was meant to encourage Christians elsewhere to resist demands of the ruling Romans that they worship the emperor.

Revelation urges Christians to stand fast because God is in charge and will bring the faithful victory. "And God shall wipe away all tears from their eyes," says Revelation 21:4 in the King James Version, "and there shall be no more death, neither sorrow, nor crying, neither shall there be any more pain: for the former things are passed away."

Over the centuries, people have interpreted the book in several ways. Some have seen it mostly as a first-century account of events that already have taken place. Others have maintained it's a coded explanation of events from the time of its writing to the end of history. Still others have seen it as a book about the future, especially the end times. Yet others have viewed it as merely a symbolic representation of good's final triumph over evil.

Koresh was certain he'd figured it out.

"Koresh is as American as apple pie in the sense that he will read the text himself and find in it all the hidden mysteries," says James D. Tabor, associate professor in the University of North Carolina at Charlotte Department of Religious Studies. Tabor worked with Arnold to help Koresh envision a peaceful way to settle the siege.

For Koresh, the significance of Revelation could be found in its Seven Seals. A figure seated on heaven's throne in the book holds a document in his right hand. It is sealed with seven seals, wax impressions used to authenticate documents. (Roman law then said a will should be sealed with seven seals of seven witnesses.)

The Lamb of God appears in Revelation and begins to undo the seals. As each is opened, some great—often violent—event unfolds on Earth. Koresh not only believed he was appointed by God to open the seals but that the world and Branch Davidians were living through the fifth seal at the time of the April 19 fire. Some Koresh followers still expect him to return before 1996 to open the remaining seals and bring history to a close. Mainline Christianity considers that a serious misreading of the Bible.

"Considered from almost every possible angle," says Brecken-ridge, "he would be perceived as departing from not only the popular Christian understanding of Revelation but an academic understanding as well. There's a long history of people reading their own agenda into this book, which is easy to do because it's so highly symbolic."

The FBI Made All the Wrong Moves
April 24, 1994

WACO, TEXAS—Federal agencies made countless mistakes here last year in assaulting David Koresh and his Branch Davidians in their rural Mount Carmel home.

But none has more implications for the future than the failure to understand the religious views of their targets.

Before the Bureau of Alcohol, Tobacco, and Firearms's incredibly botched February 28 raid—an operation even the Treasury Department admits was flawed almost beyond imagining—the ATF consulted with no experts who might have explained the sect's beliefs.

"The ATF has no internal behavioral science units," says Nancy T. Ammerman of Emory University, a religious expert the Department of Justice called on, after the fatal April fire, to help assess what happened. "It has no tradition of calling on any kind of behavioral science experts, let alone any religious studies experts. ATF simply had no information or sought no information that would have helped them understand the religious dynamics of the group. . . ."

Even the Treasury Department's report—as hard as it tried to find aspects of the ATF operation to praise—admitted "the planners should have sought assistance from psychologists and other experts" to grasp the Davidians' "extraordinary belief systems."

The report also faulted raid planners for having "underestimated the ability and resolve of Koresh and his followers." That was the inevitable result of not knowing Koresh had been preaching that the end of history would be ushered in with a government assault on Branch Davidians.

James Breckenridge, professor of religion at Baylor University in Waco, puts it this way: "The authorities were just reinforcing these people with the conviction, 'We are being persecuted, we're harassed, we're hated. And why? Because we are the faithful few that serve the Lord in a very evil world.'"

A hint of the failure to grasp the religious nature of things—either before or after the events—can be seen in the Justice and Treasury Department reports. Neither one even spells *Revelation* correctly, consistently adding an *s* to it. That may seem a small matter, but it's like trying to explain Hitler by saying you've read *Mine Camp.*

One source the ATF ignored was Bill Pitts, a Baylor religion professor who had written a history of the Branch Davidians. It begins with the group settling in Waco in 1935 as an offshoot of the Seventh-Day Adventists, which disowned (and still disowns) the sect, as does the separate Davidian sect, from which the Branch Davidians separated in 1959. But Pitts says no federal authority ever asked him about it.

Had the ATF understood Branch Davidian beliefs, even a fool would have realized the error of an armed assault—especially once raid leaders knew (as they did, despite their later denials) that Koresh was tipped off nearly an hour before the raid. The inexcusable decision to carry out the raid to serve arrest and search warrants on Koresh cost the lives of four ATF agents and six Branch Davidians.

The carnage might have ended there if the FBI—which inherited the mess and took control of the ensuing siege—had made an effort to grasp the Davidians' religious views. A few FBI experts tried to tell siege leaders the importance of knowing those beliefs, but they were, in the end, voices crying in the Texas wilderness.

Of special significance was an April 14 letter Koresh sent to his attorney, Dick DeGuerin. It's clear the FBI dismissed it as another delaying tactic. But to anyone with a grasp of Koresh's strange theology, it was key to ending the standoff peacefully.

Koresh believed he was God's anointed prophet to open the so-called Seven Seals of Revelation to usher in the end of the world. He had long felt, however, that God didn't want him to make his interpretation of those seals public. But in the April 14 letter, Koresh says God finally had granted his wish:

> I have been praying so long for this opportunity to put the Seals in written form. . . . I want the people of this generation to be saved. I am working night and day to complete my final work of the writing of "these Seals." I thank my Father. He has finally granted me the chance to do this. . . . As soon as I can see that people like Jim Tabor and Phil Arnold have a copy I will come out and then you can do your thing with this Beast.

Tabor is a University of North Carolina at Charlotte theologian. Arnold is a scholar with the Reunion Institute, a religious think tank in Houston.

As they watched the siege, Tabor and Arnold tried to think of how their own studies of Revelation might provide Koresh acceptable alternative interpretations to let him end the siege without more deaths.

Arnold met with DeGuerin several times to help the lawyer understand Koresh's view of Revelation before DeGuerin made several visits to Koresh inside Mount Carmel during the siege.

Arnold and Tabor did an April 1 radio talk show, discussing different ways Koresh might read Revelation. They sent a tape of the show to Koresh via DeGuerin when he visited Mount Carmel April 4.

"We were trying to get his trust as people who knew these materials as well as he did but were not necessarily from his group," Tabor says. "We tried to propose to him in the gentlest way, 'Well, what about this? Or what about that?' "

Almost immediately after DeGuerin's visit, the Davidians—whose practices draw heavily on the Jewish roots of Christianity—began a celebration of Passover.

"When that comes to an end," says Arnold, "the letter comes out on the 14th. Dick calls and says the letter has come out and Koresh says he'll come out after writing the seals. We're very excited and very happy. That tells us that what we did on April 1 has had its desired effect. It has contributed significantly to David Koresh saying he'll come out."

DeGuerin immediately took the letter to Jeffrey Jamar, FBI agent in charge of the siege, and Bob Ricks, FBI spokesman in the standoff.

"I got mixed signals from the FBI" at that point, DeGuerin says. "I knew what they wanted to hear. I said I was sorry, but this is what he's saying. Bob Ricks registered obvious disgust. Jamar cut him off and said, 'No, we've got all the time it takes.' And that's the last I heard from them. . . ."

"We thought anyone who understood what was going on," Arnold says, "would have understood the significance of the April 14 letter. Now, for the first time, God, who'd told him to wait, was telling him to come out, from his point of view."

Siege leaders, however, didn't wait. They got approval from Attorney General Janet Reno to launch the final attack to drive the Davidians out of Mount Carmel. Jamar declined repeated requests to answer questions about why he went ahead with the April 19 assault despite the promising April 14 letter.

"If the government had taken seriously this man and his message and his beliefs," says James E. Wood Jr., director of the J. M. Dawson Institute of Church-State Studies at Baylor, "they wouldn't have made it impossible for him to come out." The April 14 letter, Wood says, "was an important turning point."

Was Koresh just stalling, or was he serious about writing the seals and coming out?

Evidence shows he was serious. One of the Davidians escaped the inferno carrying a computer disk on which was Koresh's writing on the first seal, completed the night before.

Tabor and Arnold had Koresh's writing printed, along with their comments: "I would characterize it as fairly typical of independent Adventist groups," says Tabor. "It essentially has to do with finding yourself within the biblical prophecies. I would call it a respectable exegesis within that context. It's obviously not respectable from an academic standpoint."

Ultimately, says Arnold, he and Tabor would have had to tell Koresh that though his interpretations of the Seven Seals might be "interesting, provocative, exciting . . . we don't believe them."

But to Koresh, his writing was clearly a serious effort. Tabor, Arnold, and others believe Koresh would have finished work on the seals in a week or two and surrendered.

"What angers me," says Tabor, "is that David Koresh was coming out. I'm absolutely persuaded of this."

But when the tanks rolled on April 19, Koresh obviously decided he'd been right all along about a violent end and that Tabor and Arnold were wrong about a peaceful way out.

Given the April 19 attack, there was to be no peaceful ending. No matter how the fire was set—by Davidians, by the government, or by accident—the theological point of no return had passed. The chance to wait for Koresh to complete his writing was gone.

"David tried to tell the government about our beliefs," says Sheila Martin, a Branch Davidian who lost her husband and four children in the fire. "In the first few weeks on the phone, the FBI used to listen to David for hours. But they didn't want to believe it." In fact, they dismissed it as "Bible babble."

None of the warnings mattered. The FBI continued to treat Koresh like a terrorist, not like what he was—a religious fanatic.

"They kept pushing and pushing and pushing this person to the extreme," says Wood. "He had nothing to live for before it was over. To act in that way was the worst possible approach they could have made. This was really stupidity."

What does this mean for the future? Potentially, a great deal. Federal agencies say they're reforming the way they do business because of what they learned in Waco. For instance, Richard Scruggs, assistant to Janet Reno, says the FBI is changing procedures to reflect expert recommendations, including paying more attention to religious scholars.

This is knowledge that may be quite useful, and soon, too. For as we enter another millennium in a few years, experts expect apocalyptic fever to run high.

"I'm sure many [apocalyptic] groups that don't even exist yet will be in existence in a few years as we get closer" to 2000, says Breckenridge. "In a way, we're going to see a replay of the year 1000, when there was tremendous apocalyptic excitement."

But next time, the government needs to know about the beliefs of people behaving in ways it may consider odd. Next time, it needs to remember that whether a state is just depends in large measure on whether it protects the rights of minority groups.

At Waco, our government did not come close to doing justice. Coker puts it this way: "I don't know how it could have ended up worse than it did. It's just inconceivable."

"What Waco represents," says Ammerman, "is a failure of our system of testing out the boundaries for religious liberty."

And Timothy Miller, a University of Kansas expert on new religious movements, offers this warning: "As long as we dismiss religious conversion and commitment as properties of the lunatic fringe, we will see Waco repeat itself."

In a press conference earlier this year, Reno said one of the tragedies of Waco is that "we will never know what the right judgment was."

Nonsense.

The right judgment would have been to understand the Branch Davidians as deeply religious—however odd—and behave accordingly. Instead, our government failed us all shamefully.

Treating Gays Badly Diminishes Us All
February 7, 1993

What I'm about to say will, in some quarters, produce gasps of disbelief and vile condemnation. I can already name a few of the people who will heap calumny upon my head.

I will even admit that some of these people sincerely believe what they will say, however meanly they say it. (But I also know—and can name—a few people who will cheer what I'm about to say.)

What will light such fires? I want to share with you some of my "aha" moments about what, in a limited context, has been a subject of national debate in recent weeks: homosexuality.

I have often wondered how—150 years ago, say—white Americans who supported, tolerated, or were simply silent about the enslavement of blacks could live with themselves. From this distance, the evil of slavery seems so astonishingly clear. Why wasn't it to them?

I know that any analogy between our treatment of homosexuals today and African Americans in the last century breaks down at many points, and in some ways trivializes the black holocaust that was fueled by the slave trade. So such an analogy is, finally, an inadequate tool with which to analyze our situation today.

And yet for all that, it is true that the same kind of unexamined—almost blind—support that so many whites gave to slavery is similar to the way many of us, myself included, have approached the subject of homosexuality and homosexuals themselves in our time and place.

Too many of us have been operating in ignorance and self-inflicted stupidity. We have not carefully examined the basis—including the religious justifications—for our antigay sentiments. I am convinced that a hundred years from now—or much less, I hope—people will look back on our treatment of gays and lesbians today the way most of us now look back with horror at the way black people were treated in much of the nineteenth century and before.

Other analogies might be drawn, perhaps with greater clarity and resonance. For instance, our oppressive treatment of homosexuals might be compared to the way our androcentric culture historically has treated women. Most of us now cannot imagine an American society in which women are denied the right to vote. And yet that very foundational liberty was withheld from women even through one-fifth of this very century.

While we would not tolerate such foolish, destructive treatment of women today (the repression of them has, in most instances, become subtler than banning them from polling places, and thus harder to root out), most of us have supported or unquestioningly tolerated oppressive treatment of homosexuals, including officially banning them from military service. It's time for all of that to end.

I did not set out in any intentional way to bump up against my— and society's—ignorance and prejudices about homosexuality. My education in this area happened over a period of several years and it continues to happen, since there still is much I do not know or understand, and probably always will be.

But I now know this: We diminish both ourselves and them when we treat gays and lesbians as somehow subhuman.

This dehumanization of homosexuals is reflected in our very language, because what we fear or do not understand we tend to derogate. For instance, *The Thesaurus of Slang*, published in 1988 by Facts on File, contains no fewer than 154 slang names for homosexuals, words the book's authors readily acknowledge are either derogatory or obscene.

By contrast, the entry for the word "negro" lists only twenty slang terms, at least a few of which are not considered derogatory.

Many people base their discrimination against gays and lesbians on what they understand the Bible to say on the subject. Even my own denomination—the Presbyterian Church (U.S.A.)—refuses to ordain openly gay people as members of the clergy, though, of course, there are gay and lesbian Presbyterian ministers, just as there are and have been, despite the ban, gay and lesbian soldiers.

I will not use this secular space to discuss my recently clarified views on why I think discrimination against homosexuals based on biblical standards is a result of misreading scripture. But if you are interested in seeing this subject in a new light, I recommend a two books: *Living in Sin: A Bishop Rethinks Human Sexuality*, by John Shelby Spong, the Episcopal bishop of Newark, New Jersey, and *The New Testament and Homosexuality*, by Robin Scroggs.

To quote Spong's summary point: "Even if one is a biblical literalist [which is to say, one who believes each word of the Bible is literally and inerrantly true and historically accurate], the biblical references do not build an ironclad case for condemnation [of homosexuality]. If one is not a biblical literalist there is no case at all, nothing but the ever-present prejudice born out of a pervasive ignorance that attacks people whose only crime is to be born with an unchangeable sexual predisposition toward those of their own sex."

In his otherwise excellent book, Bishop Spong adopts—without ever quoting a source for it—the widely used figure that about 10 percent of our population is homosexual. In searching for the origin of this figure, I was inevitably led back to the studies done by Alfred C. Kinsey in the 1940s and 1950s. It appears that up to 10 percent of the males whose sexual behavior Kinsey was studying identified themselves as being homosexual to one degree or another.

The Kinsey Institute New Report on Sex, published in 1990, refers to those studies this way:

> Approximately one-third of all males are thought to have had at least one same-sex experience leading to orgasm since puberty. The Kinsey data reported that about 8 percent of U.S. males had had exclusively same-sex partners for at least a period of three years at some point in life. Only about 4 percent of men were exclusively homosexual throughout their entire lives.
>
> Among U.S. females, Kinsey found that around half of college-educated women and approximately 20 percent of non-college-educated women had at least one same-sex erotic contact past puberty; only 2 or 3 percent of these women were exclusively homosexual throughout their entire lives.
>
> Although the figures are taken from data collected by Kinsey in the 1940s and 1950s on primarily white middle-class subjects, they still provide the best estimates available.

There's a problem. We simply aren't positive how common homosexuality is. What we do know is that Kinsey ended up using a sort of sliding scale in which a small percentage of the persons studied was identified as always and exclusively heterosexual and another small percentage was identified as always and exclusively homosexual. Though by far most persons were identified as predominantly heterosexual, there turned out to be, in fact, a spectrum, or continuum, of sexuality. Which meant that even most heterosexuals had some homosexual tendencies or experiences, and vice versa.

Clearly, if we are to know what we are talking about in this area, we need more accurate figures than those derived from studying mostly white middle-class people in the uptight forties and fifties.

It also would be helpful to know what causes—if that's the right verb—homosexuality. Or heterosexuality, for that matter.

The 1990 Kinsey report says flatly: "No one knows what causes homosexuality." The Kinsey Institute is pretty convinced it knows what doesn't cause homosexuality, and that list includes all those old myths, such as domineering mothers or seduction of a child by a same-sex adult.

Some research into the subject continues, but it is, at least from a rigid scientific point of view, inconclusive. However, as Bishop Spong notes, "Contemporary research is today uncovering new facts that are producing a rising conviction that homosexuality, far from being a sickness, sin, perversion or unnatural act, is a healthy, natural and affirming form of sexuality for some people. . . . Specifically, research consistently seems to support the assertion that sexual orientation is not a matter of choice; that it is not related to any environmental influence; that it is not the result of an overbearing mother or an effeminate or absent father or a seductive sexual encounter. Some researchers are finding that certain biochemical events during prenatal life may determine adult sexual orientation, and that once set it is not amenable to change."

Whatever the cause of homosexuality, it's clear that millions of Americans are, in fact, gay. It's also clear that despite the unrealistic—and probably foolish—hopes of people who wish gays would simply make a more mainstream choice about their sexuality, they will always be gay. And it's time the rest of us acknowledge that fact, educate ourselves about this subject, and demystify homosexuality so that it does not cause us to behave in oppressive ways toward people who are, finally, much more like straight people than they are different from them.

In more than three years of volunteer work with people suffering from Acquired Immune Deficiency Syndrome (AIDS), I have met dozens of gays and lesbians, and I have come to understand in a profound way that their sexuality—like my own—only partly defines them. They—and I (and you)—are much more than sexual orientation.

In many cases they are richly talented, uniquely gifted people who have much to offer our society. It's time that they be free to be all that they can be—whether in the army or anywhere else they choose to contribute.

Ventura's Rant Betrayed a Limited Vision
October 10, 1999

I have no doubt that so-called organized religion would survive and even thrive even if no one countered the recent slam on it by Governor Jesse "the Theologian" Ventura of Minnesota.

But his remarkably ignorant statements on the subject, printed by that deeply spiritual publication, *Playboy* magazine, do offer a chance to think about the value and values of faith.

Ventura, you may recall, said this: "Organized religion is a sham and a crutch for weak-minded people who need strength in numbers. It tells people to go out and stick their noses in other people's business."

He said more, but it was even less enlightening, so I'll ignore it.

One of the first clues about someone's attitude toward faith is the term *organized religion.* It has become a code for people who have no use for mystery, faith, transcendence, revelation, or worship of what cannot be seen or fully described. So right away you know Ventura's bias.

Still, I must say that Ventura almost got part of it right. Religious faith is not just for "weak-minded people" but for people of all kinds of weakness who need strength in numbers. Strength in numbers is what those of us who are members of churches, synagogues, mosques, or other faith groups call "community." Indeed, humans are created for community, for relationship.

In a faith community one can find support, encouragement, even love. One can discover that everyone has different gifts and that when these gifts are used for the good of the whole community there is harmony and rejoicing.

The Apostle Paul, in fact, spends a good part of his first letter to the fledgling church at Corinth reminding people that they need each other because the church is a body made up of separate parts.

"Indeed," he writes beginning in I Corinthians 12:14 (in the New Revised Standard Version), "the body does not consist of one member but of many. If the foot would say, 'Because I am not a hand I do not belong to the body,' that would not make it any less a part of the body. . . . The eye cannot say to the hand, 'I have no need of you,' nor again the head to the feet, 'I have no need of you.' On the contrary, the members of the body that seem to be weaker are indispensable. . . ."

The beginning of wisdom is to recognize the many ways in which we are weak and to learn how to compensate. What we must do, in fact, is to become part of a community, a family, a group of some kind that honors both our weaknesses and our strengths and that is healthy enough to become full-bodied through the assemblage of complementary parts.

When disaster strikes, as inevitably it will, wisdom moves us to turn humbly in weakness to this community and to be enveloped by its solicitous love. When your spouse dies or your child, who will comfort you? Who will stand with you? Who will help you find the eternal perspective you need to travel from pain to hope?

When I face catastrophe, I try to turn not inward, where there is mostly empty ache, but to my family of faith. There I find comfort and the assurance that I am not alone. Jesse Ventura may call this what he will. I call it love. And the only way, it turns out, that we can either love or be loved fully is by being vulnerable enough to reveal our weaknesses.

Some people have called it the genius of the Christian faith (and others have called it the religion's scandal and foolishness) that it worships a God who came to the world in weakness, as the baby Jesus. And who died in weakness on the cross of Calvary.

This is the model Christians are asked to follow. Indeed, the idea of weakness and servanthood is found in many faiths. It is a call to live in humility and harmony with others, a call not to exploit and overpower others through misused strength and power.

But perhaps that's too difficult a concept for a former pro wrestler who probably could bench press five thousand of the ten thousand lakes in his state.

I don't deny that many people of faith get it wrong, that they can be overbearing, arrogant, and even hateful. When people really understand religious faith, however, they don't "stick their noses in other people's business," but they do recognize that the welfare of others is a big part of their calling.

Jesse Ventura can say that's crazy if he wants to. I think of it as the way God asks us to live.

Elevating Our Culture Is Not Up to Congress
October 3, 1999

Give Senator Sam Brownback of Kansas this: He worries about some of the right things, such as why our culture is plagued by coarse entertainment and a breakdown of families.

But one of his solutions—a bipartisan Senate task force to study the matter—seems unwise, even absurd. What's especially distressing is that Brownback, a Republican, may have collected enough support from leaders of the Senate's Democrats to bring the grandiosely named "Senate Task Force on the State of American Society" to reality. Not all details are set, but Senate approval of this idea will allow the task force to start operating later this year and continue until early July 2000 at a cost of five hundred thousand dollars.

It's no surprise that Brownback wants the government to worry about divorce, vulgar TV, and violent video games. People who call themselves conservatives, as Brownback does, often want the government to stay out of economic affairs but to regulate private behavior. By contrast, folks who think of themselves as liberals are happy to have the government spending money on social and economic programs but don't want the feds in their bedrooms.

And yet it appears that Brownback's idea has support from enough senators who see political value in it to move ahead with it.

But the "Senate Task Force on the State of American Society" is not a good use of government. This is true even if you agree with Brownback, as I do, that the culture is, in many ways, a disgusting mess.

The pertinent question is what the Senate can or should do about it. Should it pass a law that says people can't get divorced? Or one that gives TV six months to clean up the relentless dreck it pours into our living rooms?

Brownback is right that these are problems. I'm glad he's noticed. But the government's role in solving them is, at best, minimal. In the end, elevating our culture is up to us, not Congress.

That isn't to say there's nothing for government to do about what we might call the Roman Empiring of our culture. It can—and should—adopt laws that make it more difficult for unstable people to get guns with which to commit the violence the culture encourages. It can—and should—make sure the welfare system doesn't encourage family dissolution. It can—and should—collect and distribute figures on pregnancy rates among unwed teenagers so we know the scope of the problem.

But if members of Congress imagine their job is to tell us what TV shows are bad, what movies are too violent, or what video games not to buy, they have—as is often their wont—mistaken their role for that of parents, grandparents, and the clergy.

I am not defending our culture, although, to be fair, there is much about it—great music, soaring theater, amazing art, even inspiring sports—that elevates us. But there is far too much that demeans who we are meant to be. From putrid TV to pornographic magazines, the culture is adrift in muck.

Indeed, it can be argued that the culture degenerated even further last year when it was hard to turn on a radio or television without finding talk of oral sex in the White House. But it's not the government's job to fix what Brownback and a Democratic cohort, New York Senator Daniel Patrick Moynihan, correctly identify as "the negative cultural environment that surrounds so many children."

Brownback says the job of the new task force won't be to "prescribe cultural norms" but to "address these essential issues in a responsible, bipartisan and holistic manner and explore possible solutions."

Friends, you and I are the solution. With no threat to First Amendment freedoms, we can choose not to watch bad TV. We can choose not to buy pornography or plug into it on the World Wide Web. We can keep valueless video games out of the hands of our children. We can avoid movies that are simply vehicles for gratuitous violence. We can tell advertisers we won't buy their products if they support junk entertainment.

We don't need the government telling us how to be more decent people. We need the government to help us care for the poor, to set rational tax law, to protect our borders, our legal rights, our patents. If the Reverend Dr. Brownback wants to preach to us, let him quit the Senate and finagle invitations from churches, synagogues, and mosques.

A "Christian Society" Is a Contradiction in Terms
February 16, 1992

David Duke, Louisiana's answer to the public demand for wretchedly excessive know-nothingism, can be charitably described as confused about almost everything of consequence.

One of this presidential candidate's most wrongheaded notions has to do with church-state relations.

"We've got to begin to realize that we're a Christian society," he says. As with people who stubbornly insist that the Holocaust never happened or that the Earth is flat (two contentions of approximately equal merit), it is hard to know where to begin to refute such nonsense. Should we explain why it makes no historical sense? Should we point out why the term "Christian society," properly understood, is oxymoronic, a contradiction of terms no less awkward and amusing than, say, "civil war" or "pretty ugly"? Should we simply ignore Duke and hope he finds legitimate work?

Well, he's hard to ignore. Besides, silence in the face of lies—the choice some made when faced with Duke's erstwhile hero Adolf Hitler—can be deadly. Also, the insidiously seductive nature of Duke and his ilk means that—like biblical scholars who playfully quote from the nonexistent Book of Hezekiah—they sometimes sound like they know what they're talking about.

I have no idea what Duke means by "Christian society," and I'm sure he doesn't either. But if we search through the history of the United States, no such thing can be found. The closest we come is in pre-Revolutionary days when, as author Paul Johnson puts it in his wonderfully readable work *The History of Christianity*, America was "born Protestant."

But, as Johnson quickly notes, once Rhode Island, under Roger Williams, established itself with religious freedom as "the principle of its existence," a "decisive breach had been made." America—or, at any rate, the colonies that were to become America—moved "steadily towards religious liberty and the separation of Church and State."

In fact, well before the American Revolution was fought—and almost simultaneous with the evangelical Great Awakening—the colonies experienced what Johnson calls "the collapse of the total Christian society."

This is not to say Christianity (and, more broadly, Judeo-Christian values) did not then—and does not now—play an influential role in American culture. Surely it did. Surely it does.

(This despite the view of some mainline Christians that the values of Christians and the American society in which they live are often hostile to one another. Leonard Sweet, president of United Theological Seminary in Dayton, Ohio, expresses that view this way: "We don't live in a secular society, we live in a pagan society that is resistant to the gospel, a gospel which calls the church to perpetual criticism of the social and political order.")

Even the Founding Fathers (many of whom were not Christian but, rather, deists, whose notion of a detached God bore little resemblance to the personal God of the Hebrew and Christian scriptures) never imagined anything approximating a "Christian society." And Christians (there were some) influential in the founding of this country generally had no theocracy in mind, either.

Johnson, in fact, points out that small religious sects did not wrest from reluctant "magisterial churchmen" the religious freedom won by the revolution and guaranteed in the Constitution. Rather, that freedom was instituted by church people themselves "who saw that pluralism was the only form consonant with the ideals and necessities of the country."

Pluralism, of course, is an idea foreign to David Duke's frightened mind. That's because it embodies a notion of extreme importance to Christianity, which is this: All people—no matter what circumstance, intelligence, race, skills, or anything else—must be treated with dignity because they have been exalted by a loving God.

Admittedly, the concept that a poor black prostitute is ultimately as precious to God as a rich white priest (or even a Grand Wizard) is difficult for many people to grasp. For Duke, it has proven impossible.

Similarly, Duke shows he has no command of the difference between "society," which Christians (whom the Apostle Paul, in his letter to the Philippians, commands to be "citizens of heaven") think of as a necessary evil, and "community," the Christian ideal.

Author Glenn Tinder, in his seminal work, *The Political Meaning of Christianity*, has the best explanation of this difference. A community, he says, is "a setting in which individuals are exalted." It displays "authentic unity among human beings." It is, therefore, just an ideal toward which Christians strive.

A society, by contrast, is merely the self-protective organization we create to survive in a fallen world. It recognizes—through its laws and other limitations—that we are all sinful and need controls.

It's hard to imagine that David Duke has ever thought much about any of this. He's been too busy expectorating hate and his nincompoop theories of life and making easy money from foolish contributors. But that doesn't mean we need to let his poisonous ignorance flap around in the world unchallenged.

He no doubt hopes our silence will imbue his crackbrained pronouncements with a kind of legitimacy. That must not happen.

Buchanan's Forces Target the Wrong Dragon
March 14, 1999

Trust a crowd, says author Kurt Vonnegut, to look at the wrong end of a miracle every time.

Similarly, trust a crowd to fight the wrong wars. Almost everywhere I look I find people worrying about what both the political left and right call the culture wars, which are being fought over abortion, homosexuality, public morality, church-state separation, coarsened entertainment, multiculturalism, pornography, divorce, profanity, euthanasia, cohabitation, and on and on.

When Pat Buchanan announced his candidacy for president recently, he was direct about his desire to lead the charge against "all that pollutes our culture." To Buchanan, "ultimately, our culture war is about one question: Is God dead or is God king?"

His very wording puts him at odds with people who might, on one level, agree with his faith-based assessment but who no longer are willing to use exclusively masculine words to refer to the deity because they find it doesn't reflect the full scriptural witness and doing so is at least subtly hostile to more than half the population.

Despite the terrific heat these culture wars generate over such matters, they are, in the end, the wrong fight. I'm not saying they are unimportant. Or that there's nothing to fight about. Many of the issues (and others) deserve our best thinking and debating.

But they are secondary to the real and serious damage being done to our culture by the increasingly widespread fiction that all of us are, at base, economic creatures whose highest and best role is that of consumer.

This deception turns all segments of the media into little more than magnets to attract an audience to which advertisers may pitch their wares. It is, in fact, easy to make a case that many segments of the media rarely rise above that role. Television is the most obvious culprit, but the Internet—with its misinformation, pornography, and mere silliness packaged as vehicles for commercial messages—is often an equally ignoble enterprise.

Many of the people fighting these peripheral culture wars are, at the same time, pledging allegiance to the economic system whose abuse leads to this culture of consumerism. That is, they defend capitalism almost without qualification.

And even though it's true that an open market is, at least in its ideal, the least oppressive economic system yet devised, it is imperfect everywhere it's used and it seems to seduce some of its proponents into imagining that it's divinely ordained.

The truth is that what our consumerist culture does, in the end, is ignore the reality that we are both material and spiritual beings who have higher callings than owning the latest sports car or fastest modem.

Indeed, we are created not for consumption but for relationship. And the failure to understand that leads to an inability to grasp that there are rules about relationships that must be observed. If those rules are flouted—as they clearly were in the Clinton-Lewinsky affair (between two people with dark vacuums where their moral centers should be)—people are damaged, diminished, even destroyed.

I can be persuaded that, reworded, Buchanan's culture wars question—Is God dead or is God sovereign?—is the right one because, properly understood, it can point us toward the culture battle that should engage us. Which is the one about whether we are created first for relationship—both horizontal (with other people) and vertical (with God)—or for consumption.

But the battle cry heard on Buchanan's side of the other culture wars too often leads people to imagine that they know precisely where God stands on all issues. Armed with the arrogance of that false certainty, helmets on, pitchforks in hand, they have ridden off to slay the wrong dragons and, thus, are unavailable to fight the more sinister and insidious one.

Truths, Both Awkward and Reassuring

For All Our Progress, Are We Any More Moral?
May 30, 1993

Memorial Day weekend—a time for deconstructing memories—gives us an occasion to ask whether, in the long reach of history, humanity has made any progress at all.

It is not a simple—but neither is it a trick—question.

Progress, of course, can be defined in different ways. There is no denying, for instance, that in many fields—technology, science, medicine, transportation—we have leaped ahead a millionfold and continue to break through new barriers almost hourly.

Today I compose these words in a blip of fluid light on a computer screen. When I began in this business in the 1960s I composed on a manual typewriter and corrected my many mistakes in pencil. The machine I use now was simply not technologically possible then.

Yes, yes, we know all that and more. And seem to be less and less dazzled by it.

But what about progress of a different sort? What about becoming better people? With millennia of history and an explosion of information to teach us, are we any more moral, more noble, more honest, honorable, ethical, or decent than when our ancestors lived in caves?

Face that question honestly and your heart will sink.

Back in 1893, Senator William A. Peffer of Kansas, described as both a populist and a futurist (besides being a journalist), predicted that by 1993 war would be abolished.

"Man will grow wiser, better and purer," he said.

It is hard to imagine a more off-base, naive prediction. The twentieth century, between Peffer's words and our time, has seen the most barbarous, destructive wars in history, beginning with World

174

War I—set off, ominously enough, in Bosnia. It was a war that left the world dazed, disillusioned. But what came after that was even worse. For decades, whole cobbled-together nations were locked in ideological prisons that called themselves economic systems of "the people."

The evil of the World War II Holocaust, in a warring world gone mad, ravaged people for no greater crime than being. The evils of apartheid, racism, colonialism, sexism, and more oppressed and misused people for no better cause.

Vicious wars fought for scruffy land and bad ideas wounded the Earth as well as the psyches of generations of vulnerable people, some of whom had hardly a clue about what was happening to them.

And for half a century we have cowered in the shadow of a mushroom threat so destructive in its potential that no words can point to what its reality might be like.

Any reasonably complete list of modern human-made horrors would, in agate type, fill every page of every edition of this newspaper for the next week—and even then leave out enough evil to jam the broad road to the very gates of hell. People angry at God have it backward. God should be angry at us.

There simply is no honest way to say that all our progress—our high-tech ability to bounce electronic ideas off satellites and around the globe in a nanosecond—has made us more moral, more honest, or more loving. The graveyards we visit contain too much evidence to the contrary.

This is not news. Why, centuries ago, Hebrew prophets warned people how duplicitous the human heart is.

And yet, for all that, it is hard not to think that something good, something at least promising, has been happening to us as a result of—or at least coincident with—our technological and informational advances.

Perhaps—at a minimum—we have begun to set in place a system of information exchange that can help us make better choices and liberate people from the ignorance that produces fear, hatred, and evil.

It may be just wishful thinking, but how can hope remain dormant when visions of people smashing down the onerous Berlin Wall flash around the world and plant ideas of freedom across the land of gulags?

Who can forget—and fail to be thrilled by—the picture of that brave man in Beijing stopping an advancing tank, even though we know that, for now, the tanks have won?

Who was not profoundly moved by Boris Yeltsin standing on a tank and rallying his people against the forces of darkness? Or by pictures of young Somalis finally getting enough to eat?

Now that we can see and hear and almost touch distant spots on the globe instantly, it is harder for evil to happen unnoticed. Yes, there is the horror of ethnic cleansing in Bosnia. Yes, the Kurds live in great peril in Iraq. Yes, black South Africans are not yet free, and the Sudanese are starving. Yes, Americans still go to sleep hungry and homeless. Yes, freedom of expression in China is still only a dream.

But at least we know of such offenses now—and know immediately, too.

The difficult question in this time made for remembering is whether that knowledge will lead us to act more nobly or whether the sheer volume will deaden our nerves and let us reach for the off button of isolation.

The hope is that we can learn and change. The evidence is that we never have. But if we deny that hope altogether, it finally won't matter what we remember or, in a future we would enter trembling, what we do.

Ideal of Individualism Is, Finally, a Fiction
May 18, 1997

I was driving home the other day on an interstate highway in rush hour—I think of it as bumper cars for adults—when the harmfulness of human isolation struck me with almost physical force.

Certainly the dangers of our growing addiction to privacy had occurred to me before, but never had I felt so keenly how much that predilection goes against the very grain of who we are meant—even created—to be.

We are designed for relationship, for community, association, friendship, intimacy, alliance. Although we still honor the historically overblown ideal of rugged individualism, it is, finally, a fiction.

Few of us could survive alone. It goes against who we are. In our economy and culture, not only do we need each other to be fed, clothed, and sheltered (I can't grow all my own food, make my own shirts, build my own house), but also we need each other to fill our deep, unspoken yearning for companionship and connection.

There is something genetic about this. It's why toddlers in malls notice and move toward each other. It's why old men in small towns gather for morning coffee in cafés, even when they have little to say. It's why young mothers pushing strollers find excuses to be with other young mothers. Our deepest patterning shouts to us about our need to be connected to one another.

But there I was that day, alone in my car, surrounded by thousands of other people alone in their cars, close but out of touch. And I was heading to my single-family, detached home that I can enter with a garage-door opener, never even having to leave the cocoon of my vehicle.

Part of the reason I was thinking about some of this is that I was remembering how I used to get to and from work before a recent (voluntary and joyful) change of family circumstance mandated a move.

I used to take the bus. Every morning I would walk half a block from my front door—often seeing and speaking to my next-door neighbor as he came out to pick up his newspaper.

I would wait at the bus stop, sometimes with the same people. We grew to know each other's names. We talked about the weather and the street construction in front of us and whatever else occurred. It was rarely anything deep, but we were forced to account for the presence of someone else in our physical space, especially as we moved toward the bus door to board.

On the bus I would see many of the same faces every day, faces that eventually became names. There was Leo and Robin and Cindy and Dennis, and more. I was astonished one day—nearly twenty years into riding the same bus each day—to realize that there were hardly any strangers riding with me. I either knew or recognized almost all of them.

And even when I rode a bus full of strangers, at least I was not physically isolated. This forced me to abandon the attractive but deceitful notion that I am the center of the universe. I had to consider my place in community.

I don't want to make riding a bus seem idyllic and driving a car evil. Even though I live farther from work now than when I rode a bus, I arrive in less time. And I get to hear some news on the radio on the way. But it's clear to me that when we put ourselves in situations that force us to interact with other people, we are living closer to the way we were built to live.

Instead—especially as our affluence grows—we tend to withdraw. We abandon the bus for the car. We build fences around detached houses in gated communities. We put on our headsets and communicate, if at all, by e-mail.

We are losing the difficult balance between our genuine need for some privacy and our even deeper need for the connections of community.

And nothing good can come of that.

Huck Finn Has So Much to Teach Our World
October 4, 1992

I am no literary scholar. But I know what writers know: Words—the right words in service to great ideas—can carry the blunt and honorable freight of important truths.

So, from time to time, I open a copy of Mark Twain's best work, *Adventures of Huckleberry Finn,* and rediscover its brilliance. I listen again for the truths it can speak for our time and our place—truths it has been speaking since its publication more than a hundred years ago.

I have just finished another rereading, and I'm struck by how much our nervous, agitated, annoyed, self-centered nation needs—right now—nothing more than to sit down quietly and plumb the depths of *Huck Finn,* from which, Ernest Hemingway once correctly noted, "all modern American literature comes."

This time through showed me, among many other things, how well young Huck understands what some Christians have come to call the doctrine of the Total Depravity of Mankind. This doctrine, despite its slam-dunk name, does not say humans are bad in all ways. Rather, it says that although a good and loving God created us good, and although we carry the image of that God within us, we succumb to evil through misuse of our free will. Or at least we all get tainted with, or stained by, evil. And on our own there is no way out of it.

Huck Finn, of course, never would speak in such theological terms about the human capacity for evil. (In fact, he rightly rejects the only Christianity he knows about—a twisted religion of raging hypocrisy that finds ways to justify slavery.)

But Huck lives as though people really do have an ability to do evil, which, of course, they do. He lives, in other words, without illusions, and yet often is an illusion himself. That's because he travels under one disguise after another because he doesn't trust anyone. He assumes, on the basis of his experience (with his abusive father, among others), that people can be wicked and dangerous. He sees stupidity, arrogance, cowardice, false pride, and worse in one encounter after another. And none of it really surprises him.

In fact, what sometimes takes him back is not evil but quite the opposite—the love and caring he receives at the hands of the runaway slave Jim, truly one of literature's most glorious heroes.

Despite Huck's insightful understanding of evil, he remains essentially good-natured and capable of great sympathy and love. Perhaps nowhere is this clearer than when this uneducated young boy, a product of mid-nineteenth-century frontier America, discovers that he and Jim share a common humanity—for Huck, a stunning insight.

As he and Jim float down the river at one point, they get separated in the fog. Jim, sure Huck is dead, finally falls asleep on the raft, exhausted. But when he awakes, Huck is back and Jim is overjoyed. Huck, however, plays a trick by convincing Jim he's dreamed the whole separation.

But when Huck lets Jim in on the joke, Jim is deeply wounded: "En when I wake up en fine you back agin, all safe en soun', de tears come, en I could a got down on my knees and kiss yo' foot, I's so thankful. En all you wuz thinkin' 'bout wuz how you could make a fool uv ole Jim wid a lie."

Huck is forced to abandon the one thing that has given him status over Jim: his sense of superiority in being white.

"It was fifteen minutes," a chastened Huck confesses, "before I could work myself up to go and humble myself to a nigger—but I done it, and I warn't ever sorry for it afterwards, neither."

In some ways, Huck's action here reflects his broad capacity for living without revenge. Even people who do Huck great wrong—the rapscallion Duke and King, for instance—never elicit from him any final hatred.

In fact, when he sees those two tarred and feathered and ridden out of town on a rail, he says, "Well, it made me sick to see it; and I was sorry for them poor pitiful rascals, it seemed like I couldn't ever feel any hardness against them any more in the world. It was a dreadful thing to see. Human beings can be awful cruel to one another." But he knew he had done all he could, so he let it go, with no lingering feelings of false guilt.

What, for us, might be the implications of understanding the human capacity for evil, and of a Huck-like openness to giving and receiving kindness?

I think it would make us more clear-eyed. It would allow us to be more cognizant of our own shortcomings while not feeling stunned or utterly betrayed by the shortcomings of others. We would know better why we pass laws and build prisons to house the people who break them, but also why we need to visit the prisoners there, why we need to look for ways to reclaim their lives. It would not make us bleeding-heart liberals but, more likely, compassionate realists. We would trust in the Lord but keep our powder dry.

I want to return to Jim briefly. From time to time *Huck Finn* has been banned from libraries and schools because it contains multiple uses of the word *nigger*. This is like banning the Bible from church because it contains the word *hell*.

Some perfectly sincere people who are rightly offended by the racial pejorative cannot imagine a redemptive context for its use. But, in fact, *Huck Finn* is—even if it doesn't mean to be—a clear, urgent call for abolition of the attitudes that lead to slavery and other human degradation.

Huckleberry has grown up with the pervasive moral code of his pre–Civil War times—an era that usually saw little wrong with not only the word *nigger* but also with slavery itself. For such a boy to encounter a warm, wonderful, strong black hero and to let that encounter destroy the foundation of that bogus moral code is a thundering act of literary revolution. Twain should be applauded for his vision and courage, not criticized because he accurately captures the destructive speech that helped to buoy up an evil system.

It is hard to imagine a more remarkable, admirable hero than Jim. Clearly Twain was eager for readers to consider the possibility that what unites people like black Jim and white Huck is far more important than what seems to separate them.

Are there implications for us in this? Good Lord, yes.

We are invited not only to examine our own racial prejudices but also, by extension, all of our other biases. The example of Huck and Jim suggests that we cannot know people of different races (or genders, religions, sexual orientations, or cultures) until we live in community with them.

This is not to say we have to share a river raft together, but almost. For when we look people in the eye, sharing thoughts and dreams, our own bogus moral codes begin to erode, perhaps to be replaced by an ethic that affirms our shared humanity, with all that means, good and bad.

It sounds as if I'm urging that we read *Huck Finn* as a sort of moral guidebook, a secular Bible. No, literature—especially great literature, which surely *Huck Finn* is—must be read on its own terms. And *Huck Finn* does not set out, first of all—or maybe at all—to be a clarion call to moral rectitude and insight. (Twain, however, ironically raises that very possibility with his sardonic "Notice" at the beginning of the book that says "persons attempting to find a moral in the book will be banished.")

Rather, *Huck Finn* purports to be a story of a boy's adventures— almost picaresque in approach. And ten-year-old readers can enjoy it for that.

But if the book's ingenious contexts and dilemmas raise greater moral questions, as clearly they do, it only makes sense to try to understand how such a book can inform and shape our lives. *Huck Finn*, in the end, is not simply a boy's adventure story. Nor, for that matter, is *Catch-22* just a book about airplanes.

It is hard to write about *Huck Finn* without saying something about the river. Scholars have made lavish (oh, all right, adequate) livings writing nothing but academic treatises on the meaning of the river in Huck Finn. And though I don't know this to be true, it wouldn't surprise me to learn that some budding Ph.D. somewhere is hard at work on a paper that holds Twain up as the great environmentalist of his era on the basis of his obvious love and respect for the river.

As Huckleberry said of a bad sermon he once heard: It "give him [the preacher] a rattling reputation, because the oldest man in the world couldn't 'a' understood it." I'm sure I'd feel the same about such a doctoral dissertation.

And so it is with some unease that I even mention what struck me this time about the river in *Huck Finn*, which is that it—not unlike Huck himself—somehow remains outside of any human control, and for that reason among many, Huck loves and respects it.

The river in *Huck Finn* is nearly a living being, with fair and foul moods, with grace, with power, with a strength that elicits both caution and admiration from Huck.

If we were to respond that way to nature, the ecological implications would be legion. We would not dam up rivers willy-nilly to satisfy our craving for lakes on which to run speedboats. We would not level mountains and trees to make way for an infinite number of vacation condos. We would not, in short, live in destructive disharmony with nature if we shared the awe Huck shows for the unbridled river.

Huck Finn is a masterful work from the mind of a genius, and I've barely drawn water from its deep wells. But that, as Huck might say, doesn't put me in a sweat. I know that next year or the next, the book will be waiting on my shelf, ready to reveal other valuable truths.

Huck, at the end of the book, says that if he'd " 'a' knowed what a trouble it was to make a book I wouldn't 'a' tackled it."

If you believe that, you'll also believe that if I'd known how rich the *Adventures of Huckleberry Finn* would continue to be, I'd have read it only once.

The Basic Choice Is Empathy or Bondage
March 7, 1999

I stopped by a homeless shelter the other day to see someone I know. As I waited, I felt rather conspicuous in my suit and tie. In fact, the friendly man at the information desk asked me if I was a pastor. I chuckled.

But as I sat in the lobby waiting to see the man I came to check on, I was struck again by what may be the most difficult of all human tasks: empathy. That is, the challenge of really putting ourselves in the shoes of others.

I watched several residents of this shelter come and go while I waited, and I knew only that each of them had a unique—and almost certainly painful—history. Indeed, some of them bore the wounds of life on wearied faces that looked out at the world from the midst of a general dishevelment.

But without talking with them in detail, I could not know how they had ended up there. I had no way to feel what it must be like to live their lives. They, in turn, had no way to understand me. All they saw was a middle-aged, graying white guy in a suit. They probably imagined me as some deputized agent of a system that controlled their lives, but that's just a guess.

I think I've finally lived long enough to be able to say that our almost universal failure to appreciate either the struggle or the point of view of others is what gets us into the most trouble.

For the starkest example, we need look no further than the recent trial in Jasper, Texas, of John William King, convicted of murdering James Byrd Jr. Somehow King, a white man, had been unable to look at Byrd, a black man, and imagine anything of his humanity, which is to say his unique history.

In an odd and distorted way, that failure freed King to wrap chains around Byrd, whom he apparently saw as subhuman, and drag him to pieces behind a pickup truck last June.

It was a huge, bloody, disastrous disconnect, and it was rooted in either King's inability or his unwillingness to see the world through the eyes of Byrd or even to acknowledge that Byrd had every right to see the world differently than he saw it.

However, when a jury declared King guilty of capital murder, we saw exactly the sort of grace and empathy that might well have prevented this evil in the first place. King's father, Ronald King, telephoned James Byrd Sr., the father of the murdered man, to say how sorry he was that any of this had happened.

"I couldn't say, 'I know how you feel,' even though I'm losing my son, too," the elder King said. "I don't know how he feels. All I know is he's got to be hurting like the dickens. We all are."

Byrd, having been offered this noble gift, responded in kind: "I feel real sorry for him, really. I do. You watch your kids grow up. You teach 'em and they don't do exactly what they've been taught. I just told him I can't hold him responsible for his son."

What struck me about this wasn't just that King and Byrd had connected across racial lines. In the end, racial lines had precious little to do with this manifest empathy. Rather, each simply acknowledged the other's basic humanity and affirmed the legitimacy of the other's experience.

This represents ancient, though widely ignored, wisdom. Although Jesus of Nazareth wasn't the first to advocate this, his wording may be most famous as the Golden Rule in Luke 6:31 (as rendered by the New Revised Standard Version): "Do to others as you would have them do to you."

The "do" here should be seen as both action and attitude. This rule calls us to get into each other's skin, not only working for the other's highest good but also acknowledging in humility that the other person is of infinite value. If we fail, we figuratively—and sometimes literally—wrap each other in chains of bondage and destruction.

Where We're Free to Be Our Whole Selves
July 25, 1999

ABIQUIU, NEW MEXICO—As we drove onto the now familiar gravel road that leads to the Ghost Ranch Conference Center off U.S. 84, I felt a deep connection that began to satisfy some unnamed longing.

I said to my wife and to our friend who was joining us for a week in these remarkable red rock hills that Ghost Ranch has become one of several places that now seem like home to me.

I've been coming here to teach seminars for five or six straight summers now, and the place—its stirring land, its fascinating people—has taken root in my heart. When I'm away from this high desert country for long enough, I can feel a longing for the place pulling at my center.

This is not, of course, the only place—both around the country as well as in the Kansas City area—that draws me to it by some homing call.

Knowing that, I am moved to ask: What is it that leads us to find home in some locations but not in others? What is it we sense when we come to understand at some visceral level that we belong here or there but not, say, somewhere else?

I think home is where we are free to be our whole selves. That is, I think we feel at home in those places where we are liberated to be authentically who, at our essence, we are, with as few masks as possible.

I almost never felt that sense of wholeness in the Illinois house in which I grew up. For many reasons, my mother seemed unwilling to release control of her four children so they could discover and live out their destinies. Each of us had to do that in different ways away from the home in which we spent most of our childhoods. And it may explain why we are almost literally now scattered from coast to coast—from California to North Carolina—with just one of us within fifty miles of that house.

And yet there is something about the old house that feels like home to me. I think it's because I now understand that it was there that I first came to terms with the reality that I was not free, and it was there that I determined to be so someday. So I am drawn to that place because it remains the site of my liberating decision to find home somewhere.

Home, then, is not always someplace free of pain or anxiety. Rather, it's where distress has been confronted and, in some way, resolved—or at least understood.

The house in which my children grew up will always feel like home to me even though, as my marriage dissolved several years ago, it was the nexus of intense anxiety and discord. But despite that, the house was also where my children's mother and I reared two beautiful, healthy daughters who brought—and still bring—both of us joy.

I can think of places I've lived, however, that feel nothing like home to me today. One was the dormitory of a boarding school in India where I spent part of my twelfth year. For countless reasons, other children did not accept me there, and I felt like an unwanted alien in a strange land.

I have come to understand now much of what that was about, and I do not doubt that I could return to that school and that dorm today without bitterness. But I'm sure the place will never feel like home to me.

Similarly, there's a small studio apartment in Rochester, New York, that I once occupied for about a year. It was my first post-college place to live, but even from the first it felt like a temporary roost to me, a nest some other bird had built and in which I was trespassing. Nothing about it felt like the permanence of home.

Here at Ghost Ranch, a national Presbyterian conference center where the artist Georgia O'Keeffe once lived and painted, I am a temporary resident each year.

And yet because I am free here to be myself—and to uncover some parts of that self that get neglected in the busy-ness of most of the rest of my year—I am at home here.

Many people have tried to describe what home really is, perhaps most famously the poet Robert Frost, who said: "Home is the place where, when you have to go there, / They have to take you in."

And nearly two thousand years ago, Pliny the Elder offered this: "Home is where the heart is." I now know that Frost's observation isn't always true and that Pliny needs editing. I would put it this way: Home is where the healed heart—this side of heaven—is most free.

Where a Bit of Land Breeds Astounding Variety
March 5, 2000

ENGLEWOOD, FLORIDA—In the Cedar Point Environmental Park here, I have stopped my slow walk through the saw palmetto, slash pines, and rosary peas to read a small sign on the trail that describes another unfamiliar plant, the Florida coontie.

It is, I learn, the state's only native cycad, a group of plants roughly between ferns and palms. The coontie is an ancient plant "more complex than the fern but more primitive than the conifers like the slash pine," the signs says. Years ago people made starch from coontie tubers, but the starch is poisonous if it's not prepared properly. (I hesitate to imagine how anyone first discovered that.)

As I look around at the wild tangle of plants on these eighty-eight acres at the edge of Lemon Bay on the Gulf Coast, I am nearly overcome by the puzzling diversity of life on our planet. What is it all about? Is there some purpose to all this incredible mix? Or, instead, is it that God simply loves to be flamboyant? Even in this small patch of Earth, the variety of life is breathtaking.

In addition to the plants I've mentioned, red cedar trees are found, along with wax myrtle, cabbage palm, nickerbean, Christmas berry, smilax vine, muscadine grape vine, St. John's wort, yellow-eyed grass, hatpin (yes, hatpin), broom sedge, oak trees, shiny and rusty lyonia, coin vine, salt bush, winged sumac, poison ivy, morning glory, pennyroyal, St. Peter's wort, sea oxeye daisy, pawpaw, black needle rush, Brazilian pepper, Australian pine, and melaleuca. Amazing.

It is easy, in fact, to imagine that this kind of run-amok biodiversity resulted from some sort of divine bar bet.

"Ten bucks says I can cram dozens of weird plants onto one little patch of land in Florida," God says rather loudly. And someone takes the bet, so God has to make good. And does.

But it's not just plants that live here and not just tourists, either.

I've been looking at a male American bald eagle sitting high in a tree watching his mate in a nearby nest. She's got either eggs or baby eagles. I can't tell from where I am because the eagle trail has been blocked from tourists so this nesting process can take place without interference from curious—and often destructive—humans.

Eagles are not, of course, the only animals inhabiting Cedar Point. Take a look at this list of company: gopher, tortoise, raccoon, armadillo, rabbit, Florida mouse, osprey, seagull, great blue heron, cardinal, blue jay, red-bellied woodpecker, black vulture, black snake, yellow rat snake, anole, bobcat, gray fox, gray squirrel, palmetto rat, gopher frog, great horned owl, pelican, night heron, oystercatcher, morning dove, pileated woodpecker, flicker, turkey vulture, indigo snake, diamondback rattler, and skink. This astonishing list doesn't even include the little crabs skittering along the muddy shore.

Again, what is the purpose of all this variety? Well, there is a lot we don't know about what's now called biodiversity. But what we do know suggests that all of life—plants and animals—seems to be better off, healthier, with more variety around it. Genetic research is showing that is especially true in similar plants. For instance, if each stalk of corn planted by farmers in Iowa were a genetic twin of every other stalk, one disease or pest could wipe out the whole crop. If, however, many varieties of corn are available, disease and pests have a harder time wreaking widespread damage.

We also have learned that societies can be healthier when they include a variety of people. Communities that are predominantly homogeneous in terms of race, religion, economics, or almost any category can become incestuously weak and insulated. Their ignorance of the outside world turns them fearful, causing them sometimes to act destructively to preserve sameness.

Which is not to say that diversity automatically leads to good relations—in either the plant or animal worlds. Some plants destroy others, choking the life out of them. And, of course, some animals eat others. That's the way the world works.

But humans rise above the level of brute survival to the extent they recognize strength in variety. The lively trails through the Florida wilds remind me that differences can be accommodated into beauty.

The Problem with Get-Rich Game Shows
January 30, 2000

I know that when I condemn such popular new TV game shows as *Who Wants to Be a Millionaire*, I may be mistaken for one of those annoying Puritans whose constant worry is that someone, somewhere is having fun.

But my point has nothing to do with being against fun. Rather, it has to do with being against idolatry—an increasingly difficult concept to explain to people who accept without much question the worship of almost anything. Indeed, when a culture permits— even encourages—a multiplicity of gods, idolatry gets drained of meaning. And yet I think idolatry is a concept well worth recovering.

In early sacred history, of course, idolatry meant the worship of some material thing that somehow embodied or represented the divine. I have many memories of living in India for two years as a boy, but perhaps none so puzzling as seeing the countless stone and wood idols that, I was told, people worshiped.

The early histories of Judaism, Christianity, and Islam are, in many ways, the accounts of clashes between monotheism and the polytheistic cultures against which the values of those faiths stood.

The Hebrew Scriptures, sad to say, are full of tales about how the ancient people of Israel, with distressing regularity, would fall into idol worship. This was despite the fact that the very first— and, arguably, most formative—of the Ten Commandments forbids followers of the faith from having any other gods before the one true God.

I'm especially engaged by the description of idols in Psalm 115 (as recorded in the New Revised Standard Version) and—more—of the slam-dunk picture of those who make idols: "Their idols are silver and gold, the work of human hands. They have mouths, but do not speak; eyes, but do not see. They have ears, but do not hear; noses, but do not smell. They have hands, but do not feel; feet, but do not walk; they make no sound in their throats. Those who make them are like them; so are all who trust in them."

But what can those ancient words have to do with harmless TV game shows?

As with much of what's on television these days, *Who Wants to Be a Millionaire* and its wanna-be rivals illustrate how pervasive idolatry has become. The very name of the show almost begs for this reply: "Well, everyone wants to be a millionaire, of course, because money is good and a lot of money (which one million dollars still is, despite inflation) is better. Money, in fact, is what it's all about."

But the ultimate question about idolatry is this: What do we worship? For whatever we worship is our god.

Then the question becomes: How do we know what we are worshiping? There are many ways, but in the end the answer is always this: We worship what we live for, what we desire most, what we sacrifice for, what we work harder for than anything.

We are in a time of instant TV millionaires, of day traders who seek instant gratification in stock market fortunes, of an electorate that increasingly believes the sole purpose of government is to oversee and ensure a booming economy. "It's the economy, stupid" is not simply a presidential campaign's way of remembering to focus on the day's primary issue. It's also a reminder of what, increasingly, our culture worships.

I do not want you to imagine that I believe money is inherently evil or that it can be used only for evil, never for good. This would be foolish. Money, properly understood and used, can be a great tool for good.

But the question to ask about money is also the question to ask about material possessions, political power, and corporate ambition: Is it our god? If it is, someday our god will fail us. Someday we will inevitably experience a profound emptiness at our core.

The problem with TV's hot new get-rich-quick game shows is not that they don't entertain or intrigue us. Rather, it's that they promote the morally bankrupt idea that money represents humanity's highest value.

In the great monotheistic world religions, all sin, finally, is idolatry because all sin involves putting something ahead of God. The dubious achievement of our own culture and economy is that the list of what it worships is long, pervasive, and seductive.

Beyond that, those idols attract television audiences of millions who desperately seek assurances that what they worship will, in turn, bless them.

The Mix of Memory That Enters Our Minds
July 30, 1995

BELVIDERE, ILLINOIS—"A good memory," the voice on my car's tape deck says, "is about one-third cure and two-thirds curse."

It's a wonderful but painful line from the audiobook version of *Oldest Living Confederate Widow Tells All* by Allan Gurganus. And it strikes me—as I drive home to Kansas City from a quick trip to

Woodstock, Illinois, my old hometown just east of here—as being no more than 3 to 5 percent wrong.

On my way out of Woodstock, for instance, I drove past my high school and thought of the basketball team on which I played as a senior. Well, "played" is an exaggeration. In fact, I was the only senior on the team, the others having had their fill of an arrogant coach. But all the starters were juniors. I rarely got on the court. And nearly all our games were losses.

I remember sitting, head down, in the gym after a game and repeatedly smashing my fist into a bleacher seat, so frustrated was I at not playing and not winning. When tears filled my eyes, I left so no girls would see me.

I could tell you about the five members of our team, including me, who were tall enough (or could jump high enough) to slam-dunk the ball, and how we'd all line up together in the pregame warmups to do just that, giving our fans (and us, mostly) a thrill. But, oddly, that's not what my memory first dredged up here as I drove by. It chose curse over cure.

Just a few minutes ago I drove under an overpass with a sign telling me the name of the road above was "Twombley." And I thought of a kid I knew for a few years when I grew up—Bruce Twombley.

But that's all my memory gave me. I couldn't find his face. I couldn't remember anything about him. I couldn't even recall where in town he lived or how old we were, exactly, when we knew each other. Nor if we liked each other. I was given only his name out of the curse-cure mix of memory. And what good is that?

The countryside here in northern Illinois—cornstalks growing green and strong, barns and big-boned farm homes rising in strategically lonely spots—is almost flat. Something about its geometry, its texture, has reminded me of a stretch of road in central Illinois where, as a boy, I thought I would die.

I was riding in the backseat of my grandparents' 1948 ivory-colored Chrysler. We were, I think, heading back to their farm home in Streator from a family reunion. Grandpa (born in 1876, and this was maybe 1955) was driving.

Usually, behind the wheel, he was careful beyond reason. But today he elected to pass a car on a two-lane rural road. I looked down the flatness that was ribboned out before me and saw another collection of rolling steel aiming at us from only a few hundred yards away.

I gripped the seat. As we got closer, I gripped my little sister next to me. We were next to the car we were passing but not making much progress against it. And the oncoming car kept getting bigger and bigger.

Just before what I knew would be a deadly crash, I tightened all my muscles and closed my eyes. As I did, I felt us jerk to the right, and heard the oncoming car flash by us inches away.

I remember the hot-dread rush of adrenaline and the sweat. And I heard Grandpa telling my sister and me not to make that kind of noise anymore. It bothered him, he said, and he needed to pay attention to the road. Apparently he hadn't imagined anyone was in danger.

Out on some of the most fertile and beautiful farmland in the world, I am reliving a near-death experience because of the curse-cure nature of memory.

Some people wipe out all their bad memories, creating a falsely optimistic picture of the past. Some wipe out most of the good memories, perversely clinging to a darkly unrealistic history. Most of us wrestle with a skewed mix of both, and our balance in life depends on not letting curse overwhelm cure.

Feeling Somehow Omnipresent
July 10, 1994

ATLANTA—A sense of place is easy to lose in our culture.

Not only does one Motel 6 look like another Motel 6, but the speed with which we pinball around causes us to lose our bearings. It happened to me just a few minutes ago.

I was sitting on an airplane here in Atlanta, waiting for the bump that says we are backing out of the gate for takeoff. As I waited, I was reading a collection of work by newspaper columnists all over the country.

The piece I happened to be in the middle of was by the *Atlanta Constitution's* great Celestine Sibley, who has written for the paper for more than fifty years. She was talking about all the construction going on in downtown Atlanta and moaning that "landmarks I knew have tottered and fallen and been crushed and hauled away."

About midway through the piece, I paused and looked out the window of the plane. Suddenly it occurred to me that I was reading about Atlanta while actually being in Atlanta. I was jarred. While reading, I had been, well, nowhere. I had been suspended, untethered to any geography.

It's easier and easier to do. Watching TV and reading can transport our brains hither and yon while we sit in a chair. We're all familiar with the sensation of, say, jumping out of the chair to cheer a touchdown, only to be reminded that we aren't in a football stadium but under our own roof.

In Kurt Vonnegut's wonderful book *Slaughterhouse Five*, the main character Billy Pilgrim becomes "unstuck in time." The problem modern people increasingly face is becoming unstuck in place. And the fast growth of technology adds to our sense that because it doesn't much matter where we are, we could be anywhere. And maybe we are.

I first wrote some of these words in a notebook on an airplane in Atlanta. I then shaped and completed them on a computer in my Kansas City office. But I could have done that work as easily on a computer at home or on a laptop computer in Florida or Kansas or, well, anywhere. Similarly, a year or so ago I traveled in one day from Kansas City to Atlanta to New Orleans to Dallas and back to Kansas City. With that sort of movement, it's easy to become unstuck in place.

The information highway, unlike concrete roads, doesn't lead from one place to another so much as it leads everywhere at once. It's possible, through the Internet, to be connected to people in Chicago, St. Paul, Vancouver, New York, and New Delhi all at once. Place becomes less and less important.

Years ago—it must have been in the mid-1970s—I read an engaging John McPhee piece in the *New Yorker* about Bill Bradley, now a U.S. senator from New Jersey, then a great basketball player for the New York Knicks.

McPhee's point, as I recall it nearly twenty years later, was that what made Bradley such a marvelous player was his uncannily accurate sense on the court of exactly where he was. He would not, thus, turn to fire a fourteen-foot jump shot and realize halfway up that he was sixteen feet away.

Some internal gyroscope let Bradley know at all times precisely where he was in relationship to the basket—which was, after all, ground zero.

It's the ability to locate ourselves not just geographically but also intellectually, spiritually, and emotionally that I sometimes think we are losing. Part of it is that the Atlanta airport looks like the Dallas airport, which looks like the St. Louis airport. And that we move around so much. And part of it is that our phones and faxes and modems make place seem less and less relevant.

But whatever the cause, I'm not sure anyone has given much thought to the consequences of a whole people becoming unstuck not in time but in place. If we become geographically rootless, do we also drift into intellectual, spiritual, and emotional rootlessness?

And then where are we?

Ringling a Reminder of Fanciful Need
June 24, 1994

SARASOTA, FLORIDA—It is easy here in this pretty Gulf Coast city to remember the wonderful words of the late artist Sister Corita Kent: "Damn everything but the circus."

This is, after all, where the late John Ringling used to bring his circus to spend winters. And it's where the Ringling Circus Museum operates today to remind us that no town is so good and happy that it can't be improved a little by the arrival of the circus.

I've always liked circuses, though I'm not exactly a wild aficionado of them. That is, I don't drive miles and miles at the drop of a bowler hat to see one. Still, one of the problems with the world is that it has a critical shortage of the sort of real circuses memorialized here at the Ringling Circus Museum.

The circus, after all, is the embodiment of the mind's playful fantasies, of which we need more.

Our mind, for instance, perhaps not on its best behavior, says to no one in particular, "I wonder if it's possible to shoot someone out of a cannon." And the circus, always a willing accomplice, replies, "Maybe. Let's try."

So here in the museum there is an old silver truck mounted with a long silver cannon barrel out of which men and women—and maybe, for all I know, children and ponies—used to be launched into the electrically expectant air of circus tents.

This particular cannon is spring-loaded. More modern versions use compressed air. I feel bad telling you that, however. It's a like giving away a magician's trick or drawing back the wizard's curtain to find a wimpy little guy pulling levers.

Still, it's the business of circuses to turn our harmless fantasies into realities and to let us laugh at and thrill to the results. That sometimes requires the simple physics of coiled springs or exploded air. Or the chemistry of greasepaint, such as the tubes displayed here that used to transform Emmett Kelly's face from whatever it looked like when he woke up in the morning to the wonderfully sad clown face we all loved because we know sad faces tell more fascinating stories than happy faces.

The circus is not just for the eyes. It's also for the ears. So in the museum one of the charming old circus wagons—colorful carriages of dreams and tigers—pumps out airy, bouncy calliope music, endless bars of "The Sidewalks of New York."

This small museum does not, however, do enough to recreate the sights, sounds, smells, and feels of the circus. The costumes, wagons, chariots, and trinkets are displayed without much imagination.

Which is odd for a museum that should understand its primary goal to be the celebration of the imaginative circuses created by John Ringling, whose nearby old mansion, for heaven's sake, named Ca'd'Zan (Venetian dialect for "House of John"), has dancing couples painted on the ballroom ceiling and organ pipes hidden behind huge and gaudy tapestries on the second floor.

Not that there was nothing "serious" about the man. Heck, he became fabulously well-to-do and bought a hundredyskillion seriously wonderful paintings (he was big on Peter Paul Rubens), now displayed here in a lovely gallery.

But paintings are, at least in part, entertainment for the intellect. The circus is entertainment for the heart, the imagination, the funny bone. It is an exploration of the limits of realized whimsy.

And the circus museum here, whatever its faults, is a way of reminding us that people are easier to live with if, now and then, they honor their childlike fantasies by saying with Sister Corita, "Damn everything but the circus."

Art Speaks to the Silence of Our Souls
October 19, 1997

If you like, you may think of this as a hypothetical question to which there never will be a universally satisfying answer, but I intend to wrestle with it nonetheless: Can people with mental illnesses or developmental disorders create real art?

In some ways the 1996 movie "Shine," about the mentally ill pianist David Helfgott, raised this question. But the answer the movie provided wasn't very enlightening, at least to me. Helfgott became a draw on the concert tour and was widely admired for his charisma and ability to thrill audiences.

And yet music critics applying the rigid standards of their trade found Helfgott's piano playing woefully lacking. To their trained ears, his work—never mind what he had to overcome to produce it—was simply awful.

Yet it was clear that Helfgott drew from his audiences an almost visceral response. And it has always seemed to me that art is art only if it somehow speaks (often in silence) to the silence that lies at the epicenter of our souls, the silence that snuffs out words as inadequate intruders on truth.

So I was disposed to imagine that Helfgott's work, no matter what the critics said, met a crucial criterion (mine, anyway) for being called art.

This whole matter resurfaced for me recently when I volunteered at an art show sponsored by an agency that works with developmentally disabled people. Pottery and paintings, mostly, were for sale. The pottery tended to have a rough finish. There were, for instance, glazed plates with dark reds, greens, and speckled blues on moon-textured surfaces. Some of it was quite striking.

Finger painting—bold, flashy strokes—had been framed, and some of it seemed so energetic that it threatened to burst its artificial borders.

I looked at all this, and then looked again. And again. And I kept asking myself whether what I was seeing—whether what was making that silent place inside me resonate—was really art.

I don't know why I worry myself with questions like that. I am, I confess, an artistic illiterate. I've never taken an art class, nor even a course in art history. I cannot draw anything more complicated than stick figures and have no training in art theory that would allow me to discern whether what other people have drawn meets any accepted artistic standard.

And I don't want to minimize those standards. There must be standards, rules, criteria. After more than thirty years in the newspaper business, I certainly can tell a quality piece of journalistic writing from the kind of flabby schlock that too often fills the columns of the nation's newspapers. And part of the way I judge that is by the rules of grammar and syntax, style and spelling, punctuation and voice.

So I am not one who advocates playing anarchistically, without rules.

And yet I do know that some pieces of mediocre writing can and do touch the hearts of readers. That may, of course, say less about the quality of the writing than it does about the discernment of the readers. How, after all, do you explain the popularity of "poets" like Rod McKuen or Helen Steiner Rice if not by public preference for sentimentality over insight?

And yet for people who are stirred by McKuen or Rice or Robert James Waller's tedious prose, isn't the writing in some core sense art?

In the same way, if I am moved or instructed or shaken by a work produced by someone with mental or developmental disorders, can I not call it art? My own simple rule, I've decided, is to call it art if I would respond to it in that way even if I didn't know a thing about the artist.

Probably art professors in colleges around the country would find my rule completely indefensible. Well, let them. But if that's their reaction, I find it artless.

Humor Helps Us Survive Journeys through Pain
July 19, 1998

ABIQUIU, NEW MEXICO—She doubted that she would live and was sure she'd never felt anything like the emotional pain that had extinguished her senses and curled her into a fetal ball of raw hurt.

Though Jill is not her real name, that's what I'll call this remarkably direct, deeply wounded, but vibrant woman who is—thank God and humor—on her way to wholeness again.

Jill's husband, whom she had loved faithfully for more than thirty years, had found someone else and was—with no notice, with hardly a thank-you—leaving. By the time she found out, he'd already retained a divorce lawyer. She was stunned.

He wouldn't consent to counseling, but some primal instinct told her she needed to. She made an appointment and asked her best friend to drive her there, so unsure of herself was she that she even doubted her ability to maneuver a car to an office building. I'll call Jill's friend Ramona.

On their way, they drove by a prison. Ramona, somehow knowing how to touch Jill's pain, admonished her not to do anything violent to her husband that would land her in the clink. Ramona knew Jill was a voracious reader. Indeed, Jill belongs to three book clubs, and one time—she swears this is true—she spent so many hours in one position (lying on the floor, hand supporting her chin) reading a book that she required surgery to fix two disks. The surgeon, amazed, said he planned to write up the case for a medical journal.

As they passed the prison, Ramona explained why Jill should restrain her instinct to kill the jerk.

"For one thing," she said, "you've already read every book in that prison. And if I have to come visit you I'm not going to bring you any new books, and you will be miserable."

So there it was. In the midst of this crisis, Jill smiled at Ramona. Then she laughed a little. Ramona's humor had broken through Jill's grief, given her at least the hope of hope, reconnected her to that place where her senses could work again, where she could feel something besides pain.

She isn't whole yet. She still cries, is still angry, still—some days—wants to drive a stake through the heartless heart of the man who threw her away like yesterday's omelet. But it's getting better. And humor is helping.

I suppose I've never doubted that laughter can heal, but I'm certain I've never had so much proof of it as I saw recently when I taught a week-long seminar called "From Pain to Hope through Writing" here at Ghost Ranch, a national Presbyterian conference center.

I hadn't known what to expect from the dozen or so people who came to confront their pain and, in a Christian context, search for hope through writing about it. I knew that writing about pain had helped me pass through my own shadowed valleys and emerge whole on the other side. But I wasn't sure whether others would or could share my experience.

As the week unfolded, it became increasingly clear that if any one thing could point the way out of bleakness—or at least alert the one in pain that the hurt wouldn't last forever—it was humor.

Another woman here—I'll call her Jean—is an accomplished writer and lay preacher. But she had never tried to write about one of the oldest, most intense aches of her life, an abusive mother who, with a slashing belt, would make blood run down Jean's little girl legs.

So Jean screwed up her courage and wrote an account that she shared privately with another class member, who had the wisdom to recognize that the writing had healed almost nothing, had simply recounted the pain. It contained no hope. And she saw why: It contained no humor.

Don't rewrite it, she told Jean. Start over.

So Jean began again. And this time there was wit. This time there was a little girl leaping with astonishing agility over couches and under beds to escape her furious mother, outrunning the rage until her mother wore out. This time there was more than a victim in the story, there was a tiny heroine who knew in her heart's deepest hiding place that she would survive and, one day, become whole.

Verse four of chapter three of Ecclesiastes in the Hebrew Scriptures tells us there is both a time to weep and a time to laugh.

What it does not say is that often they are the same time; often (maybe always) the path of laughter is the only way through rage. I know that's true because I have witnessed it. And it filled my eyes with tears.

The AIDS *Phenomenon*

AIDS: A Truth behind the Stories
June 16, 1991

Endlessly fascinated by anniversaries, the media earlier this month were full of stories about the fact that Americans have been aware of and struggling with AIDS now for ten years.

This milestone was calculated from June 5, 1981, when the Centers for Disease Control in Atlanta published a nine-paragraph item in its epidemic bulletin, saying five young homosexual men had contracted a rare form of pneumonia. Two of them, by then, already were dead.

The term *Acquired Immune Deficiency Syndrome* was not coined until later, but by mid-1981 it was clear that something vicious and mysterious was doing its destructive work.

I don't want to repeat all the facts and figures of a decade of AIDS. But, for the record, official figures (you should be hesitant about accepting them as literal truth and, instead, consider them reasonable but conservative estimates) show AIDS has afflicted nearly 175,000 Americans, of whom some 110,500 are dead. In addition, 1 million or more people are infected with what is termed the AIDS virus—called HIV, for Human Immunodeficiency Virus. But this is a moving target. The numbers grow daily.

Worldwide it's estimated that 1.5 million people have AIDS, while up to 10 million others are infected with the virus but haven't yet developed the full-blown disease, though they almost surely will.

AIDS is transmitted primarily through sexual contact or through the shared use of contaminated intravenous needles. The people who have contracted this killer have predominantly been gay men or IV drug abusers. Which has meant it has afflicted mostly people outside society's mainstream.

In fact, one early theory (announced almost as divine revelation) among some of the more fundamentalist Christians was that AIDS

199

is God's punishment for the sin of homosexuality. It was a stunning conclusion, demeaning the very God these people worship, and it hasn't died out yet. I heard a man put it in exactly those stark terms only last month.

If, on the other hand (and to follow the logic of the God's-punishment crowd), AIDS were a white-collar-crime-transmitted disease, the infected would be legion. Or if AIDS were, for some odd reason, contracted primarily by people who commit the sins of pride or slothfulness or greed, say, the American population would lie in ruins today.

As it turns out, the high-risk behaviors leading to AIDS run more toward the kind of conduct mainstream America finds easy to hate.

My point in raising that old issue—and the larger truth about the outcast nature of most people with AIDS—is simply to say that even now, ten years into our experience, many Americans have little or no personal experience with people who have AIDS.

And the media—with a few exceptions—have not helped much. They have tended to focus on AIDS statistics and on research aimed at finding a cure. Though there has been some effort to humanize the AIDS story, persons with AIDS remain, for the most part, one-dimensional social pariahs to many Americans.

This has had the effect of concealing a larger truth: Many of the people with AIDS are creative, interesting, warm, generous, and caring. If their sins have been different from the sins the rest of us commit, they are, for that, no less human.

Not counting my professional interest in the developing story of AIDS over the years, my own life was first touched by the disease when a friend died of it early in 1989.

After that, my family and I, with others, began to study and discuss AIDS in the context of what the church in general—often slow in responding to such crises—(and our church in particular) should do about AIDS.

Out of that study and discussion has grown an AIDS ministry group at our church. It has sought to educate its members about the disease and to try in various ways to assist individuals and families touched by AIDS, as well as to help with the work of some local secular AIDS service agencies.

To me, the most interesting work in all this has been our connection with a recently opened AIDS wing at a nursing home. We simply visit patients there, providing some outside human contact (and, it turns out, occasional support for the dedicated but sometimes stressed nursing staff, too).

We go not to convert anyone to our particular faith (we are Christian, most of us Presbyterian), nor to discuss theology, nor to tell patients everything is going to be all right. (It almost certainly isn't going to be all right.)

Rather, we go to be of some companionship, to try to meet whatever limited needs we can. We talk with patients. We bring them puzzles and videotapes. We listen to them. We're simply there when we can be. That's all.

And in the course of that we discover anew the profound truth that we all share a common humanity. No matter who we are, we are puzzling through the mysteries of life together, and we must respect each other's dignity or we will cause both ourselves and others immeasurable harm.

Our work has introduced us to a wide variety of patients, not all of them young gay men. There also has been a young mother, a grandfather, a grandmother, and a middle-aged mother. So in an important sense, those of us who volunteer in this AIDS unit—and countless other volunteers in other AIDS-related programs and agencies—are simply meeting ourselves, which is to say brothers and sisters in need.

Part of our job, of course, is education. And we do what we can to teach others about the disease and behaviors that put one at risk of contracting it. But when we are face to face with AIDS patients, the question of how they acquired the disease is moot. We are there because they have needs we can help meet. And that is reason enough.

AIDS, though slowed recently in its rate of increase, will continue to be a terrifying problem for years to come—even if there's a quick medical breakthrough, such as the recently announced vaccine turning out to be a surefire cure (unlikely). It will demand public and private resources and will test us severely.

We will fail that test if we convince ourselves that AIDS patients are marginal people who deserve what they have. If that were to be the recommended attitude, we would have no compassion toward people whose smoking has given them lung cancer or whose gluttonous diets have produced heart disease.

Clearly we should speak a word of warning about smoking and diet, but that must not be done as an I-told-you-so message to people who are dying. When people are seeking to live out their last days with some sense of order, our call is simply to stand with them.

AIDS has been a brutal teacher, but we must learn again the lesson it offers: When others are in pain, all of us hurt, and we must do what we can to align ourselves with the forces of healing, reconciliation, and personal dignity.

To do less would be unworthy of us all.

Many Are in Magic's Shoes
November 9, 1991

The night Magic Johnson announced he had the AIDS virus I was talking with a young man who has the fully developed AIDS disease. He was grateful for the forthcoming way Johnson had decided to talk about the disease.

"Bless him," the man said.

I agree but am, nonetheless, discomforted that once again we need a celebrity to make AIDS dinner-table conversation. Why does it take Magic's courage to get us to think about AIDS? Why hasn't it been enough that people I've known have died of it—people exactly as precious in God's sight as Magic?

People like Ted. Or Clay. Or Ron. Or May. Or Hal. Or Rhoda. Or Steve. Or Jimmy. Or Lisa. Or Michael. Or Joseph. Or David. Or Louis. Or Larry. Or John. Or Bruce. Or Gary. Or Dean. Look again at each of those names. A few years ago—in some cases a few weeks ago—they were all alive. Today they're gone.

I could name more but that's enough, I hope, to help you understand the suffering behind on the numbing statistics that reveal more than 120,000 deaths from AIDS in the United States since 1981. Another million-plus are in Magic's shoes—they have the virus but not yet full-blown AIDS. Worldwide the estimates run as high as 10 million carriers of the virus.

The question, then, is why it takes a Rock Hudson or a Ryan White or a Kimberly Bergalis or a Magic Johnson to make Americans care about HIV or Acquired Immune Deficiency Syndrome. We seem unable to see the value of each individual if the person who acquires the virus is without fame and fortune. Shame on us for that.

But surely that isn't the only way we have failed in the AIDS crisis.

As author Randy Shilts makes painfully obvious in his book *And the Band Played On*, the government and the health research industry it funds were almost criminally slow to respond when the AIDS virus first appeared in the United States more than ten years ago.

AIDS, when finally identified, was viewed then—and often still—as simply an odd gay disease. Some arrogant fools even called it God's judgment on homosexuals. What, then, is it today? God's judgment on basketball players?

The word AIDS almost never passed Ronald Reagan's uptight lips when he was president—a monumental failure of courage, leadership, and decency.

Perhaps if our leaders had possessed even half the wisdom and vision of former Surgeon General C. Everett Koop—a voice reason and sanity on AIDS in the reprehensible Reagan wilderness—Americans today would be better educated and fewer would be dying.

Ultimately, of course, it's up to each individual to know what sort of behavior puts him or her at risk of contracting this disease. And, thus, it's up to each individual to avoid such behavior. So any clear-eyed analysis must conclude that a bright, gifted man like Magic Johnson should have known how to avoid being exposed to the AIDS virus.

But that's exactly my point. Magic is no different from any of the other people who've tested HIV-positive. He didn't think it would ever happen to him. Apparently he was like so many sexually active teenagers (and others) today who think they're utterly bulletproof. But there he was on TV, telling the world, "It can happen to anybody. Even me."

If six-foot, nine-inch, handsome, rich, MVP, married, famous, talented Earvin Johnson is not bulletproof, nobody is. You aren't. I'm not. Our kids aren't. Our parents aren't.

It angers me that it takes someone like Magic to get people to see AIDS for what it is—a vicious, heartbreaking disease that will kill anyone without regard to gender, sexual orientation, age, race, religion, or nationality.

But, thank God, Johnson was unwilling to pretend he doesn't have the virus. He was willing to share his vulnerability with us. Maybe it will help us see our own vulnerability more clearly and to care for and about those who, because of the AIDS virus, are, like Magic, face to face with their own mortality.

Final Remembrance Is out of Our Hands
May 10, 1992

Ted Warmbold, a friend who died of AIDS in 1989, has two panels in the growing national Names Project AIDS Memorial Quilt.

When part of that quilt was in Kansas City recently I saw them for the first time. One, using masthead type, lists all the newspapers and magazines for which Ted had worked. (At his death he was editor of the *San Antonio Light*.) Another uses colorful artwork to reflect Ted's interest in collecting Central American folk art.

Both reflections are true—and were created with skill and love. But this is what struck me: How any of us will be remembered, if at all, is almost utterly in the hands of others.

We can leave precise funeral arrangement requests. We can leave long diaries. We can leave bulging photo albums. But finally it is up to others if the world is to remember anything about us.

And there are no guarantees. The world, after all, is a busy place. There isn't much time for remembering. Imagine all the people alive 150 years ago. What do we know of their individual lives? How many of their names do we even know? We can walk through cemeteries and look at headstones. But what do they tell us?

As I write this, I am preparing to travel to my hometown to help my mother pick out a headstone for the grave of my father, who died in January. What can be said about this man's eighty-two years of active life on a small slab of granite? Almost nothing.

I am, for that reason, increasingly grateful that fifteen or so years ago, Dad and I did an oral history of his life and work. The original rough transcript, which I am cleaning up this year, runs 222 pages and contains important details for Dad's survivors.

But as my wife was proofreading the new version recently she noted, correctly, that it fails to capture the man's cornball sense of humor. So even such a lengthy (and rare) project as this is no guarantee that our essence, our soul, our core, will be remembered accurately.

Talk of headstones and writing brings Harry Truman to my mind. His grave marker at the Truman Library and Museum in Independence lists the elective offices he held. But that, of course, tells us practically nothing of who he was.

It is true that Truman has been the subject of much writing. I am, at the moment, reading a review copy of David McCullough's huge (nearly a thousand pages) new biography of Truman—called, simply, *Truman*. And I am struck by how even so singularly important a life as Truman's can be squeezed into something you can hold in your hand.

Can any biography tell the full story of anyone? No. The general semanticists have it right: No one can ever say all about anything. Much less anyone.

The most famous person who ever lived—Jesus of Nazareth— was the subject of no biographies (that have survived, anyway) written by contemporaries, and Jesus left no writing of his own.

The four Gospel accounts of his life in the Bible not only weren't meant to be primarily biographical (and aren't), they disagree with each other in some ways. They aren't complete accounts, either. The last verse in the Gospel of John, in fact, says that if everything Jesus did in his short life "were written down, I suppose that even the whole world would not have room for the books that would be written."

What are the implications of knowing that we will have almost nothing to say about how we are remembered?

There are several, no doubt, but perhaps the primary one is that we must not be consumed with what the future will recall of us. Rather, our task is to make a positive difference now in the lives of others. Let the unborn bury the dead.

Though the beautifully crafted Ted Warmbold quilt panels help us remember an important life, they can never be a substitute for that life itself or for my memory of how he used that life to encourage other journalists to speak clearly, accurately, and forcefully— especially on behalf of the voiceless.

The irony here is that if we spend our lives myopically focused on how we'll be remembered, we may not do much worth remembering at all.

AIDS, Like War, Slices Down Young Lives
June 26, 1994

The evening of that steamy Sunday a few weeks ago stayed warm and humid. Rain couldn't decide whether to fall.

I went to a city park with a couple of hundred other people for a vigil to remember the bright lives AIDS has extinguished, lives that were more than numbing statistics. To us they were faces and personalities. They had names—Harry and Dean, Don and Kip, Michael and Woody, Lisa and Wayne, on and on.

A pastor was reading a familiar passage from Isaiah 61: "The Spirit of the Lord God is upon me, because the Lord has anointed me to bring good tidings to the afflicted; he has sent me to bind up the brokenhearted . . ."

As the prophet's ancient—though somehow fresh—words floated across the green park, a jarring sound from across the street interrupted. It came from a restaurant. It was music. Was, in fact, "Happy Birthday."

The irony and pain were both clear and immediate. All the lives we were remembering—David's and Hal's, May's and Bill's, Tom's and Steve's, Larry's and Louis's—had been cut off from the possibility of more birthdays. These young people had been erased in midstride.

Which is part of what makes the AIDS epidemic so frustrating and painful. It's the incongruity, the cruel way it breaks the traditional patterns and natural rhythms of life.

Acquired Immune Deficiency Syndrome, whatever else its characteristics, is, in its effect on life's cadences and tempos, life's boundaries and blueprints, not unlike war, which slices down young lives before they can progress to the three score and ten years described as normal by the same Bible read that evening.

The world has just completed a moving commemoration of the fiftieth anniversary of D-Day. Pictures of cemeteries—carefully tended rows of crosses and stars—are fresh in our memories. Those stones mark the burial places of thousands of young men killed before their natural time. In their absence we are left to imagine how life for all of us would be different had they lived long lives.

The thousands of people who have succumbed to AIDS, on the other hand, are not buried together in neat rows on a single plot of land somewhere. So, unless we see a display of the national Names Project quilt, the gathering enormity of the AIDS disaster—the stark and stunning way in which life's ordinary rhythms have been interrupted—is not as immediately apparent as it is in a place like the American cemetery at Colleville-sur-Mer.

Nonetheless, the families, friends, and caregivers of those whom AIDS has cut off have in their minds a space where they carve out the names of their dead—Frank and Ron, Billy and Joe, Clay, Larez,

Bruce, John, Jimmy, Ted, Christine, Jim, Robert, Herman, and on and on.

In many ways this growing internal space is as compelling and breathtaking, as well-tended and sanctified as a military cemetery. And it welcomes daily visits.

Recently I have begun to write a series of poems about people I've known who have died of AIDS. It is slow, painful, relentlessly inadequate work, and I'm far from satisfied with it.

But it has hardened in me the realization that some kind of evil hand grenade, some viral equivalent of a claymore mine, has exploded in the midst of a generation, and—not unlike the way war changes things—it has forever scrambled the pattern of life.

Because of that evil confusion, everything will be different from this time on. Everything. Even hearing "Happy Birthday."

Some Hopeful Signs among the AIDS Stricken
November 29, 1996

As people around the globe commemorate (celebrate is nowhere close to the right word) the ninth annual World AIDS Day on Sunday, those of us who have been active in the struggle against this evil disease find ourselves on the edge of awkward hope.

We want, most of all, to believe that the recent good experience some of our friends with AIDS have had taking new drugs called protease inhibitors really will mean an end to the death sentence Acquired Immune Deficiency Syndrome has pronounced.

We hope medical and political authorities are right when they say we are rapidly getting to the point at which AIDS can be considered a chronic ailment that can be lived with and managed over the long term.

But for a decade and a half we have seen so much death, so many lives—mostly young men—snuffed out, that we are cautious. Some say false hope is better than no hope, but I disagree. Although some people I've known with AIDS have reached for any hope with a desperation bordering on panic, most persons with AIDS want the truth, however harsh it is.

Still, I see people living longer and longer with the Human Immunodeficiency Virus that causes AIDS. They are active, fully engaged people who contribute enormously to the world around them. One such friend, in fact, will play the organ at my wedding this evening. So there is hope—hope that holds its breath, but hope none-theless.

And yet the very fact that AIDS patients are living longer also contributes to a growing awareness that we are not running a sprint here but a marathon. Even if no one in the whole world were in-fected with HIV after today, it still would take decades to handle the disastrous medical, social, economic, and political effects of the pandemic.

After all, some 20 million people on the globe now live with HIV or AIDS. The cost of treating them will continue to be enormous.

And the question some of us worry about is where the next generation of volunteers will come from. The first generation came together in a sense of crisis and anger. The aura of crisis—though plainly not gone—seems diminished. And it takes more effort and understanding to get and remain creatively angry about a chronic illness that people can live with for decades than about a rapacious killer that wipes out beautiful young lives in a few months.

My experience, however, does not leave me in despair. Some weeks ago, at Hope Care Center, a newly opened Kansas City AIDS nursing facility at which I volunteer, there was a meeting for po-tential volunteers. The room was so crowded there weren't enough seats.

To be sure, some old, familiar faces were there. But also included in the gathering was a teacher nearing retirement who'd never done this work but expected soon to have time to devote. And there were two high school girls who spoke of believing that the God they worship has called them to be with others in pain.

The group at Hope Care Center may not be representative of vol-unteer numbers around the world. I suspect, in fact, that the reality is grimmer elsewhere.

But one thing is certain on World AIDS Day 1996—the long-term need for volunteers to help alleviate the loneliness and devastation of AIDS may be greater than ever.

AIDS, after all, is an extraordinarily expensive disease that drains financial and personal resources out of the health care industry and requires constant focus and energy from patients trying to cope with its effects. Without volunteers to help ease the burden, the already deeply stressed system would simply be overwhelmed.

As I say, what is becoming clearer to volunteers is that, despite (or maybe, ironically, because of) recent good medical news, there is no end of need in sight. And if you can't run this marathon yourself, you can at least support and cheer on those who can.

St. Mary College Shoots the Messenger
April 30, 2000

I wasn't angry so much as profoundly saddened to be told recently that the board of trustees of St. Mary College in Leavenworth was withdrawing an invitation for me to deliver the commencement address there May 13.

The president of the small Catholic college, the Reverend Richard J. Mucowski, and a board member, Robert Arter, came to my office to tell me the board made this decision because a few months ago the newspaper I work for had printed a series of articles on AIDS in the priesthood that many board members found offensive to the Catholic Church.

Father Mucowski, who did nearly all the talking, clearly was uncomfortable delivering this retributive message. He chose his words carefully—even pastorally—but I concluded he disagreed with the board. As well he should. As well the St. Mary students should. As well the faculty and alumni should. And not because of me. No, they should disagree because the decision was narrow-minded, misguided, punitive, and unworthy of the values of a liberal arts college.

Indeed, the decision reveals nothing about my own failures as a journalist or a person (they are legion). But it reveals much about the human inclination to control truth, avoid difficult subjects, and blame the messenger. I am prone to all those faults, though I've learned that avoiding conflict nearly always results in worse discord later.

The fact is, I had not planned to speak about AIDS or the *Kansas City Star's* AIDS series. Rather, I was going to do something surprising for a Protestant—speak about Mary, the name the graduates will carry with them (whatever their religion) for the rest of their lives. I was going to try to draw out of the biblical witness what we could learn about the mother of Jesus that might help us as we try to "live value-centered lives of learning, service, and character," as the school's own mission statement says.

The 2000 class at St. Mary will never hear that speech (though it was written before the cancellation came) because the school's trustees, out of fear, anger, and vindictiveness, acted dishonorably. The lesson for the graduates—indeed, for all of us—is that almost anything we do from spite will be destructive and have unintended negative consequences.

I had nothing to do with the *Star*'s AIDS series, but I thought it was an important work that spoke much truth. Indeed, after it ran, I drew on my own decade-long participation in an AIDS ministry and wrote the newspaper's unsigned editorial that tried to point out how Acquired Immune Deficiency Syndrome has wounded not just the Catholic Church but many faith communities. Avoiding the issues AIDS inevitably raises, I wrote, "may be a comforting short-term strategy, but in the end that approach only produces the kinds of profound problems the Catholic Church now faces."

What I find so exasperating is that in seeking to punish the newspaper by withdrawing the speaking invitation to me (officially extended after the series had run), the St. Mary board has offered yet another example of a short-term strategy that produces more problems than it solves. Think of it as the board firing the organist because the priest delivered an objectionable sermon.

Part of the reason that makes me so sad is that I have tried hard in recent years to encourage better relations among the segments of Christianity's divided house. As a Presbyterian, I'm shaped by the faith's Reformed tradition that's at the root of my denomination. But I have used my column and spent my personal time in various ways to try to bring harmony out of this discord. Last summer I cotaught a weeklong seminar about doctrines that divide the church. My partner was a friend who is a Catholic priest and Trappist monk. We found considerable common ground that week; it gave me hope that reconciliation can be achieved from the ground up.

Both the media and religion have what I call prophetic voices. I don't mean prophetic in the sense of foretelling the future but, rather, of calling others to do what is right for the greater society. Any good editorial page, in fact, inevitably shares much of its agenda with religions that seek to lift people up and give them hope.

I'm certain, therefore, that my goals—and the goals of this newspaper—are in tune with the larger purposes of the St. Mary board. So

I don't question the board's motives. Rather, I question the myopic see-no-evil, hear-no-evil approach it adopted.

When the angel Gabriel told Mary that God wanted her to bear the Christ child, Mary had a choice. With courage and faith, she said yes. How sad that the board of a college bearing Mary's name today has not acted with similar openness and trust.

Wars and Rumors of Wars

Those 911 Prayers for Peace
January 15, 1991

The old saying that there are no atheists in foxholes reasserted itself with a vengeance as America prepared for war in the Persian Gulf.

The Associated Press, for instance, reported that people across the country over the weekend were seeking "divine help" to avert war. And Cardinal John J. O'Connor of New York spoke these rather remarkable words: "We must pray like we never prayed before and let us pray with our deepest sincerity."

Just what is going on here? It was people who started this mess, and now they want God to get them out of it. They are playing the prayer card, hoping the creator of the universe will rescue them like some heavenly Superman.

Before I offend everyone here, I want to say two things: I believe in prayer and I believe God is sovereign. By implication, then, I believe divine intervention is possible. But let's be clear about what is happening.

Although the name of God often is invoked as a justification for war, God did not invade Kuwait. People invaded Kuwait. God, in response, did not order hundreds of thousands of troops to Saudi Arabia. People sent them. God did not set the January 15 deadline. People did. God did not decide that our culture and economy should be dependent on oil. We decided that.

But now that the ripple effects of these—and countless other—decisions have brought us to the rim of war, we want God to rescue us. And so we pray like we never prayed before and, like frightened children, try to pray with our deepest sincerity, as Cardinal O'Connor suggested.

Although I, too, think it would be wonderful if God intervened and brought peace, I think these 911 prayers are arrogant if unac-

212

companied by an acknowledgment of who really is to blame and a request for forgiveness and mercy.

As often as not, such last-minute prayers reveal our failure to be in consistent relationship with God. They are like the cries of a juvenile delinquent to a parent when the child's foolish decisions have landed him in police custody once again. The parent loves the child, but perhaps there comes a time when the most loving thing to do is to allow the child to suffer the consequences of his behavior.

There is biblical evidence that God loves us in just that way, in effect allowing us to punish ourselves by misusing our freedom. In Jesus' parable of the prodigal son, for instance, the father (who represents God in the story) allows one of his sons to take his inheritance. As Luke tells the story in the Revised English Bible translation, the young man turned what he was given into cash and "left home for a distant country, where he squandered it in dissolute living."

The father's willingness to give his son his freedom turned out— because of the foolish way the son used that freedom—to be the vehicle for punishment and, thus, justice.

Similarly, we now confront the consequences of actions we took in freedom. What actions? We and others have chosen to sell arms to countries throughout the Middle East. Why do we feign shock that they would be used?

As undeniably evil as Saddam Hussein's capture of Kuwait was, there are no innocents in this conflict. Not one. And our cries to the Lord now to set things straight would sound more credible if we first acknowledged that we need God's forgiveness for our complicity in social, political, economic, and cultural systems that oppress and coerce people and inevitably lead to war.

To beg God's favor otherwise strikes me as disingenuous and arrogant. For our sakes, I hope it does not strike God that way.

Our Discordant Hearts Carry a Message
February 3, 1991

When the Reverend William Sloane Coffin was in our office the other day talking about the war, he used a revealing phrase: The crisis has made us people of "divided hearts."

Coffin—for decades a national voice of liberal political positions informed by theological understandings—may be starry-eyed about some things, but I think he's diagnosed our (or certainly my) current condition accurately.

As patriots we want to support our troops, win the war, and be done with Saddam Hussein. Those are understandable—maybe even noble—aims.

Yet we hate war. We feel pangs of pity and (can we even whisper it?) sympathy for the Iraqi people. And we suspect there was a way other than war.

I've decided, finally, that we need to pay attention to this ambiguity, this division in our hearts. And we need feel neither guilty nor wishy-washy about it. Instead, we should recognize that our discordant hearts are trying to tell us something important.

They are asking us to reexamine our ultimate loyalties and acknowledge that we, too, even if unintentionally, contribute to evil in the world. This very awareness of our own culpability—which is a quite healthy and necessary discernment—leads to divided hearts. Maybe we should worry about ourselves more if our enthusiasms run rampant. Tempered fervor indicates we are grasping the complexities involved.

Divided hearts reflect the almost infuriating predicament of the human condition. Events that pinball around us—often outside our control—affect us and cause us to do (or think) things we'd rather avoid or even that we regret. And, worse, we often know even before we do them that we will regret them and do them reluctantly.

That very predicament—and the frustration of it—comes close to what some people have understood as the inevitable result of Original Sin. Which is to say that we are affected by what's happened before us and cannot live untouched by that history and its spider-web effects.

If our hearts are divided, we may be close to the political stance recommended by Glenn Tinder: "humane and engaged but also hesitant and critical." Tinder, a political science professor at the University of Massachusetts and author of *The Political Meaning of Christianity*, says such a stance allows us to evaluate claims of political leaders with more objectivity and to decide whether our final allegiance is to country or to a higher authority. It allows us to acknowledge the gray in what some would have us think is all black and white.

In the hot fire of war, we must guard against a facile view of the world. That leads to the belief that Saddam Hussein is subhuman and that God is entirely on our side, just as, in a different time, it led to the frantic imprisonment of some of our own citizens who happened to be of Japanese extraction.

And we must remember that if average citizens are capable of slipping into this hyped-up rhetoric, our political leaders feel almost compelled to engage in it. Their job is to rally the nation behind war. So they paint simplistic pictures of a reality that's anything but simple.

What we finally must remember, I think, is that there's nothing unpatriotic about divided hearts. Being humane and engaged does not forbid us from being hesitant and critical—especially of ourselves.

And it's in the very wrestling with these dilemmas that we are most fully human.

Human Drama Missing in the Gulf War
February 17, 1991

The day friendly fire hit Confederate general Stonewall Jackson near Chancellorsville, Virginia, the allied commander in the Persian Gulf, General H. Norman Schwarzkopf, was on TV saying the Iraqis were "capable of the most heinous acts."

I know this sounds impossible, but I'm in the odd position of reading a Civil War history while trying to follow the Gulf War. So the day I read author Shelby Foote's description of the wounding of Jackson, I also heard Schwarzkopf's indictment of Iraq's troops.

It has been eerie and disorienting but also instructive, my two-war life. One is a low-tech (from this distance; in the 1860s it wasn't), unthinkably bloody affair, the other a high-tech, oddly veiled (despite TV) war.

Foote, the eloquent historian so prominent in last year's PBS Civil War series, writes with passion and insight, telling a monstrously large story in very human terms.

A small scene: Just before the Chancellorsville action—a battle in which outmanned rebels forced a Union retreat—Jackson (a Presbyterian deacon) and General Robert E. Lee (married to the great-granddaughter of George Washington's wife Martha) met at night in a grove of trees to make plans. Then they tried to sleep.

> They lay down where they were, in separate quarters of the grove, spreading their saddle blankets on the pine needles for a bed and using

their saddles for a pillow. Both were soon asleep, but Lee was wakened presently by an officer he had sent to look into conditions on the turnpike to the north. "Ah, Captain, you have returned, have you?" he said, and he sat up slowly. "Come here and tell me what you have learned on the right." It was the same young man from Jackson's staff who had wakened him two mornings ago to tell him [Union general Joe] Hooker was crossing; J. P. Smith was his name, a divinity student before the war.

It's that human scale of the story I find so striking: Legendary generals sleeping in woods, soldiers on opposite sides singing together or simply yelling insults at each other before battle, officers with little information to go on save what scouts spot through spyglasses or riders in a hot-air balloon see above treetop level.

And Foote makes clear how crucial the will, wit, skill, and courage of individual generals was to the outcome of battles.

In the Gulf War, the human scale has been lacking. Oh, we get occasional images of Iraqi civilians yelling about what the military antiseptically calls "collateral damage" from bombs. And now and then we get talking soldier heads describing how it felt to "kick some butt," as they say so incessantly and inelegantly.

But we're left to imagine the perspective, the revealing vignettes. Even the little stories that get through military censors stand unconnected to any broader vision of what's happening—a vision that, in fact, can come only with hindsight and the historian's selective eye for relevant detail. Maybe this detachment is the inevitable result of the air war and the eerily silent video replays of laser-guided bombs following crosshairs to targets.

In Foote's Civil War narrative, by contrast, we get the sounds: Stonewall Jackson moaning "My own men!" with his now-useless shot-up left arm dangling, and what an anesthetized Jackson described as "the most delightful music"—the singing of the bone saw a surgeon used to amputate that arm.

The night the Gulf War broke out, three CNN correspondents crouched in a Baghdad hotel room and let us hear the awful sound of technologically proficient death machines. It was a small taste of war's relentless terror. But since then, this war has mostly played with the mute button on.

Only years from now, when some future Shelby Foote regathers the frightful noises of this war, will we have an accurate sense of the human scale of what's going on.

I hope for long life. But having read Foote, I don't want to be around to read that horror.

War Pattern Indelibly Engraved on Life
March 3, 1991

Like bruises on an apple, the dark stains of war mark my life.

World War II still had most of a year to run when I was born. The Korean War raged when I was in grade school, and I still remember the *Weekly Reader* announcing its end. Or at least its cease-fire. The Vietnam War was the vicious, heartbreaking background against which I lived my college and young adult years. Now the brief and furious Gulf War is imprinted on my midlife.

This periodic pattern of war is not, of course, unique to me. But, like most people confronted by overwhelming events, I look for meaning first in personal terms. I have come to uneasy terms with the reality (almost the inevitability) of wars—perhaps because I've never had to fight in any of them.

The war pattern by now is so indelibly engraved on my life that when it renews itself it grieves—but does not astonish—me.

But what wounded my restive heart the other day was the realization that this same terrible pattern of war has settled on the lives of my daughters, too.

One was born at the height of the Vietnam War, one as that war shut down. Until now, war for them hasn't been much of a reality beyond their history classes or talks with their maternal grandfather, who fought in France in World War II.

Now that has changed. People they know were sent to the Persian Gulf. War has been daily on their radios and TVs and in their newspapers. It's personal for them now. One took yellow ribbons to her school and went to the airport to say goodbye to a boy bound for the war. One wrote a story for her college newspaper about members of a medical unit called up to active duty.

It's now clear there is no saving them from the war pattern that overlays my own life. We have stained yet another generation with humanity's failures. For what is war, after all, if not an admission of failure?

Oh, I understand that some wars are just and that there is a long and carefully thought-out tradition defining when wars properly may be so deemed. But calling a war just—even if it is—doesn't obviate the conclusion that we have failed to achieve our goals by other, better means.

I don't know why I was so struck by the recognition that periodic wars now are a pattern in my children's lives as well as mine. The same pattern has been a reality for almost all people for almost all time. It must be like the difference between an understanding that we all die and the reality of losing one's own child.

People sometimes speak of these moments of stark maturation as a loss of innocence. Probably it would be more accurate to call them a loss of the delusion of innocence. For nearly all our innocence is mere hallucination.

"The heart is deceitful above all things and beyond cure," the Old Testament prophet Jeremiah said. "Who can understand it?"

My head has known this biblical truth, but my own deceitful heart did not start to grasp the comprehensiveness of it until the Gulf War touched my children. And now I have begun to understand that their innocent generation, too, is ensnared by human evil.

Since the Age of Enlightenment much of humanity has chosen to see history as progress and people as perfectable on earth. Those are foolish conceits.

And however much we hope and pray and work for peace, we must acknowledge how pervasive and relentless war is. The test of our character and commitment, I suppose, is whether—in the face of that awful reality—the hope, prayer, and work continue just as relentlessly.

Only the Narrow Think Globalization Is New
January 2, 2000

AIX-EN-PROVENCE, FRANCE—The day Henry Eli died, June 2, 1945—"Mort Pour La France," as a sign on his grave says—I was not quite five months old.

"Mort Pour La France" is a lovely sentiment but it's a pathetic understatement, if I have things figured right.

The almost certain fact is that Henry Eli, whose remains lie here in St. Pierre Cemetery, also died for me. And for you. And for everyone else who lives in freedom today as a result of the Allied victory in World War II.

It is an astonishing thing to be standing at the end of the 1900s in the cool air of Provence, the sun warming the back of my neck, and to see the black-and-white photo of Henry Eli on a memorial plaque attached to his grave.

He represents to me the hundreds of thousands of French, British, American, and other soldiers who died so that someday, in liberty, I could visit France, stand in front of Henry Eli's grave, and say a quiet thank-you for a stunning gift from a man I never knew.

In the photo, Henry is wearing a military uniform. His hat cuts through the middle of his forehead and his eyes stare out at the world with an odd mixture of determination and uncertainty.

I can only imagine what he feared.

I know nothing of Henry Eli's life, save that he died for France nearly a year after D-Day. I also know nothing of his death, save that it, and so many others, allowed civilization to continue its uncertain struggle forward and not drop indefinitely into an unspeakably bleak abyss.

Under Henry's picture is a French flag, but the original tricolors are so worn they are nearly gone. That, I'm afraid, is also the condition of the historical memory of many of the people for whom Henry Eli died.

Indeed, here in this crowded cemetery in the south of France I am left to wonder who even among the dead knew Eli, who understood what he did for them.

Just up the path from Henry's grave lie the remains of Andre and Marcelle Atger. Andre was not quite sixty years old when he died in 1965, so he lived through both world wars. Marcelle, seven years Andre's junior, survived until 1997, which accounts for why Andre's photo on his grave shows a man with dark hair and a Jimmy Stewart smile, while Marcelle's picture reveals an old woman with basset-hound eyes, evidence of the kind of relentless sorrow widowhood sometimes brings.

Did either of the Atgers know Henry Eli? It would take me a year of research, probably, to learn the answer, if there is an answer. And then what would I really know?

And what about Serge Royer, who was barely sixteen when he died in 1971 and who also lies in repose not far from Eli: Did this young man have any clear idea why the France he called home was not under the cruel fist of victorious Nazis and their monstrous ideas about eugenics, drawn from social Darwinism run amok? Did young Serge ever come to St. Pierre Cemetery and see Henry Eli's picture? Did Serge play in the nearby park, where today young boys ride skateboards with a recklessness that makes it clear they have no sense of their own mortality? I do not know. I know only that we are all so oddly connected.

It often is said that just in our time the world economy has gone global. That the world is shrinking. That the Internet finally is stitching us together in a seamless network built on a technology that knows what Albert Einstein knew—so much in the physical world depends on the constancy of the speed of light.

For all their truth, these are statements of incredible arrogance and historical ignorance. The fact is the world has been shrinking for centuries. We were global when World War I doughboys perished in French fields. We were inseparably knit together when Allied troops shot their way ashore at Normandy as young Americans less than half the age I am now ate the speeding bullets of the enemy, and Henry Eli—wherever he was then—cheered the news that his native land was being liberated from darkness.

Henry Eli, the young French soldier with the determined, slightly baffled eyes, died for France, yes. But because we can do almost nothing in this life that does not touch others—often profoundly—Henry Eli also died for me. And here where he lies, I offer my presence today in gratitude for so costly a gift.

Sports and the Rest of Us

One More Time, Quisenberry Bears Our Burdens
June 7, 1998

When more than thirty thousand people, including me, gathered recently for no other reason than to cheer a famous man who is dying, I had trouble at first imagining what drew us to this spectacle.

Did we really care about Dan Quisenberry, once a fabulous relief pitcher for the Kansas City Royals, now a middle-aged man most of the people there had never met in person? Were we there just to thank him for all the games he saved more than a decade ago now that the team finally was inducting him into its Hall of Fame?

Were we there to encourage him as he battles the loose, wandering fire of cancer that has rooted its evil self in his remarkably creative brain? Were we simply curious to see a once-strapping athlete now stripped mostly bald by the treatments marshaled to bludgeon his run-amok cells?

Did we gather to thank him for reminding us in clever and funny ways that sport—even at the highest professional level—is not to be taken with full-bore seriousness?

No doubt we were there for all those reasons, and more, including Dan's being a civic and giving spirit. But many of us had another motive for coming.

We were there, I think, because we understood in some silent, primal part of our being that death terrifies and mystifies us, so we have deputized Dan Quisenberry to die for us. Which is to say, we want him to give us the nerve to face our own end.

Dan, after all, has borne other burdens for us. He saved crucial games to allow our baseball team to become world champion, giving Kansas City a reason for pride and community spirit. Did we ever feel better about ourselves than when the Royals won the 1985 World Series?

Dan has kneecapped the dragon of boredom for us, the dispir-

221

iting mood that destroys the balance wheel of eternal perspective. (Who else grew the best tomatoes in the bull pen? Who else, on hot Sunday afternoons at the ballpark, thought to get out the hose and spray down baking fans in the bleachers? Who else told gullible sportswriters after a game that his final pitch was an overhand curve?)

Through his own writing he has grappled with the terror of incomprehensible poetry for us, creating verse at once lovely and accessible. And he has been a charitable volunteer for us, as well as a man committed to marriage, family, and religious faith.

So it's no surprise that now we would ask him to die for us. I don't mean that we have ever said that to him. And probably Dan himself—who hopes not to die at all for a long time—does not see things in quite the way I've described.

But the more I think about why we were all standing there cheering through our tears, the more I'm convinced that we hope Dan can at least distract death for a time so it won't find us.

As I get older, I understand in increasingly profound ways that until we understand our death we cannot hope to understand our life.

The mainline Christian faith tradition that Dan Quisenberry and I share rejects the astonishingly popular old Greek idea of the immortality of the soul. Rather, our faith tells us that no part of us is in any way able to survive death. Resurrection, in which we believe with so much certainty and hope, has nothing to do with who we are but everything to do with who God is.

The miracle of resurrection is not that we have an eternal soul but that a loving and sovereign God can choose to give us the gift of eternal life despite our death. That everlasting life, in a critical sense, comes out of our death, and no words can fully exhaust the meaning of this mystery.

But however we think of death, we remain frightened children staring into a dark, terrifying cave. We say to each other, "You first."

That's what we are saying to Dan Quisenberry. You first, Dan. And if you can die with the dignity, humor, and grace you've always shown, maybe we can, too.

If Dan were writing this, he'd almost certainly now say something light and witty, like his wonderfully famous line, "I have seen the future, and it's much like the present, only longer."

Well, we all know that our individual futures may not be long at all. That's what cheering Dan causes us to remember. So our hope is that Dan will look into that uncertain black hole for us and offer something like this version: "I have seen the future, and it's much like the present, only better."

We are asking Dan Quisenberry, after years of saving big games for us, to save that hope for us. It is, of course, a hugely unfair, ridiculous request. But it's what we expect our few remaining heroes to do for us. And it's because Dan is doing it so well that we cheer and cry for him—as well as for ourselves.

Dreamin' in Real Time at Hoops Tourney
July 26, 1993

It's raining—the steady, soaking, summer-flood rain we in the Midwest have had up to our tailbones.

Instead of hiding from it, however, I've surrounded myself with it. It's early Sunday morning. I'm standing on a downtown street doing nothing more sane than dribbling and shooting a basketball, getting ready for Day 2 of the annual Easter Seals Hoops 3-on-3 Basketball Tournament, an in-your-face, streetwise competition that draws thousands of players.

Our team is, of course, in the over-forty division—known to other divisions as the Almost Dead Guys.

I want to tell you something about this experience that's strange. I skipped church to come down here this morning, fully aware I might be killing myself. Not because God will get me for missing church. No, God and I have a deal. We cut each other some slack. Rather, it has to do with my 48.5-year-old body.

The ball of my left foot has a painful blood blister from the first round of games played yesterday on hot, boil-your-soles pavement in this concrete canyon.

And I'm still recovering from a persistent thigh muscle pull or tear from last year's unsmashing softball season. I've never had an injury hang on so long—unless you count my looks.

And my shoulders—oh, my poor shoulders. They've been killing me for weeks. My health care providers haven't figured out whether it's bursitis, arthritis, or bovine radial keratotomy suture syndrome. They've given me pills. The pills haven't helped.

Plus, I'm wearing an old pair of glasses here in the rain so I won't destroy my expensive new bifocals by placing them in the way of a flying elbow. There's more wrong, but you get my drift.

"I'll either cure myself or die," I tell my wife as I leave for the games. She's headed for church. Her presence there comforts me.

So here I am. Creaky, hurting, half-blind, and soaked.

But the strange part is this: In abandoning myself to this wonderful game on this shiny wet street, I'm not feeling any of my troubles. Somehow I've cast off pain and age and worries.

The basketball arcs through the raindrops, seeks the bottom of the net, and—with astonishing consistency for someone of my modest abilities—finds it again and again. I am, for now, a little boy splashing through forbidden puddles—and lost in the joy of it.

What can be happening here? Is my lanky, goofy body giving itself one last bath of natural endorphins and dopamine before it turns itself in, overdue, in the drop-off box of God's library?

Well, maybe, but I don't think this is entirely chemical or metaphysical. I think this has to do with giving myself permission to dream in 3-D real time.

I've never been a great athlete. Some games—including basketball—I've been able to play with occasional flares of competence. And once in a great while there have been moments of incomprehensible brilliance—an inexplicable running catch to end a softball game in the early 1970s, a night of couldn't-miss jump shooting on a YMCA basketball team about that same time, and a hole-in-one with a borrowed 8-iron in 1991.

The dream of such moments of grace dies hard.

Out here on the gently sloping street this morning, water trickling down my glasses, it feels as if anything might be possible. I have come to one of those moments Kurt Vonnegut once described as "Everything was beautiful and nothing hurt."

The day plays out. We win, win again, and again, and yet again. My jump shot, though not completely reliable, falls from time to time. My teammates play with heart and even some actual skill, which I didn't know was allowed in this division.

The sun comes out. It gets warm, steamy, but not ridiculously so.

Somehow we make it to the finals, having lost only our first game yesterday. If we beat this unbeaten team twice, we're champs.

Well, look, not all dreams come true. We lose by four points. They were a little younger. Each time our six-foot, eight-inch center got the ball they tackled him. Besides, they weren't bad.

I pack up, head home. I need a shower. I'm suddenly aware that my shoulders are killing me.

But maybe if they heal themselves by next summer, I'll enter the slam-dunk competition—if officials agree to lower the rim by a foot or two.

One of Life's Rare, Perfectly Complete Acts
September 13, 1998

For most of this strange baseball season—a year of diluted pitching talent and a juiced ball—the race to break Roger Maris's thirty-seven-year-old single-season home run record has hypnotized fans and casual observers alike.

As the now successful, muscle-enhanced Mark McGwire plus Sammy Sosa, Ken Griffey Jr., and others have clobbered the poor ball, launching it on a few trips that still may not have ended, I've been trying to understand why the homer—the round-tripper, the four-bagger, the tater, the jack—has always engaged our hearts.

Finally I have figured it out. It's because the home run is one of life's rare, perfectly complete acts. In an oddly self-referential way, the home run fulfills itself. It is whole, exhaustive, unabridged. It is comprehensive and, thus, cannot be added to. It can only be celebrated.

It is, beyond that, an individual act cocooned within the context of a team game. And yet even when it accounts for the only run in a 17–1 drubbing, say, it is never meaningless. Its swift beauty and awesome irrevocability give it a sweetness, a ripeness, a finality—a prime-numberness, if you will—that refuses to be discounted.

There simply are not many events in life that can compare with the wholeness, the completed essence of a home run. It is baseball's equivalent of golf's hole-in-one, of football's hundred-yard kickoff return, of marriage's simultaneously achieved sexual orgasm.

What can people say after such consummate fulfillments except "Wow!"? And often even that should be withheld in favor of the respect shown by simple silence.

We spend much of our lives seeking experiences as full and autonomous as the home run but find ourselves settling much more often for the equivalent of base hits, ground-rule doubles, or birdies.

Yet all the while we know intuitively how lovely it would be to go deep, to pound one out of the park.

Perhaps one reason the home run so appeals to our sense of completeness is that we both start and finish at—where else?—home. And what is home sweet home if not where, in the end, we belong? What is home if not where the heart is? If not our castle? If not the place where, as Robert Frost said, when you go there, they have to take you in? If not the place it took a heap o' livin' to make? If not the place, be it ever so humble, there's no other place like?

And how, in baseball, do we get back to home once we've left after a home run swing? Why, we circle—ah, circle—the bases. And what's a circle—even on a diamond—if not a perfect shape? What is a circle if not, as Ralph Waldo Emerson called it, "the highest emblem in the cipher of the world"?

Even when we cannot understand the whole of which we may be a part, a circle is a sacramental sign of the very fullness we seek. It is why, in Christian theological insignia, the Trinity often is represented by three intersecting circles.

And the home run—which, in fact, the runner does not complete by following the hard right angles of the base paths but, rather, by softly rounding those angles into something like a circle—contains within itself enough meaning to stand alone, even if, in the context of a game, its adjacent team meaning is unclear.

It is true, of course, that the home run has become so common in the big leagues that even ninth-place hitters now tag a dozen or more per season. That murderous year when Babe Ruth hit sixty homers in 1927, his regular teammates contributed only ninety-one more, and Lou Gehrig had forty-seven of those. In the World Series that year, Ruth had the only two homers hit by either team.

But however routine the home run has become, nothing can alter the finished nature of it. And as people who often are fragmented, distracted, and unfulfilled, it is precisely that completeness for which we yearn. And for which, in this remarkably charming season, we cheer and cheer.

Honoring Brett for the Magic Moments
September 29, 1993

I did something the other night I've never done.

I paid good money (well, nine bucks) for no other purpose than to honor a man who is younger than I am, unimaginably richer and more famous than I will ever be, and who wouldn't know me from Adam if we were to meet on an otherwise empty sidewalk.

But even in retrospect I'm not embarrassed by it. George Brett is worth it.

I moved to Kansas City three years before George did, so I've been able to watch his entire Hall of Fame career with the Kansas City Royals, for whom he'll now serve as a vice president, having announced his retirement as a player Saturday.

In George's twenty-one years with the team, I watched him play in person at least 250 times. When his appearances on my TV are counted, I can't even calculate how often I've seen him play, except to say, sadly, not often enough.

What is it about this sometimes temperamental, sometimes inarticulate, sometimes annoying man that would bring me to the ballpark for one last look, a final, personal thank-you?

Baseball, for me, has always been a peculiarly American experience. It's a game of grace and rhythm. It is simple enough in its fundamental thrust to follow easily—like a NASA rocket lifting off—but complex enough in its subtleties—again, like a rocket—to engage the intellect (and the spirit) almost endlessly.

At the major league level, it requires awesome skills from superbly conditioned athletes able to beat huge odds of nanosecond timing. It is, nonetheless, a sport of great fun and timelessness, in the sense that each game has at least the potential to last forever.

Baseball is, of course, also a business—often a heartless one that can chew up a young man's dream and spit it out without remorse.

Brett certainly knew about the business aspects of the game. Occasionally he would act like a petulant little boy when he wanted to renegotiate his contract. Sometimes I wanted to tell him just to shut up and play.

But for all that, he never forgot that baseball is to be played full-tilt boogie, without a throttle. It is a game to which a man of his talents could give himself with utter abandon, the type of individual about whom, in a different context, a poet once asked, "How can we tell the dancer from the dance?"

Is Brett the most naturally gifted man ever to play the game? Not even close. He isn't even the most naturally gifted player in his family. That honor always went to his brother Ken, who had an unremarkable career as a big-league pitcher.

What George had, however, was pluck, persistence, and focus. He learned that if he took his God-given talents and worked like crazy to make them his own, he could make it to the big leagues and hold a job.

He could have quit after reaching a career 3,000-hit level late last season, a total achieved by fewer than twenty of all the thousands who've ever played in the majors.

But that would have been like stopping before reaching first on a grounder. No, he clearly had one more season in him, a season in which he'll finish at or near the team lead in homers, runs batted in, and hits.

So on this chilly late September night I came to watch George Brett one last time, to say a personal thank-you for all the magic moments he created by sheer force of will.

It didn't matter that he went 0 for 5 on this particular night. After all, he'd gone 21 for 21 when you count seasons, doing as well as he could for as long as he could without embarrassing himself.

In fact, he did better than he could. He overachieved. In the biblical parable of the talents, he would have been a servant who was given 1 but who returned 150 to his master—along with a high-five.

For that rare model, I honor the man.

Pulling for a Very Classy Hometown Hero
June 10, 1996

With the cruel mental preparation of being a long-time fan of the Chicago Cubs, I had been ready for my favorite pro-golf team, Tom Watson and his putter, to go another several decades without winning a championship.

My Cubs, after all, have not even been in a World Series since the year I was born, 1945, and have not actually won a World Series since the year before my late father was born, 1908. Indeed, Dad lived eighty-two years without once seeing the Cubs win a series. (I wish I cared as little as he did.)

Watson, by comparison, had gone only nine years without a tour victory before winning the Memorial Tournament in Ohio recently. Nine years, however, must have seemed practically forever to a man who, prior to that, was golf's equivalent of the 1927 Yankees.

I must say I'm proud of myself for being a steady Watson fan. I'd watch him on TV every chance I'd get and would try to speak telepathically to his nerves on those pesky three-foot putts that seemed to drive him crazy in recent years.

And I think my stellar behavior in this matter over the long course of his victory drought should be a model for how we as a culture approach other aspects of our lives.

For instance, never once did I publicly suggest that Watson trade himself for a player to be named later.

Heck, if a baseball player these days has one bad month, to say nothing of a rotten decade, fans galore want him outta here. That's not how I responded to Watson's decade of discontent. I stuck with this Kansas City lad, partly because he has more class than a whole dugout full of designated hitters.

Besides, I was afraid that if Watson did trade himself, those of us who live in Kansas City might end up with some fancy-pants showoff golfer or, worse, some erratic goofball.

No, sir. A steady, middle-of-the-road, traditional-values sort of midwestern place like Kansas City—a place half the world thinks is in Kansas and, therefore, ipso facto boring—should have a decent, upright (and, my female friends tell me, cute) golfer like Tom Watson. And we do.

A guy like John Daly would be to Kansas City what William "The Refrigerator" Perry once was to pole vaulting.

As I say, my steady, unwavering support of Watson throughout his no-win years reflects an attitude that the rest of the country would do well to emulate in other areas. But Americans seem unwilling to give anyone a honeymoon period anymore. Why, I bet if Bob Dole gets elected president, his honeymoon will last even less time than Bill Clinton's twelve-hour free ride did in 1993.

If a new college football coach loses the first game of the season, hordes of alumni descend on the campus in search of his scalp. A new corporate CEO gets maybe forty-five minutes to turn around a badly managed company before stockholders start unloading their equities and filing class-action suits. One mediocre sermon is enough to turn an entire congregation against a new preacher. Come on, people.

Do you think Tom Watson wanted to lose all those golf tournaments he played in since 1987? Do you think Buddy Bell, rookie manager of the Detroit Tigers, wants to have far and away the worst record in baseball this year?

Do you think this Congress wanted to waste all that time on political posturing this session instead of getting things done? Yeah, so do I.

But that doesn't mean others don't deserve the slack I gave Watson. Others like me, for instance. And maybe you.

Baseball Is Behaving with Raging Stupidity
February 13, 1994

The first baseball players will show up in big-league spring training camps in a few days. Normally this would make me glad. Fresh, hopeful beginnings, great expectations, all that.

But Major League Baseball—besides experiencing the normal trauma that comes when such class players as George Brett and Nolan Ryan retire—is suffering all kinds of self-inflicted wounds. It is behaving with raging stupidity. If I didn't love the simple grace and beauty of the game itself, I would give it up. Baseball is trying my soul.

Its first problem is that it's leaderless. It hasn't had a commissioner since owners forced Fay Vincent to quit on September 7, 1992. And those same owners now have given up choosing a commissioner anytime this season.

This is like trying to run the federal government without a president. This is big-league dumb.

The trouble seems to be that the owners don't want anyone with any smarts or any willingness to tell them their ideas stink. Imagine the damage that can be done by a run-amok group that includes the likes of Marge Schott and George Steinbrenner. Lordy, lordy.

So baseball will go through another sad summer without a commissioner, jerking around with all the akimbo grace of a headless chicken.

If there had been even a half-bright commissioner on the job last year, he or she (ha! baseball has almost no tolerance for women anywhere) never would have allowed owners to institute the new three-division system that will be used this year to expand post-season play to another round.

"No!" he would have said. "Don't be idiots! You adopt this mess and I quit!" They might have adopted it anyway, but not without the kind of public fight it deserved.

The new system is little more than an overly complicated money grab. It will allow second-rate teams to participate in post-season play, thus diluting the meaning of the season, the playoffs, and the World Series.

Under the old system, a team had to play well enough for 162 games to win one of four divisions—two in the American League and two in the National. Then winners of a playoff series between division champs—in a seamless and sensible continuation of the season—advanced to the World Series.

But this year each league will have three divisions. Each division winner plus a wild-card team will go to the first round of playoffs. That's eight teams, not four, and it cheapens the whole process. It means a team that didn't play well enough to make it to the playoffs in 1993 quite possibly will rise to the post-season occasion and win two playoff series and the 1994 World Series.

The whole drama of the cumulative season—from the early chill of April openers through August's scorching afternoons and into brisk October evenings—may be short-circuited.

And why? Not because it improves the game. Not because it's fairer. Only because adding another level of playoff games means more money.

Look, it's not that I'm just discovering the big business aspect of pro sports. Of course baseball is a business, and there are even a few civic-minded owners—the late Ewing Kauffman of the Royals was one—willing to lose lots of money to retain the countless peripheral benefits that accrue to a city with a big-league franchise. But there's a difference between improving baseball and exploiting it mindlessly for greed.

Why do you think the Chicago White Sox are giving Michael Jordan a shot at spring training this year? The same reason they gave a mediocre player like Bo Jackson a shot.

We deserve better from our national pastime. Baseball is adrift. The people in charge of it are sliming the game.

Where have you gone, Mickey Mantle? Oh, yeah. To the Betty Ford Clinic. Sigh.

Can Baseball Come Back?

March 5, 1995

*Whoever wants to know the heart and mind of America
had better learn baseball.*—JACQUES BARZUN
(French-born American teacher, historian, and author)

The national pastime, baseball, has been ailing because of the national preoccupation, greed.

It's clearly been a serious illness, though maybe not terminal. And it has threatened a central—if often misunderstood—element of our culture.

The fight between spoiled players and short-sighted—at times petulant—owners has raised the question of why it's important to have major league baseball played at its highest possible skill level.

A few years ago, in his slightly hyperventilating book about baseball called *Men at Work,* columnist George F. Will came close to the cultural essence of the game.

There is, he wrote,

a civic interest served by having the population at large leavened by millions of fans. They are spectators of a game that rewards, and thus, elicits, a remarkable level of intelligence from those who compete. To be an intelligent fan is to participate in something. It is an activity, a form of appreciating that is good for the individual's soul, and hence for society.

Proof of the genius of ancient Greece is that it understood baseball's future importance. Greek philosophers considered sports a religious and civic—in a word, moral—undertaking. Sport, they said, is morally serious because mankind's noblest aim is the loving contemplation of worthy things, such as beauty and courage. By witnessing physical grace, the soul comes to understand love and beauty. Seeing people compete courageously and fairly helps emancipate the individual by educating his passions.

Quite simply, in its simultaneous and edifying demands on fans and athletes, there is no other sport like baseball. And when the level of the game is allowed to slip below what is possible—as a result, say, of using less skillful replacement players—the entire enterprise is diminished and, in some way, the republic is wounded.

Using replacement players in major league games, in fact, is akin to hiring the star of a high school Thespian play to be leading lady in a Merchant-Ivory film. It is expecting T. S. Eliot but getting Rod McKuen. It's like asking track fans to be impressed by a five-minute mile.

Tom Seaver, when he was pitching, got it right: "So many of the owners think of me and all the other players essentially as laborers. They have no appreciation of the artistic value of what I do. . . . How can they be in baseball and not see what it's all about? Pitching is a beautiful thing. It's an art."

But pitcher Warren Spahn had it right, too, when he said baseball is "a game of failure." And yet an acceptable level of failure at the major league level (a mediocre batter failing to get a hit 75 percent of the time, say) still requires extraordinary skill.

A batter facing a pitcher hurling 90 mph fastballs, for instance, has perhaps half a second to decide what to do, to get that message from his brain to the bat in his hands and to drive the ball to a location within the foul lines that won't result in an out.

The fact that some players can last decades and hit above .300 for a lifetime under those conditions is not simply a reflection of their skill, it's a miracle. Which is why—however they behaved off the field—the careers of such hitters as Ty Cobb, Willie Mays, Pete Rose, and George Brett are so breathtaking.

Former Phillies pitcher Curt Simmons once expressed his appreciation of such skill this way: "Throwing a fastball by Henry Aaron is like trying to sneak the sunrise past a rooster."

It's the game's physics and geometry, its grace, pace, and beauty, that raises baseball to an intellectual level not approached by other sports. But appreciation of these elements must take into account the game's incredible complexity.

Even when nothing seems to be happening on the field, a lot is happening. Indeed, defensive players must continually receive and evaluate information about what's going on in front of them (or behind them) before every pitch. It is no exaggeration to state that there can be—and often is—a perceptible difference between the first foul on a 3-and-2 count and the fifth foul on the same count by the same batter.

Nine defensive players must process data and prepare for what to do in the event that x, y, or z happens. But the often troublesome truth is that the possibilities are never limited to x, y, and z. They are, instead, almost infinite.

Infinity plays a subtle but important part in baseball, and it helps to differentiate it from other sports. Each baseball game is potentially endless. There is no time clock. Some games have lasted twenty or thirty innings.

The major league norm, of course, is nine innings played in roughly three hours. But the fact that one game may last an hour and forty-five minutes and be a no-hitter, while the next game can last five hours and ten minutes and be a 26–25 slugfest, makes the concept of an "average" game almost meaningless.

Careful listeners to veteran baseball broadcasters will notice that at least once every two weeks, they will say something like, "In all my time watching baseball, I've never seen anything like that." Indeed, baseball is new every day.

One day it may be Bo Jackson of the Royals firing a ball from the left-field corner to home plate, on the fly, to nail a runner. Another day it may be Kevin Mitchell of the Giants turning and twisting in the outfield and eventually catching a fly ball bare-handed. The next it may be Larry Biitner of the Cubs losing a baseball in his hat in the outfield. Right. In his hat.

Or the daily newness of the game may be expressed in the almost indescribable grace of a deftly turned double play. Or in the perfect placement of a suicide squeeze bunt. Or the monstrous power of a home run.

For each discipline or art there is a special language. Painters talk of advancing and retreating colors, of cissing, of cubism, of grisaille. Musicians speak of codas, of cadence, of embouchure. Jazz dancers refer to glissades and pelvis rolls.

And so it is with baseball, except that so much of the language has entered the vocabulary of the entire culture. We speak of hitting grand slams and getting to first base, of shutouts, striking out, and getting thrown a curve. And as we do, we confirm the place of baseball at the core of the American experience.

But the baseball we have in mind—in addition to the fun game played by amateurs at picnics and by minor leaguers hoping for a shot at the big time—is the game Ted Williams played, and Babe Ruth, the game Brooks Robinson played, and Ernie Banks, Mickey Mantle, and Bob Gibson, Ozzie Smith, and Roberto Clemente, Hank Aaron, and Nolan Ryan.

Second-rate replacement baseball, while it may have its amusing moments, simply isn't what this country is about.

The Media's Soft Underbelly

Good Riddance to a Disgrace and Liar
June 28, 1998

SAN DIEGO—Regina Brett is fighting breast cancer with courage, chemicals, and—as the recently elected president of the National Society of Newspaper Columnists—with wrath.

She wears a baseball cap to cover her once-beautiful hair, now gone. And she's intimate with cancer's terror. Which is why this *Akron (Ohio) Beacon Journal* columnist is so angry at *Boston Globe* columnist Patricia Smith, if that's her real name.

Smith has wounded Regina, me, and every other newspaper columnist by doing precisely what we are required never to do: pass off fiction as fact. She's now admitted it and lost her job. Good riddance.

"When I first heard what Patricia Smith had done," Regina told the NSNC's recent annual conference here, "I felt sorry for her for sabotaging such an incredible career. But then . . . as I was trying to put in my contact lens, my lower eyelashes came tumbling out. My eyes would soon be as bald as my head, thanks to the chemo that is trying to eradicate the cancer in my breast.

"The tears fell, probably washing another ten eyelashes out. But instead of feeling sad, I began to feel outraged—outraged at how a writer could make up a cancer patient, make up what it feels like to live with cancer, to lose parts of yourself bit by bit, hair by hair, eyelash by eyelash.

"How dare Patricia Smith pretend to know what it is like, pretend to know so well? . . . What arrogance to think she could be more eloquent and accurate in expressing the fear, pain, and despair the diagnosis brings."

No wonder we elected this eloquent columnist our NSNC president. She's right. Smith has betrayed not only the trusting readers of the prose she crafted with apparent grace and beauty (and, we now know, guile), but she has betrayed the very profession Regina and I practice and try to improve and challenge through the NSNC.

Smith is like the scientist who fakes research to receive continued grants. She has forced other columnists—just as the phony scientist forces other researchers—to defend their craft, to ask readers not to imagine her deceit is typical of our work.

It would be understandable, of course, if readers simply assumed now that all columnists routinely make up quotes and create nonexistent people so we can do what Smith called "slam home some salient point."

I won't claim Smith is the only guilty columnist ever, but I will say that the hundreds of columnists I know and respect would never try to slip some undisclosed fiction past readers. Such deception is not at all like major league pitchers throwing spit balls or hitters corking their bats—sins everyone winks at. Nobody in my profession who cares even a little about ethics does what Smith has admitted to doing.

Please understand that I'm not saying columnists don't sometimes have fun saying goofy things for humorous effect—things they and their readers know to be false. Heck, I myself have called William Shakespeare Greek. I've said Warren G. Harding wrote the Constitution.

That sort of silliness goes on a lot, and readers recognize it, especially because we always tell them what we're up to, either directly or indirectly. Dave Barry of the *Miami Herald*, in fact, does this so often he's forced to tell readers when he's not making up some fact.

But that's not what got Smith in trouble. Rather, in serious pieces about serious subjects, she simply created people and their quotes ex nihilo.

It's tempting to wonder what sort of overly trusting editors Smith had. Or to puzzle over why someone didn't catch on and confront Smith about writing fiction. But it finally doesn't matter who let her sins slip through. She's to blame.

We in the newspaper business have nothing without our credibility. And we forfeit it far too often by erring through laziness. But those are sins of sloppiness, not deceit.

Smith's colleague at the *Boston Globe*, Pulitzer prizewinner Eileen McNamara, who was our NSNC keynote speaker, said this well: "Credibility is all we have. It's absolutely the currency we exchange with the public."

Good column writing requires risks. We must be willing to offend readers as we do our most important job—making them think. As Neil Morgan of the *San Diego Union-Tribune* says: "If you don't get out ahead of your readers there's not much reason to come to work. If you get too far ahead there's no reason to come to work."

But that balancing act should never lead a columnist to give readers fiction masquerading as fact. Columnists who do that are a disgrace.

Smith says she will "write as long as I breathe, despite the dire predictions that this indiscretion spells the end of my career." There she goes again. It wasn't an "indiscretion." It was lying. And if she writes again, it should not be for a newspaper. She has forfeited that privilege.

A Great Columnist, but No Role Model for Writers
April 18, 1999

Ernie Pyle, an authentic giant in column-writing, died fifty-four years ago today at age forty-four. While serving as a war correspondent on the little Pacific island of Ie Shima off Okinawa, he took a Japanese bullet in his left temple.

Pyle, who wrote about World War II from the perspective of men in the trenches, did many things well as a columnist. He got out of the office and did real reporting. He avoided the trap of writing only about big-name personalities or quoting only muckety-mucks. Beyond that, he was smart enough to tell obtuse editors who wanted him to cover breaking news to go to hell. If they didn't recognize his strengths, he did. (James Tobin notes all this in his book, *Ernie Pyle's War: America's Eyewitness to World War II*.)

Those were enough reasons for the National Society of Newspaper Columnists to have selected Pyle's death date to be National Columnists Day. I feel a little responsible for that. When I was the society's president a few years ago, I asked one of our members to find an appropriate date for my idea of having such a day, and he recommended April 18.

So today I honor Pyle as well as all good columnists—the ones who understand that their job is not to get famous enough to be a talking head on TV but, rather, to make readers think in fresh ways.

Nevertheless, I hope nobody imagines that columnists—or anyone else—should seek to imitate Pyle's life. Even if Pyle had not been killed while trying to hide in a ditch thousands of miles from his native Indiana, he already had paid much too high a price for the work he did.

Consider: He was on the road relentlessly. His married life usually was in shambles. He was childless, partly because of his own sexual dysfunction. He drank too much. His wife, whom he eventually divorced in great angst, was mentally ill and also consumed far too much alcohol and medication. Pyle, not a brilliant craftsman of words—but nonetheless direct and clear in his writing—often struggled with whether he could produce even one more word. Some role model.

Imagine having someone say of you what Lee G. Miller, one of Pyle's editors and author of *The Story of Ernie Pyle,* wrote of Pyle and his wife, Jerry (Geraldine): The mental distresses she suffered may have been because of "something in her relationship with Ernie; during some of their years together, theirs was a non-physical union, due to a functional incapacity on Ernie's part which was eventually redressed. Conceivably, Jerry was affected by an unrealized jealousy of Ernie's growing importance. . . . Whatever the cause, something malevolent was gnawing at her."

Jerry, in fact, had been reluctant to get married at all and later insisted they tell none of their friends.

Imagine having someone say of you what Pyle said of himself and Jerry before he left to cover the war: "Our visits to Washington seem almost like dreams. When people over the country ask us where we live, we say Washington, D.C. . . . Yet we really have no home at all. . . . [O]ur visits to Washington are so infrequent and so brief that each one is like a daze. . . . We realize at the end that we have talked to lots of friends, yet individually we have talked to nobody. . . .

"Always, after we leave Washington, we have a little talk to ourselves, and we visualize the day when disappointment in us will have wearied all of our old friends, and we see ourselves eventually returning to Washington with nobody at all to speak to us."

Or imagine writing this, as Pyle did about himself: "my life is purposeless and tortured, and soon my ability to carry on and make a living will be impaired, and that will be the beginning of the end."

Or this: "I feel that my capacity ever to produce the column again has died."

What column is worth that? None. What career of any kind is worth that? None. Pyle told much truth, and we honor him for that.

But the English man of letters Cyril Connolly was right: "Better to write for yourself and have no public," he said, "than to write for the public and have no self."

Despite what our culture would have us believe, throwing oneself on the pyre of personal sacrifice in pursuit of professional advancement in any field is not honorable at all. Rather, it is distressing evidence of a sad confusion between what is of lasting value and what is ephemeral.

Newspapers Face Daunting List of Problems
June 6, 1999

The newspaper industry has been staring at its navel lately and not liking what it's seeing.

No wonder. We do a lot badly. But when polls tell us the public distrusts us and that people are getting their news from other sources, we tend to blame everyone but ourselves.

Newspapers are not the cause of all their troubles—distrust, falling circulation, disinterested young readers, and more. Indeed, when people criticize the "media" they often mean that television and radio talk shows go beyond the bounds of decency or that Web sites pretending to offer journalism can't tell a fact from a rumor.

Newspapers suffer guilt by association with such outlets. Despite that, newspapers—even while offering invaluable nuggets of gold to readers—are among their own worst enemies.

Too often they forget why they're in business. Or they don't do at all what only they can do. Or they do badly what they should do best. It's painful to turn state's evidence on my own profession, but after more than thirty years of laboring in these vineyards I know where some of the bodies are buried. And it will do us all good to acknowledge them.

Since November 2, 1920, when Leo Rosenberg broadcast the Harding-Cox election returns over the nation's first commercial radio station, KDKA in Pittsburgh, newspapers have been losing the immediacy battle. Now, of course, there's TV and the Internet. Newspapers printing hard news stories that are ten hours old by the time they're read too often are suffering from a lack of imagination and admitting they don't know what else to do.

This is foolish. Because of radio, TV, and the Internet, can newspapers ever again be first at anything? Yes. We can be first at offering a sense of context to the news, analysis of what the news means. When trouble first breaks out, we can give you a primer on Kosovo. When the U.N. War Crimes Tribunal indicts Slobodan Milosevic, we can give you a history of war crimes trials. We can analyze whether our military is really able to fight the frustratingly limited wars it's been asked to prosecute. We can print exclusive investigations of public corruption. And we can offer the personal voices of columnists who engage readers by sharing their own hearts and minds.

Indeed, in this explosive Information Age, offering just such fare is the primary job of newspaper editors. But many of them don't do it at all or they do it badly. Why? Well, part of the problem is that too often newspapers have tried to survive by cutting the very staff that can give readers the in-depth coverage needed to compete with more immediate competitors.

Worse, much of the remaining staff is ordered to produce what columnist Russell Baker once correctly called popcorn—mindless junk about our celebrity-infatuated culture. It's not that all entertainment news is illegitimate. It's that newspapers, by their fawning coverage, tend to give cultural legitimacy to what, in the end, are simply ways to make money from numbskulls who imagine their highest calling is to be consumers and fans.

Even when editors offer solid coverage of important events, they too often tell readers, by story placement, they don't think the news is worth much. The day after the recent release of the alarming report about Chinese espionage, for instance, the follow-up story in this and too many other papers got bumped off the front page. Editors who make such questionable decisions (often because they edit by formula, not by instinct and art) can't expect to be taken seriously.

When all of that is coupled with the industry's continuing failure to recruit and promote a staff representative of the communities newspapers try to cover, the trouble multiplies.

In 1997, for instance, the percentage of Asian, African American, Hispanic, and Native American newsroom employees at America's daily papers was just 11.46 percent. By 1998 it had crept up to 11.55 percent. True, it was only about 4 percent in 1978, but the U.S. minority population now is more than 25 percent. In a diverse world, our industry is out of synch, and it's costing us readers.

This is far from an exhaustive catalog of problems confronting papers. But even this list will go unsolved as long as we think the blame lies elsewhere. Some does, but until we meet these challenges, we won't know if we can survive on our own considerable merits.

Sometimes, the News Tells You Too Much
November 14, 1999

I keep telling myself there's nothing ultimately harmful in the relentlessly squalid celebrity news that takes up more and more space in many newspapers these days.

It's an accurate reflection of our arid culture, I say to myself, and part of our job as journalists is to hold a mirror up to society.

It attracts mindless readers who might, if only inadvertently, learn something of value while they're flipping through the paper, I say.

It makes people feel better about themselves in the same way watching guests on Jerry Springer's TV show accomplishes that by offering assurances that our own lives, pathetic as they may be, will never be so shabby.

But I'm wrong. Newspapers seem to have become addicted to the worship of celebrity in a way that violates their responsibility to provide useful news. They simply have elected to wallow in unredemptive titillation—imagining, probably correctly, that people want this rot.

Just recently, for instance, on the cover of the "FYI" section of our own paper, there was a short item about an actress named Holland Taylor, of whom, I confess, I had never heard. The story said Taylor plays a judge on *The Practice*, a TV show I've never seen. Here's what Taylor, fifty-six, was quoted as saying: "[I've] never been promiscuous, but I certainly love sex. I'm very, very viable in that department."

What I don't get is why anyone thought it necessary to write down that quote (even if she said it), to put it in a story, to distribute it on a national news wire or to commit the resources of computers, editors, ink, paper, printing presses, and delivery trucks to distribute it.

I'm simply at a loss to explain why any newspaper—much less my own, of which I'm often proud—would publish this kind of debris. Does it inform in any useful way? Does it shed any light on any issue of the day? Does it somehow touch the human spirit?

Similar to the Holland Taylor item was a recent note in the *San Francisco Chronicle* that repeated a quote from actress Suzanne

Somers in *Time* magazine: "Now I never have gas, I can proudly say. It's a great thing not to have gas."

I give just a little more leeway to this stupefying bit of cultural detritus because it appeared in a column by Leah Garchik, who does a nice job making fun of celebrity nincompoops, and no doubt that was her purpose here. I'd have argued, however, with Leah about including the Somers quote because it offered us no new insights about her, acting, or anything else.

Another recent example appeared in our "FYI" section's "Star-Gazing" feature. Actress Rita Wilson, wife of actor Tom Hanks, was quoted as revealing the secret of a good marriage. Her final comment: "you gotta have lots of tantric yoga sex."

The unspoken assumption is that somehow readers should care whether Wilson and Hanks have sex and, beyond that, what kind. We should care whether Suzanne Somers has gas. It should matter to us that Holland Taylor is sexually "very viable."

I can hardly think of three pieces of information that matter less to me. But what matters to me personally is not the point, for I readily concede that I remain purposefully detached from much of popular culture because I find it so barren, unimaginative, dispiriting, and devoid of important values.

Rather, what should matter to all of us is why newspapers, on which so many of us depend for news and analysis, have so lost their way as to be devoting precious resources to such dreck.

I don't mean to say that papers don't print lots of wonderful and useful words and pictures. They do. And many of their World Wide Web sites offer supplemental material that can deepen our understanding of terribly complex questions.

But why would papers devote even a word to Taylor's orgasms or Somers's flatulence when children are shooting each other, adults are abusing their own offspring, schools are failing, health care is in need of reform, and urban sprawl is chewing up the countryside?

What can editors be thinking?

And what can you as a reader be thinking if you aren't complaining about this lowest-common-denominator journalism and demanding, instead, excellence? You, after all, are the market. And if you're buying, someone will always be willing to sell. It's both the genius and the flaw of capitalism.

Television Is Teaching All the Time
November 15, 1998

More than fifty years after commercial television invaded American life, an obvious question is why so much of it—especially on the networks—is so arid, vacuous, and bleak.

A less obvious question is whether the soulless sex- and violence-laden dreck that fills prime-time TV matters any more, given the explosion of alternative information and entertainment choices. (Yes, it does, but maybe not as much.)

The broadcast industry, after all, has atomized. This means more people can ignore the insipid debris on commercial TV by choosing instead to plug into satellites, get specialized cable channels—the History Channel is a wholesome example—and surf the Internet, sometimes on a medium-blurring device called Web TV. Although, of course, those sources also harbor sludge amid more uplifting offerings.

The hopeful evidence, as ratings show, is that some formerly heavy TV viewers may be making better choices, leaving behind the network offal of murder and body fluids as entertainment.

"Americans," says Henry Labalme, executive director of a nonprofit advocacy group, TV-Free America, "are finally moving beyond the old debates about whose show is better than whose and recognizing that all TV watching displaces interactions and activities that are simply healthier, more productive, and more fun."

In short, some folks are discovering a liberating truth: Much of commercial TV is cultural pollution. Indeed, says Labalme's group, this past April a record 5 million people joined in National TV-Turnoff Week.

"Nobody," he says, "ever lay on their deathbed wishing they had spent more time watching Geraldo Rivera or Rosie O'Donnell."

Repugnant situation comedies and violent dramas may be a smaller percentage of what's on network TV today, but they're still there, drawing millions of viewers. Why? No doubt for many reasons, but one is compellingly clear: Much of our culture—because it relies on lowest-common-denominator commercial success—is equally vapid and disheartening. How else to explain brand loyalty to products that clog arteries or cause lung cancer?

The sobering reality is that commercial TV offers a reasonably accurate picture of who we are—a people mired in a culture of celebrity, afraid of life-affirming risk, leery of real creativity, and willing to do almost anything to avoid hard questions about ultimate meaning.

Cowering in living rooms, demanding to be anesthetized by cheap, tawdry entertainment, people who watch the drivel on commercial TV get what they deserve because they buy the products for which the medium creates demand.

And let's be clear: Commercial TV's main function has not changed from the late 1940s, when Jack Benny and Milton Berle were becoming its first stars. It exists to sell brand-name soap. Well, soap, beer, and cars, not to speak of aspirin, computers, and soft drinks. It is nothing less than a magnet advertisers use to attract a critical mass of customers. Everything else is secondary. Everything.

This role explains much of the astonishingly puerile, stupefying prime-time shows I watched recently to reacquaint myself with the sort of bilge I have refused to watch for decades. They all seem to be about nothing but irresponsible, casual sex. Some highlights:

On *Suddenly Susan,* an NBC show, a sidekick character observes star Brooke Shields's unmarried character's out-of-the-ordinary breakfast and concludes it means but one thing: "You're having sex! Way to go!"

Shield's lying response: "The closest thing I have to a sex life is when my Thighmaster slips."

On ABC's *Home Improvement,* the unmarried sister of star Tim Allen's TV wife has sex in Allen's house with Allen's unmarried TV brother. Allen dismisses it as inconsequential. Allen's wife tells him, "You'd be comfortable doing it with a relative in the room."

On *Clueless,* a UPN show on which actors without skill recite lines without meaning to advance a story without plot, a euphemism for sex is "going downtown." When the female star—who cares what her name is?—gets interrupted while waiting for a kiss, she says, "Hello! Girl and tongue waiting!" The to-be-continued episode ends when fake human feces (soon eaten by an actor) in a swimming pool breaks up a party.

Spin City, an ABC show, opens with star Michael J. Fox's unmarried character telling a slim, unmarried model, "Look, just because we've been on a couple of dates doesn't mean there's any pressure."

She responds by removing her blouse. We next see her lying on a bed in just her bra and panties. The actual intercourse, bless ABC, occurs off camera.

"That was amazing," he says afterward. She yodels, explaining,

"I like to yodel after sex." He responds, "I prefer the wave," and raises both his arms. Later she complains to him, "You don't know anything about me."

But already I know too much: She has apparently unprotected sex with anyone she wants, then wonders why her sex partners don't get to know her. Such people once were called tramps and wolves; now they're stars.

Notice I've said nothing about daytime TV's lurid soap operas or the animated Comedy Central hit *South Park,* in one episode of which the muffled, elementary-school character Kenny uses vulgar anatomical language to describe female body parts he likes.

What a sad use of a potentially, and sometimes an actually, marvelous medium. If, as one A. C. Nielsen study shows, children watch nearly four hours of TV a day (other studies report the time has fallen to ninety minutes), it's no wonder that 95 percent of Americans between the ages of thirteen and seventeen can name the actor who played the Fresh Prince of Bel Air on TV (Will Smith) but only 2 percent can name the chief justice of the United States (William Rehnquist).

"Television," Marshall McLuhan once said, "is teaching all the time." Indeed, one of its lessons should be this: Art doesn't require a laugh track. But a recent *New Yorker* article quotes Jamie Tarses, ABC Entertainment president, as essentially saying viewers are idiots: "People will wonder, Am I supposed to think this is funny or serious? People need the comforting aural cue of laughter."

The technology to deliver all this is improving rapidly. We're moving toward wide availability of High Definition Television, Digital Video Discs, and "Flat TV," which uses plasma, or charged gas, to light color pixels that make up images.

But what difference will that make if we burn time watching this still-vast wasteland's rubbish?

Nearly sixty years ago, the author E. B. White saw a demonstration of TV and declared, "We shall discover either a new and unbearable disturbance of the general peace or a saving radiance in the sky."

Forget the saving radiance. After all, commercial TV's spiritually empty role is to collect zombies to buy the advertised products, a job built on the lie that more stuff will make us happy. But whether TV continues to be an unbearable disturbance is up to us. Our job, after all, is to be discerning and responsible in this new era of choices.

Surfing for Meaning in the E-Maelstrom
November 10, 1996

The Internet—high technology's web-footed, precocious child—is proof that something profound is being born. But what? Nobody seems to have more than the vaguest notion.

What many of us suspect is happening in cyberspace, however, fills us with anxiety—along with perplexing hope.

That's because the Internet, while promising to connect us one to another, turns out to be a soulless tool that must employ phony "emoticons"—an example is :-) as a sideways smiley face—to indicate feelings in electronic mail.

To grasp the unsettling dimensions of what the Internet is becoming, it may help to ask how we created this global, if U.S.-centered, network of computer networks. And, beyond that, what its implications are for how we live.

The Internet's tender roots can be traced to 1969 and the Pentagon's "ARPANET" system for fail-safe communication in nuclear war. In 1974 the Pentagon adopted a common transmission method, allowing readier connection among scientists and academicians. The spread of modems and personal computers caused an explosion of Internet connections in the 1980s and '90s. Every figure purporting to say how many people are connected is outdated, but it's clearly in the tens of millions.

The Internet umbrella covers such diverse elements as the graphically jazzy World Wide Web, Usenet, and the Gopher system. And if the net doesn't first fall of its own weight, its potential is astonishing.

"We are in the middle of the most transforming technological event since the capture of fire," says John Perry Barlow, a founder of the Electronic Frontier Foundation, formed to protect civil liberties in cyberspace.

I have been connected to the Internet for two years and find it to be an occasionally wonderful tool for research and communication. I have obtained almost instant access to full texts of bills in Congress. In less time than it takes to eat a cookie, I acquired the Unabomber's thirty-five-thousand-word Luddite manifesto. And I have electronically wished my niece in Minnesota happy birthday.

So experience convinces me the Internet can be a tremendous resource. This is true even though it contains hard-to-find, badly organized, and misleading data.

The Internet offers what one critic calls "an ocean of unedited data." And it sometimes acts like what another calls "a carnival gone awry."

"The thoughtful and the thoughtless coexist side by side in the Internet's electronic universe," says Vinton G. Cerf, a member of the board of directors of the Internet Society. "We have but one tool to apply: critical thinking."

In fact, the huge variety of information on the net raises disturbing questions about the Information Age itself. If the information we collect is untrustworthy, how can it lead us to wisdom? And if it doesn't do that, what's the point? If the Information Age doesn't eventually produce the Wisdom Age, won't it have been for naught?

That issue, of course, won't be settled for a long time. But other prickly concerns demand quicker resolution.

These include privacy, fair access, censorship (of pornography and other data), and encryption, which is a way of coding data to protect its security in passage. In fact, the Internet probably has little commercial future without a strong system of encryption, and the fight over that still rages.

The question of who has access goes to the heart of the fear that we are creating information haves and have-nots. The haves are on the Information Superhighway. The have-nots (most people in the world) are in a ditch of off-line ignorance.

And the related issues of privacy and censorship have huge implications.

Indeed, the very existence of nation-states with defendable borders may be compromised if the Internet grows relatively unfettered and if its data become well organized and dependable.

That's why such nervous and oppressive countries as China and Singapore do their best to restrict their citizens' Internet access. That, of course, is a fool's game. They cannot forever be insulated from the astonishing wave of data—including truth—sloshing around the world. There is, finally, no Great Wall high enough to keep out truth, even if people on-line have to sift through junk to find that truth.

"The nation-state," says Barlow, "is doomed and ought to be." Even if that's exaggerated—and it is—it's clear that China represents the old computer model of a huge mainframe with a central processing unit. By contrast, current-generation computer systems employ "massive parallelism," which breaks processing power into many smaller processors. Decentralization, in fact, is the nature of the Internet.

The in-vogue phrase for this is "distributed intelligence," and Vice President Gore correctly notes that it "offers an insight into why democracy has triumphed over governments that depended exclusively on a central authority."

Gore, the administration's technology point man, also rightly notes that Congress often addresses science and technology "with all the wisdom of a potted plant," putting research and development in jeopardy just when we need them so desperately. As Jim Barksdale, Netscape's chief executive, says, "A lot of people in the government haven't seen the football since the kickoff."

Even setting aside these cosmic issues, we find that the Internet still is affecting us in ways we don't fully understand. Spelling and grammar, for example, are changing because of the net.

Columnist Charles Stough argued in a recent New York Times News Service piece that much as Johann Gutenberg's fifteenth-century printing work led to standardized spelling and grammar, the Internet is contributing to their destandardization by allowing the many hands typing on it to ignore rules.

Stough says we are entering the age of "unprinting," which is "undoing all the rules." Is this a good idea? IMHO, no. (IMHO, as you may know, is Internet shorthand for "in my humble opinion." It's entering the lexicon with other "netisms.")

This sloppy system encourages quickness over depth or reflection, resulting in impudent, thoughtless responses—including nasty notes called flaming. But beyond that, the growth of the whole Internet is so quick there seems to be no time to ponder its implications. We may regret that far more than injudicious e-mail.

For the truth is we don't know where technology is leading. Never have. Probably never will.

What we do know so far is that the Internet reflects our venality, our arrogance, our greed—even as it also reflects our most magnanimous hopes and dreams. Indeed, if we have learned anything in the Internet's brief life, it is that—even if it can entertain and inform us—it cannot save us. Whether it can destroy us is unanswered.

President Clinton, in a speech soon after the 1995 Oklahoma City bombing, was exactly right when he said that "the forces that are lifting us up and bringing us together contain a dark underside of possibility for evil. . . . The great challenge for the twenty-first century will be how to see the opportunities presented by technology, by free movement of people, by the openness of society, by the shrinking of the borders between nations without being absolutely consumed by the dangers and threats that those same forces present. . . . Because evil has not been uprooted from human nature."

Our experience with high-tech evil and failure should prepare for the reality that the Internet disappoints us and causes us angst about its vacuousness, its frustrating unreliability, and its capacity to transmit malevolence and lies at top speed.

It is much the same failure we sense with television, technology's mixed blessing of high art and low taste, great ideas and insidious emptiness, useful information and destructive coarseness.

But we are relentlessly foolish enough to imagine that new technology will be different. Well, the Internet clearly is different from TV, but not in its endless capacity for idiocy.

We seem seduced by Al Gore's inviting Internet vision: "Empowered by the movable type of the next millennium, we can send caravans loaded with the wealth of human knowledge and creativity along trails of light that lead to every home and village."

But the reality is messier. Included in the caravans are infojunk and lies. And the trail so far leads only to people wise or rich enough to be plugged in.

Which is not to say we should shut down the Internet. Not at all. Besides, we're way too late for that stupid move.

But it is to say we would do well to pay more attention to what we are creating and to acknowledge that in our globally connected village we often can't even name the pain our next-door neighbors are in.

And it is to say we should recognize that the Internet will fail to meet our highest goals for it if we cannot make it function in an ethos of universally valid values—such as human rights and dignity, liberty, and the principle that political power ultimately belongs to the people.

Can we do this? The odds are dreadfully against it. But not to try would be the greater failure.

Epilogue

The typesetting of this book was nearly completed when the September 11, 2001, terrorist attacks on America occurred. One of those who died that day was my nephew, Karleton Fyfe, thirty-one, of Brookline, Massachusetts. This is the column I wrote about him. I include it here as a way of honoring his life—as well as the lives of everyone who died that evil day.

Bill Tammeus

One Precious Life among Many
September 15, 2001

I will tell you how terrorists think. They think like Joseph Stalin. This is what Stalin once said about the value of human life: "One death is a tragedy; a million deaths are a statistic."

Now I will tell you how decent, rational, and loving people think. They think the people who died in the terrorist attacks on New York and Washington were not statistics, no matter what the final number of them turns out to be. They think each of them was a real person with real families, real dreams, hurts, joys, and, above all, real histories.

And they're right. I can't tell you about each precious life erased in this despicable madness. But I can tell you about one of them. I can tell you about my nephew, the only son of one of my sisters and her husband. He was on the first flight to hit the World Trade Center. Maybe my words about Karleton Douglas Beye Fyfe can, in some inadequate way, illuminate all the lives annihilated by darkness.

This, and more, is who Karleton was: loving and cherished son, husband, father, cousin, brother, uncle, nephew, and friend. He was gentle but clear-eyed, analytical but whimsical—as you might expect from someone whose dual majors at the University of North Carolina were economics and, of all things, philosophy.

251

He maintained an intriguing philosophical approach to life even as he went on to Boston University to get his MBA while working for Fidelity Investments, before transferring to John Hancock. The cosmic questions of life—and the absurdities—fascinated him, and he looked forward to working out answers as he grew older and wiser.

But now the killers have made that impossible.

Karleton loved—simply loved—life. To him it was a puzzle to be solved, a gift to be opened excitedly, a party to enjoy with family, which meant everything to him. He looked forward to nothing more than living out a full, long life with his wife, Haven, and little boy, Jackson (who will turn two years old in February, five days before what would have been Karleton's thirty-second birthday).

But now the killers have made that impossible.

Karleton was born in Texas the year his parents moved from there to North Carolina. His father is a biochemical researcher, his mother (my sister) a registered nurse. One of Karleton's two sisters has two children herself and lives near Atlanta. His other sister just got married this summer (the last time I was with Karleton) and also lives in Boston, where she and her brother loved to spend time together.

But now the killers have made that impossible.

When Karleton went to college, he made huge numbers of friends, all of whom, it seemed, showed up at his wedding in 1994. What fun we had that day. How we laughed later about one of his groomsmen collapsing in a heap in the middle of the service when he thought he'd lost the ring he was holding. What good, loving, wonderful people came into Karleton's circle. How he looked forward to staying in touch with them.

But now the killers have made that impossible.

When Karleton took a job as a financial analyst in Boston, it was clear he was a quick study. He moved up rapidly. Even his doting mother could hardly believe her boy was doing so well in a field that many of the rest of us in his family would have found tedious and mysterious.

He was able to infuse the world of finance with meaning and import because he understood that decisions made by major investment houses ultimately can have a terrific influence on people he loved. He looked forward to creating a career that would help people achieve the financial freedom to allow them to devote their lives more fully to family and to helping those in need.

But now the killers have made that impossible.

What joy Karleton brought to me personally. When he was a boy he would visit my family in the summers. We'd go on trips. We'd play catch in the backyard. One day while working on his curveball, he put a baseball through my neighbor's garage window. And, at age eleven, he offered to pay for it.

How much in recent years I loved getting his strange, spontaneous e-mail. For no reason at all, he'd flash me a note that said, simply, "Did you know how incredibly handsome and tall I am?" I wanted this to go on for decades.

But now the killers have made that impossible.

And all of us grieve with all the families who have lost all these precious Karletons.

About the Author

Bill Tammeus is an editorial page columnist for the *Kansas City Star,* where he has worked since 1970. He has done freelance reporting for numerous publications, including the *New York Times* and the *Washington Post. A Gift of Meaning* is his first book.